Pentecostalism: The World Their Parish

RELIGION AND MODERNITY

Series Editors: Paul Heelas, Linda Woodhead; Editorial Advisor: David Martin; Founding Editors: John Clayton and Ninian Smart
University of Lancaster, University of Lancaster, University of Boston, University of California – Santa Barbara

The **Religion and Modernity** series makes accessible to a wide audience some of the most important work in the study of religion today. The series invites leading scholars to present clear and non-technical contributions to contemporary thinking about religion in the modern world. Although the series is geared primarily to the needs of college and university students, the volumes in **Religion and Modernity** will prove invaluable to readers with some background in Religious Studies who wish to keep up with recent thinking in the subject, as well as to the general reader who is seeking to learn more about the transformations of religion in our time.

Published:

Don Cupitt – *Mysticism after Modernity*
Paul Heelas, with the assistance of David Martin and
    Paul Morris – *Religion, Modernity and Postmodernity*
Linda Woodhead and Paul Heelas – *Religion in Modern Times*
David Martin – *Pentecostalism: The World Their Parish*

Forthcoming:

Steve Bruce – *God is Dead*
Juan Campo – *Pilgrimage and Modernity*
David Smith – *Hinduism and Modernity*

Pentecostalism:
The World Their Parish

David Martin

BLACKWELL
Publishers

The moral right of David Martin to be identified as author
of this work has been asserted in accordance with the Copyright,
Designs and Patents Act 1988.

First published 2002

2 4 6 8 10 9 7 5 3 1

Blackwell Publishers Ltd
108 Cowley Road
Oxford OX4 1JF
UK

Blackwell Publishers Inc.
350 Main Street
Malden, Massachusetts 02148
USA

British Library Cataloguing in Publication Data

A CIP catalogue record for this book is available from the
British Library.

Library of Congress Cataloging-in-Publication Data

Martin, David, 1929–
    Pentecostalism : the world their parish / David Martin.
        p. cm. — (Religion and modernity)
    Includes bibliographical references and index.
        ISBN 0–631–23120–X (alk. paper) — ISBN 0–631–23121–8
    (pbk. : alk. paper)
        1. Pentecostalism.   I. Title.   II. Series.
    BR1644 .M37 2002
    270.8′2—dc21

                                                        2001001525

Typeset in 10 on 12.5 pt Meridien
by Graphicraft Limited, Hong Kong
Printed in Great Britain by TJ International, Padstow, Cornwall

This book is printed on acid-free paper.

for Dick and Cally Fenn
our Good Companions

contents

preface

The World Their Parish aims to complement my *Tongues of Fire*, published by Blackwell in 1990, by putting Pentecostalism, and its charismatic penumbra, in global context, and taking off from the initial template that may be offered by Latin America.

The book came about through the happy coincidence of being asked to contribute a global overview of contemporary Evangelicalism for an Oxford conference in the Summer of 1999 (under the aegis of Brian Stanley and the "Currents in World Christianity" project at Westminster College, Cambridge) and a period generously made available to me the following Autumn with the theology department and the Institute for the Study of Economic Culture (ISEC) (director Peter Berger) at Boston University.[1] Through writing this overview and having this time it became clear that a mass of material collected as complementary to my work on Pentecostalism in Latin America could not be assimilated in that context and was in fact available for a book on global Pentecostalism. The overview itself is to be published in Donald M. Lewis (ed.), *Evangelical Christianity in the Twentieth Century in the Non-Western World* (Grand Rapids, MI: Eerdmanns, 2002).

A book of this kind is likely to relate to various other writings, notably two books published by Cambridge University Press in 2001: Simon Coleman's *The Word and the World: the Globalization of Charismatic Christianity*, which concentrates on that sector of the movement propagating a "Faith Teaching," and Paul Freston's *Evangelicals and Politics in Asia, Africa and Latin America*, which concentrates, as its title suggests, on politics rather than culture. By contrast this book deals mainly with Pentecostalism, and mainly with cultural change, though I sketch some few instances of incursions into politics to illustrate of what kinds these may be. Freston's book provides the only comprehensive coverage of political aspects and offers an exacting complement to what is provided in these pages. However, I do offer a comparative analysis of Pentecostal and Catholic political styles in chapter 7 of my *Does Christianity Cause War?* (Oxford: Oxford University Press, 1997) and more broadly-based comment in my *Reflections on Sociology and Theology* (Oxford: Oxford University Press, 1997).

The argument offered here closely complements my *Tongues of Fire*, utilizing much material appearing since its publication over a decade ago, but extending the scope globally. In common with that book the focus is on studies of contemporary cultural change. I have not repeated the extended treatment of Korea in the earlier book, though in the Asian context the Korean case is of great importance. The wider context, more especially in chapter 2, is my *A General Theory of Secularisation* (Oxford: Blackwell, 1978). I apologize for these backward and sideways references to my own work, but there is an extended project here, indeed a life's work, in which the present book is necessarily embedded.

This is the appropriate point at which to acknowledge the founding fathers in this area of scholarship, above all Bryan Wilson, Emilio Willems, Christian Lalive D'Epinay, José Miguez Bonino, and Walter Hollenweger. At a broader level I have largely eschewed debates about globalization, modernity, etc., though I have read such scholars as Peter Beyer, Roland Robertson, and Gustavo Benavides with admiration and profit, and there is some relevant material on these matters in chapter 3. In the chapter on Africa I have not felt it relevant, nor do I have the competence, to enter debates involving such major Africanists as John Peel, Terence Ranger, Adrian Hastings, and the Comaroffs. At the broadest possible level I have drawn sustenance from Adam Seligman's *Modernity's Wager* (Princeton, NJ: Princeton University Press, 2000) and I think Danièle Hervieu-Léger's *Le Pélerin et le converti* (Paris: Flammarion, 1999) highly relevant.

One of the pleasures in reading the most recent literature, which I would like at least to note in passing, is the diminution in the blanket suppositions infecting even the scholarly world only a decade ago. Quite apart from what has been the unhappy adoption and deployment for varied purposes of journalistic rag-bags like "fundamentalism," I notice in particular the shrunken status of views which set the expansion of Pentecostalism under the rubric of American hegemony and which treated its widespread adoption by indigenous peoples as a uniquely unfortunate trespass on authenticity. The last two articles I read before final dispatch of the typescript of this book, by Stephen Hunt and Luisa Elvira Belaunde in *The Journal of Contemporary Religion* 15:3 (2000) (footnote 16, chapter 1; and footnote 12, chapter 5), indicate where we are now with regard to those particular moral panics. And Steve Bruce's authoritative *Fundamentalism* (Cambridge: Polity Press, 2001) conspicuously does not sweep Pentecostalism under that label. Slowly the Sunday supplement view of the world is being undermined, though it certainly exacted its costs when first challenged. Moral panics, even liberal ones, are poor guides to the complexity of the contemporary world.

A further complementary volume is *Betterment from on High*, written by myself and Bernice Martin, to be published in due course by Oxford

University Press. This is a study in depth of the life-worlds of Pentecostals, and especially their economic ethos, in Chile and Brazil, and is the more direct consequence of the ISEC funding following *Tongues of Fire*. A key to the argument of that book, and a useful sidelight on the present one, is provided in three articles by Bernice Martin: "New mutations of the Protestant Ethic among Latin American Pentecostals" in *Religion* 25 (1995); "The Pentecostal gender paradox" in R. K. Fenn (ed.), *The Blackwell Companion to the Sociology of Religion* published by Blackwell in 2001; and "From pre- to post-modernity in Latin America: the case of Pentecostalism" in Paul Heelas (ed.), *Religion, Modernity and Postmodernity*, published by Blackwell in 1998. I should also say that chapter 3 in this volume is a revized version of an unpublished joint paper written by David Martin with Bernice Martin, for a conference arranged in Costa Rica by Larry Harrison. Obviously much of that paper is by Bernice Martin, notably the sections on contemporary capitalism, and I hope I have not too much abbreviated her careful scholarship and extended references to the literature. Her detailed treatment of economic context and gender will be available in *Betterment from on High*.

One of the problems in a book such as this is the constant appearance of new material, in this case in the quite short space of half a year between writing in October–November 1999 (with further revision in the early Spring of 2000) and a final overview after comments in August 2000. In the end one has to let it go "with all its imperfections on [its] head." But I could have made more of the rise of charismatic Catholicism especially in Latin America, which has received attention recently from Peter Clarke and Andrew Chesnut. The neglect of that topic by comparison with liberation theology is easily explicable, and tells us what we already knew about the way sympathy and hope for the poor affect objective assessment of influence. Anthony Gill's *Rendering Unto Caesar. The Catholic Church and the State in Latin America* (Chicago and London: University of Chicago Press, 1998) is illuminating and incisive on that matter, as is Manuel Vásquez's *The Brazilian Church and the Crisis of Modernity* (Cambridge: Cambridge University Press, 1998) frank – if obscurely couched – reassessment from within.

On a rather different point put to me – about the usefulness of life histories and the sense they give of people embedded in everyday activities – some have already been published in David Martin, "Bedevilled," in R. K. Fenn and D. Capps (eds), *On Losing the Soul* (Albany, NY: State University of New York Press, 1995), but most are reserved for *Betterment from on High*.

Late in the day, one also comes across important new materials which have to be slipped in footnotes, for example articles and critiques sent me by David Maxwell touching on the debates over Pentecostalism in

Africa and involving such distinguished scholars as Paul Gifford and Harri Englund. I have also been sent fresh material by Patricia Fortuny on La Luz del Mundo and have encountered more of the work of an emerging Pentecostal intelligentsia at Selly Oak (Birmingham University) under the aegis of Alan Anderson, and at the Oxford Centre for Mission Studies under Vinay Samuel. The "World Christianity" project centered on Brian Stanley at Westminster College, Cambridge has been a stimulus and major resource.

With regard to the Pentecostal intelligentsia, I have had helpful contacts with Douglas Petersen (El Salvador), Arturo Piedra Solano (Costa Rica), Ivan Satyavrata (India), and Joseph Suico (Philippines). They have obviously owed much to Walter Hollenweger as pre-eminent father of Pentecostal Studies, as well as to José Miguez Bonino, and to the more recent stimulus provided by Harvey Cox in his insightful and lively popularization *Fire From Heaven* (New York: Addison-Wesley, 1994). One would like to know what future trajectories are suggested by Alan Anderson and Walter Hollenweger (eds), *Pentecostals After a Century. Global Perspectives on a Movement in Transition* (Sheffield: Sheffield Academic Press, 1999), by Douglas Petersen's *Not by Might nor by Power. A Pentecostal Theology of Social Concern in Latin America* (1996), and by Robert Beckford's writings on Pentecostal liberationism, such as *Jesus is Dread* (1998).

What I have not done, lacking "world enough and time," is fully to acknowledge a wide penumbra of ancillary reading in the historic and contemporary varieties of Pentecostalism and the charismatic movement generally. I think in particular of Edward Cleary O.P., Andrew Walker, Donald Dayton, William Abraham, Irving Hexham, Karla Poewe, Martyn Percy, Margaret Poloma, Russell Spittler, Gary McGee – and Peter Hocken (of *Pneuma: the Journal of Pentecostal Studies*). Happily Grant Wacker's new book, *Heaven Below. Early Pentecostalism and American Culture* (Cambridge, MA: Harvard University Press, 2001), is about to throw major new light on what has been an obscure cultural history.

The hope is that students will find this volume a useful guide to a major contemporary movement, and so it may help finally to say something about its arrangement. The opening in chapter 1 is rather abstract simply because there has to be some indication of the theoretical problems raised, and the second chapter is very extended because one of those problems has to do with "European Exceptionalism." A simpler but still viable version of the book can be read by reading first the last section of chapter 1 and proceeding straight to chapter 3 which, in dealing with global capitalism and the megacity, etc., provides a platform for the wider comparative analysis. Rather than provide an extended bibliography I have indicated some key books and some key bibliographies, in particular that by André Corten. I am also very grateful indeed to

Paul Freston, David Maxwell, David Lehmann, John Walsh, Robin Gill, José Casanova, Gustavo Benavides, Grant Wacker, Grace Davie, David Hempton, Linda Woodhead, and Paul Heelas. Bernice Martin has heard it all, and I owe her in this, and in all else, my gratitude. And what Bernice most kindly heard, Yvonne Brown most kindly typed.

DAVID MARTIN, MARTINMAS 2000

"I don't think God plays well in Sweden," he said.
"God sticks pretty close to the equator."

John Updike, *Bech at Bay*, p. 126

"I look upon all the world as my parish."

John Wesley, *Journal*, 3 July 1759

proposed argument

The World Their Parish: Pentecostalism as Cultural Revolution and Global Option

The book deals with the largest global shift in the religious market place over the last 40 years: the astonishing rise of Pentecostalism and its associated penumbra of charismatic Christianity. The first chapter deals with the sheer size of the phenomenon, which on a conservative estimate includes about a quarter of a billion people, mostly concentrated in the developing world. It then analyzes its roots in Methodism, treated as an earlier mobilization in the North Atlantic world. Following on from that it shows how the religion of poor whites fused with the religion of poor blacks to create a potent amalgam capable of crossing the cultural species barrier and taking off on a global scale. The chapter concludes with the kinds of social niche most receptive to Pentecostalism: the respectable poor seeking to enter the modern world in Latin America and Africa; the new middle classes of West Africa and South-East Asia, including the Chinese diaspora; minorities tucked away from the main centers, for example in the Andes or Nepal or inland China. A comparison is offered with global Catholicism, the main Christian rival, setting out their different advantages.

The second chapter is theoretically the most demanding because it seeks to frame the very different situations in North America and in Europe, compared to the developing world. In North America Pentecostalism proper is subordinate to Evangelicalism and various new forms of charismatic movement, and that pattern is repeated in the "old Commonwealth" and Britain, though with smaller proportions of population involved. In Europe neither Pentecostalism nor Evangelicalism make much impact except in parts of southern Europe (Italy, Portugal) and Eastern Europe (Romania). To explain this requires an examination of European secularity under the rubric of "European exceptionalism," that is, why Europe is so resistant to religious movements compared to everywhere else. An explanation requires a further enquiry into why Latin America is so receptive compared to Latin Europe.

Thereafter in the rest of the book these problems are followed through, beginning in chapter 3 with setting Latin American developments in the context of global capitalism and the rise of the megacity. In chapter 4 various themes are followed through, such as healing, religious development agencies, the economic and political ethos of Pentecostalism, comparisons with base communities, the special appeal to women, and the reform of the nuclear family. Chapter 5 deals with the appeal to minority peoples, initially in Latin America, a theme that is repeated in other contexts in chapters 6 and 7. Chapters 6 and 7 deal respectively with changes in Africa and Asia. In Africa Pentecostalism appeals to young men and women disembedded from traditional contexts and anxious to embrace modernity. In Asia it appeals to emergent middle classes in Singapore, Korea, etc., and to Chinese making the great trek to the megacity. The final chapter brings all these themes together.

CHAPTER ONE

a cultural revolution: sources, character, niches

The most dramatic development of Christianity in the century recently concluded has been Pentecostalism and its vast charismatic penumbra. While Pentecostalism has spread primarily among the poor of the non-western world, the charismatic movement has had a more middle-class provenance, clearly so in the West but also globally. How you estimate the overall numbers involved depends on the criteria you apply, but on a fairly conservative estimate we are dealing with a quarter of a billion people, and so with the most widespread form of non-Roman Catholic Christianity. Broadly understood, Pentecostalism includes one in eight of the Christian "constituency" of nearly two billion, indeed more given how much of that is dormant, and one in twenty-five of the global population. It has therefore to be placed in the context of other massive religious mobilizations, notably those within Islam but also within Hinduism and Buddhism.

For some observers such huge shifts, Christian, Islamic, and otherwise, can be assembled together under the rubric of "Fundamentalism" but there are good reasons for rejecting this catch-all category, quite apart from its journalistic misuse and its pejorative overtone. One is that while Pentecostalism is indeed attached to Christian "fundamentals" and to a conservative understanding of Scripture, the heart of its distinctive appeal lies in empowerment through spiritual gifts offered to all. Another is that whereas Islamic revivalism pursues an organic relation between law, society, and faith, Pentecostalism represents a fissiparous and peaceable extension of voluntarism and competitive pluralism. A third reason relates to understandings which view "fundamentalisms" as reactions against modernization. However, in those parts of the world where Pentecostalism is most expansive, notably Latin America and Africa, any extension of pluralistic voluntarism is arguably a manifestation of modernity. Nor, as will become clear, is that the only respect in which Pentecostalism manifests and advances modernity.

There are even more difficult issues to be canvassed than nomenclature and categorization, which have to do with models of secularization. If Pentecostalism advances pluralism in Latin America and voluntarism in Africa (and elsewhere) then it not only has historical links with the USA, but represents a variant of the North American model of secularization in areas where such a development seemed unlikely. That model is one in which differentiation separates church from state, from territory and local community, and exhibits a partnership between voluntary denominations (including revivalist movements) and modernity.[1]

The question posed is obvious. If indeed secularization according to this model is proceeding in Latin America, then it may be that the very influential Latin European model, which it recapitulated up till quite recently, is historically temporary and geographically local. According to the Latin European style of secularization, there is intense conflict between church and state, and between Catholic clerics and enlightened radicals, and a relation between religion and nationalism varying between mutual support and outright warfare. That, after all, is the context in which the hard version of secularization theory, taken as a package, made most sense, though very significantly modified (as I have argued in my *A General Theory of Secularisation*) for the varied conditions of establishment and partial establishment in non-Latin and non-Catholic Europe. If then European secularity taken as a whole, and not only the southern Latin version, is localized, then it makes sense to discuss the very modest impact of Pentecostalism in Europe under the rubric of what Peter Berger has called "European Exceptionalism." Chapter 2 attempts to do precisely that.

Unfortunately complexity multiplies, because not only does the North American model exhibit a partnership between modernity and voluntary competitive religion, but there is a partial shift in the later stages, round about the beginning of the last century, from Evangelical to Liberal Christianity, most dramatically exemplified in the evolution of Methodism. Such a shift implies that Evangelical Christianity (of which Pentecostalism is a version) belongs to a phase in the process of modernization, with the corollary that the Pentecostalism now so expansive in the modernization of the developing world is likewise a phase. Put crudely, Pentecostalism in the developing world is likely to follow a trajectory of incline and decline, until its devotees all too successfully better themselves, relax their rigor, and "go to school."

However, complexity multiplies again, because it now appears that the Liberal Christian adjustment to modernity in the USA, seen as somehow natural, itself runs into trouble, undermined by its own logic of pluralism, individual choice, and tolerance. The matter is endlessly debated, especially as it impinges on the character, timing, and extent of secularization in the USA, but there is little doubt as to the vulnerability of Liberal Christianity, however big its battalions. At the same time there is some modest agreement as to the reinvigoration of Evangelical Christianity.[2] One stresses the modesty of this agreement because there is a subsidiary debate as to whether yet another sequence of liberalization is proceeding within this reinvigorated Evangelicalism. Given that we are considering an extension of the North American model in the developing world, at least by analogy if not diffusion, these debates clearly bear on the course and future of Pentecostalism in those areas. We have to ask whether Pentecostalism follows the Liberal trajectory in the style of the early twentieth-century USA, emulating in particular the evolution of Methodism from which it partially derived, or alternatively whether that trajectory is itself historically contingent and local.

Nor are such questions straight alternatives, since it is quite possible, even likely, that the Liberal–modern nexus may be *partly* local and contingent, just as the European experience may be partly local and contingent. After all, post-modernity (if one takes that seriously), and the doubt about continuing enlightened hegemony (if one is likewise serious about that), together suggest the old presumptions about sequences of development no longer hold. As the confrontations of earlier stages of modernization in "the West" recede, the alternative logics which evade the more restrictive protocols of reason may reassert themselves. As the academic and intellectual strata lose their grip on the socialization of the young is the world really to be made-over in the image of the faculty club? One way and another it may turn out that universal western predictions are local extrapolations.

Something of the mixture of local and contingent with the universal is implied by the difference between Pentecostalism in the developing world and in "the West," more particularly North America. The contemporary situation is roughly as follows. In the developing world we observe a mobilization of "the damned of the earth," not in the "enlightened" Marxist form so long anticipated (e.g. Ethiopia), but through religion, and so far as Christianity is concerned that means pre-eminently through Pentecostalism – or else through Catholicism, to be discussed below. Liberal Christianity is clearly under pressure in the developing world, even among the elites. However in North America, Liberal Christianity retains a massive hold, especially in the denominational directorates, as does an older non-Pentecostal Evangelicalism. Insofar as Pentecostalism spreads it does so principally through a charismatic movement partly inside the older churches and partly "breaking bounds" in every sense, even displaying faint affinities with New Age "spirituality." Though classical Pentecostalism is vibrant in North America, it remains subordinate. That particular pattern is repeated throughout the North Atlantic world, though the degree of evangelical-charismatic invigoration decreases as one moves from the USA to Canada, Canada to Britain, and Britain to Western Europe. Clearly this gradient needs to be analyzed, a task taking up the rest of chapter 2.

Beyond that, one observes how the charismatic version of Pentecostalism, partly within the historic churches and partly breaking bounds in Neo-Pentecostal and other forms "with signs and wonders," also emerges in the expanding middle classes of the non-western world. These are often part of a transnational business culture with considerable exposure to American cultural radiation, and their adoption of a softened form of Pentecost with more porous boundaries could be fitted into a modified version of standard developmental sequences. Conceivably they too are in a queue awaiting liberalization. Emerging in parallel with them is a Pentecostal intelligentsia, still small, but also open to American cultural radiation, and perhaps ahead in the same queue. One waits with some interest to see how they will handle themselves.

There is a final and important question to do with the relation between the cumulative global impact of the successive Anglo-American empires, an impact which has been as much in the cultural as in the political sphere, and the uprising of (some of) the damned of the earth in the form of the redeemed. The answer to that question is as intriguing as it is unexpected. It lies in a fusion of a populist Christianity, originally coming out from under the Magisterial Reformation of Luther, Calvin, and Cranmer, with a black spirituality, including in that the Afro-Brazilian strain. That has in turn fused with a layer of shamanism from the Andes to Korea and inland China.[3]

This is where the perspective dramatically extends in time as well as in space, and one envisages links with the pneumatic Christianity of the Primitive Church. In the precise sense of the word Pentecostalism is "primitive" Christianity as it emerged two millennia ago on the despised margins of the Roman empire: lay empowerments of the Spirit in alliance with aspirations to holiness and wholeness. These intermittently simmered in the Catholic matrix, which for a millennium acted as the unifying holy ghost of a fragmented Roman imperium, and in the skirts of the established Protestant churches. Eventually they found opportunity to break loose from the constraints of the Magisterial Reformation in Northern Europe, especially as establishments started to cave in across the English Channel and finally to break up across the Atlantic Ocean. On these Anglo-American marches and margins, as I argued in *Tongues of Fire*, radical primitive Christianity expanded as part of successive downward mobilizations, until it reached poor whites and poor blacks, each in different ways moved and "transported." Finally it crossed the cultural species barrier to germinate among the poor, especially poor women, in Harare, Seoul, Lagos, and São Paulo.[4]

That bears restatement because it is crucial. Somewhere in the successive and increasingly unsponsored mobilizations of *laissez-faire* lay religion, running to and fro between Britain and North America, especially between their respective unruly margins in Ulster, Cornwall, Scotland, and Wales, and in Kentucky, Kansas, Texas, and (finally) California, there emerged a many-centered mobilization. In the pullulating matrix of American experimental religion, stomping alongside American modernization, there emerged a potent variant capable of stomping alongside modernization world-wide. It met life-threatening and feckless disorder with personal discipline and collective ecstasy.

What happened following the explosive star-burst at the end of the trail in Los Angeles in 1906, and equally following all the other parallel star-bursts world-wide, was a hurling of people in every direction, carrying with them a fusion of the faith of culturally despised poor blacks with that of culturally despised poor whites. This reached down through semi-stabilized upper crusts of religiosity to a primal layer of spiritual energy. Under intense pressures the modernizing upper levels fired the deep structures, allowing the upward draught of a universal "holy" Spirit to suck a multitude of ambiguous spirits into its inclusive ambit. No wonder that Pentecostalism is so potently ambiguous, because (as I argued over a decade ago) it brings together the most ancient and the most modern, and unites the modernizing thrust to the deep structure of spiritual "animation".

Once this fusion is properly recognized then the combination of Anglo-American genesis – Mow Cop, Staffordshire, Gwennap Pit, Cornwall, the Kingswood miners, the Keswick evangelicals, Kansas poor whites and Los Angeles blacks, backwoods Appalachians, circuit riders on the frontier – with many-centered, near-contemporary and semi-independent manifestations from India to Santiago, Chile, makes sense. So also do the links between American provenance and rapid indigenization, and between a ransacked global English and a polyglot translation of the Hebrew and Christian Scriptures into a myriad languages. David Lehmann has insightfully distinguished between a Catholic cosmopolitan universality, relating itself by accretion and absorption to cultural context, and of recent years consciously pursuing "acculturation," and an unsponsored Pentecostal globalism without such sensitivities (and, indeed, as will be illustrated later, anxious to break out of local context into wider more modern worlds).[5] However, precisely that distinction, perhaps overdrawn, needs to take account of what is *already* "acculturated" in Pentecostalism, as well as that crucial escape from sponsorship which Lehmann rightly emphasizes. (Implicitly, of course, his point raises the question: who are we, if our relativism is genuine, to define authenticity for others, or to deny their capacity actively to appropriate as creative agents just because their choices are not ours?)

In my *Tongues of Fire* I used the metaphor of a "walk-out" from the linked mediations of socio-ecclesiastical hierarchies, into a movement led by energetic cadres of God-made men, trained through long years of practical apprenticeship among those of their own kind.[6] This is how it comes about that we are now hearing the raised voices – the "tongues" – of those not heard from before, sometimes pushy, even brash and nepotistic in the leadership cadres, but ingeniously pragmatic in using every resonance of modern communication to make their presence felt. They, quite literally, have got the microphone and the electronic synthesizer in their own hands.

To understand this walk-out, which has already in some places become a walk-in, so fast is the pace of change, one has to understand how faith works. Faith gives divine permission to speak without certification through the authoritative offer of new names and re-formed identities. It issues open-ended and pressing invitations to come off the highways and byways to forge a new "respectability" in a deep sense of that misused word. It initiates participation in a bounded social space of the like-minded through the exercise of an outrageous religious entrepreneurship. It creates a mobilization from the bottom up by "unlearned and ignorant" men. The fissiparous star-burst that follows has traditionally been accounted the Achilles heel of Protestantism because it leads to a Babel of disjointed rival movements, but in today's rapidly changing world, with its demand for constant adjustment, it can also lead to a jostling Pentecost.

All this means that it does not make much sense to regard Pentecostalism as an imported package, especially in situations – the vast majority – which are replete with multi-cultural transfers, and where there has long been a changing market in the gods. Rather it is a repertoire of religious explorations controlled, though sometimes barely, within a Christian frame and apt for adaptation in a myriad indigenous contexts. In that it resembles the Bible, also controlled, if barely, within an ethical and monotheistic frame. People link their own stories and their group experiences to a narrative moving from slavery to liberty, exile to restoration, and also from the dark dominion of the powers through the engagements of spiritual warfare to the empowerments of the kingdom. The kind of reverential and close reading of the Bible found among Pentecostals makes them familiar with its landscape, intimate friends with its characters regarded as people like themselves, and able to find all kinds of resonances in its dreams, healings, and deliverances, its rebirths, prophecies, and expectations of future transformation. At the same time, Pentecostals will often engage in a luxuriant and mimetic redeployment of local practices, including its modes of authority, but reassembled under a Christian aegis. This is not a kind of promiscuity because boundaries are retained and rigorously marked out. The antecedent forms, and the deep structures of "the archaic," are brought together in an unbroken continuum opening on to modernity. People can dance their way through the rebirths of a great transition, bringing the whole person to bear rather than a split-off segment of the rational self. People are moved as they move, inner drama matching outer. The past is carried forward even as a line is drawn under it. That is why some acute observers mistake it for a recrudescence of popular religiosity – a significant misidentification all the same because antithetical to the charge of being an imported package.

Reworking the Methodist Linkage

In almost all these ways Pentecostalism is an extension of Methodism and of the Evangelical Revivals (or Awakenings) accompanying Anglo-American modernization. However, it inclines more to the American than the British way because British Methodism ran into an upper ceiling of established religion which blunted it, whereas in the USA Methodism was merely self-limiting in ways to be indicated later.

Methodism can be seen, in terms of the suggested sequence of downward mobilizations, and of the groups to which it appealed, as in every way inter-mediate. It traveled in the ambit of a mobile society, a global movement prior to globalization, above all on the American frontier but also on the British frontier in Africa, Asia, and the Pacific islands. In Methodism one sees the ancient territorial emplacements of religion begin to dissolve into fraternal associations, so that John Wesley could genuinely claim, "The world is my parish." As its circuit riders traveled they offered universal good news for the personal choice of multitudes in a way analogous to and even presaging the offer of universal citizenship. However much the believers saw themselves as mired in sin they might still by grace aspire to a Christian perfection, assurance, and holiness, and become "fulfilled" with God. "All things are possible," wrote Charles Wesley and in that claim one recognizes an exuberance which with only a change of key can yield a theology of success and power.

Because Methodism had escaped the social and ecclesiastical hierarchies linked to territory, to automatic belonging, and to state power, it was a cultural revolution rather than a political one. It might exploit this or that political affinity according to its social placement, as when it aligned itself with late-nineteenth-century British Liberalism and later with the Social Gospel, but its primary and original sphere of action was finding the supernatural in the fabric of everyday life. It revised biographies and belonged to the expanding networks of voluntary association between state and individual – that is, to what we now call civil society – as well as creating a zone of peaceable order over against disorder and fecklessness.

Nathan Hatch, the distinguished Methodist historian, has put it as follows, and it is instructive to tick off one by one the different kinds of consonance with a Pentecostalism which (through the holiness branch of Methodism) eventually took over from it.[7]

> Methodism in America transcended all barriers and empowered common people to make religion their own. Unlike Calvinism, which emphasized human corruption, divine initiative, and the authority of educated clergymen and inherited ecclesiastical structures, the Methodists proclaimed the breathtaking message of individual freedom, autonomy, responsibility and achievement. More African Americans became Christians in ten years of Methodist preaching than in a century of Anglican influence. Methodism did not suppress the impulses of popular religion, dreams and visions, ecstasy, unrestrained emotional release, preaching by blacks, by women, by anyone who felt the call. It was under Methodist auspices that religious folk music – white and black spirituals – prospered.

Hatch goes on to note the ways in which Methodism used to be unacceptable just as Pentecostalism is now unacceptable, in particular through loud singing, groaning, bouncing, and sighing. It appealed to aspiring upstarts making up the first wave of competitive religious entrepreneurship. Yet the self-limitation which it eventually encountered even in the USA came about as it began to build Gothic churches and to create universities, one of whose objects was to train its professional ministry in the old east-coast manner. By 1900 it had become the largest and wealthiest Protestant denomination, and the time was ripe for Pentecostalism to pick up Methodism's "unfinished task."

Unacceptability takes many forms, and Hatch comments that even the history of Methodism has been passed over as somehow too close to the American spirit to be distinctive and worthy of note: the primacy of practicality over theory, of sincerity over manners, and of experience over doctrine. Since historians prefer to deal with intellectual history they have found Methodism uninteresting compared with Puritanism. Furthermore, their commitment to ecumenism has motivated them to overlook the way raw dynamism gives rise to splintering, rivalry, and aggressive conversion. Here Hatch emphasizes, as I have done with regard to Pentecostalism, that Methodism represented religious organization taking market form.

In almost every respect Pentecostalism replicated Methodism: in its entrepreneurship and adaptability, lay participation and enthusiasm, and in its splintering and fractiousness. It did so also in the place it offered to blacks and women and that in spite of the splintering over color which occurred in both movements, and in spite of the lack of endorsement for equal ministry as between men and women. Where the two movements differed was in the "third blessing" of Holy Spirit baptism, in the intensity of millennial expectation, and in a shift to a Christ of power rather than the Man of Sorrows. In reality the third blessing and the millennial expectation were closely linked because the gift of tongues presaged the last days. During the time remaining, one was not passively to await the end but to "work while it is still day."[8] Yet such differences may not be all that great. So far as millennial expectation is concerned, we find it present in early Methodism, and one cannot be sure how prominent it remains in contemporary Pentecostalism. As for the shift from Christ crucified to Christ triumphant, that is yet another possible source for a shift to a theology of success – and power.

Harold Bloom, the literary critic, extends Nathan Hatch's analysis by characterizing Pentecostalism as a quintessentially American shamanism in its ecstatic embrace of power. He says that of all versions of the American Religion, Pentecostalism is experientially the most daring in "trespassing upon so many taboos." He sees it as a wild affirmation of self and an acute devaluation of social concerns, without being necessarily identified with the most right-wing among American denominations. It is this spirited relativization of contingent circumstance which gives Pentecostals their appeal to the insulted and injured. (Hence the title of Robert Mapes Anderson's book *Vision of the Disinherited* (Oxford: Oxford University Press, 1979).) As Bloom puts it, "To attend a Pentecostal service, where the Spirit descends upon and among the congregation, is to hear and see the unloosing of authentic forces that seem to emerge from the recesses of being. . . . My one experience of a Hispanic Pentecostal service was a humbling and informative occasion."[9]

In expressing himself with this evident degree of empathy and ambivalence, Harold Bloom belongs to a group of agnostic commentators who clearly recognize a primal presence but who wonder what the upshot may be. André Corten, for example, in recounting his own empathic experience of "the opium of the people," also characterizes it as a form of "theological romanticism" with the authoritarian potentials to which that has sometimes led.[10]

If commentators of the distinction of Hatch, Corten, and Bloom comment on the unacceptability of this kind of religion then one has to pause and ask why this is so, without recourse to such stock literary stereotypes of the evangelical as Sinclair Lewis's Elmer Gantry, Dickens's Chadband, or Augustus Carp. One has to ask why the affluent arbiters of secular and religious opinion should be hard on a religion which is so much the option of the poor, especially of the black female poor. Why should they ignore or at best satirize a faith exuberantly achieving the holism to which they themselves awkwardly aspire?

Such unacceptability is as much a Durkheimian "fait social" as anything else, and as much requiring explanation. Clues already touched on include Pentecostal indifference to notions of authenticity and the way the gains of participation are linked to the vigorous exercise of authority. However, perhaps the major clue lies in the way many Pentecostals embrace social quietism at the expense of analytical social criticism, though they recognize well enough the injustice of their situation. Again, in the turbulent developing world they are viewed as too often inclined to political obedience rather than the romanticism of revolutionary violence.

For them the "world" and "nature" are swallowed up in an ecstasy which divides believers from a secular reality dominated by the age-old Enemy of Mankind. A dualism of faith and world reanimates a primitive Christian vocabulary of spiritual warfare "against wickedness in high places." Perhaps it is this terminology of spiritual war that arouses suspicion, at least by comparison with "struggle," though it can hardly come as a surprise to Catholics, or indeed to anyone steeped in St. Paul, John Bunyan, Charles Wesley, or the cantatas and Passions of Bach. Victory is clearly at the heart of the Christian lexicon and once one has heard a vast congregation of mainly black Pentecostals in Brazil shouting "Gloria" in the Hallelujah Chorus – following close on a performance of "Thanks be to God which giveth us the *victory*" from *Messiah* – the long-term cultural genealogies are hardly in doubt.

The Pentecostal virtues of betterment, self-discipline, aspiration, and hard work are those which in the western experience are assigned to the first, harsh phase of modernization. Though they clearly assist the survival of the poor and help forward fledgling economies, they are dismissible as mere "capitalist work discipline" and have so far resisted translation into contemporary liberal attitudes. Pentecostals belong to groups which liberals cast in the role of victim, and in every way they refuse to play that role. By contrast with those social milieux in which people admire either communitarian obligation or individual autonomy, they obstinately adhere to the disciplines of the nuclear family. As people remote from the political and educated classes and with few resources, Pentecostals concentrate their efforts on "doing good to them that are of the household of faith."

There is also a different though supplementary source of unacceptability emanating from the historic churches. Partly it has to do with dualism in various forms, by which is meant an emphasis on the supernatural, including the miraculous, rather than the orderliness of nature. This is linked, of course, to the recovery of a "primitive" Christianity. However, it has also to do with the kind of theodicy (or justification of the ways of

God) which can be latent in classical Pentecostalism and often manifest in Neo-Pentecostalism. This theodicy spans the whole cultural range from an instrumental attitude towards divine power present in what (for want of agreed acceptable terminology) has to be called "folk" or "primitive" religion, and a consumerist attitude towards faith found on the debatable margins of post-modernity.

This fusion of instrumentality and consumerism is particularly evident with respect to healing from diseases and bedevilments, and includes an implicit or explicit bargain with Providence: give in order that you may receive; have faith and God will save you from the ills that threaten you. This can, of course, simply express a law of spiritual existence to the effect that those who surrender themselves reap an abundant harvest of grace and fulfillment, but quite slight changes of intonation easily lead to major changes of emphasis. One may, for example, recognize that greater bodily and internal well-being follow from a disciplined and faithful life (especially where psychosomatic ills are rife) but then shift towards an inherent link between virtue and achievement, or between faith and a form of Christian body-building. In Neo-Pentecostalism this kind of slick theodicy can play a major role. What had been a consequence of virtue turns into its evident proof, with the corollary that those who fail or fall ill have also failed in faith. Inner devastation follows. Thus the "empowerment" of "the poor," which is usually "acceptable," becomes an embrace of power per se, and of a "God of power and might," most obviously on the part of leaders, which is conspicuously "unacceptable." The "miracles" of restoration undeniably observed among the poor can be redeployed as tinsel advertisements for itinerant wonder-workers.

Resources and Paradoxes of Autonomy and Dependence

The relation of Pentecostalism to modernity as well as to a deep structure of shamanistic power and healing energies should be clear enough. Such a relation, whether direct or indirect, includes internalized conscientiousness and a portable integrity at home and at work, as well as an eminent pragmatism as to means, the principle of voluntary choice and voluntary association in matters of faith, and an aspiration to rise above fickle fortune. But simply to note the consonance of Pentecostalism with modernity (and especially perhaps with the initial phases of modernity) is to place this particular cultural revolution in far too shallow an historical and sociological perspective. It is to deal only in the historical foreground, and to neglect the more profound social dynamics such as those of autonomy and dependence.

After all such central themes as inwardness and a portable and all-embracing integrity were broached millennia ago, not merely in the Reformation, but in early Christianity and the Hebrew Scriptures. This is not to say that these are their only sources or that those who put them forward intended them just as we understand them today. It is to say that they have lain latent in the particular religious ensemble we have inherited, awaiting the successive releases afforded by social circumstance, and what is more, their existence has been an active factor in bringing such circumstance about. The latter point is, of course, crucial in that religion creates latent platforms in consciousness from which new initiatives can take off. They then prove their ability to fly far from their original base without their Christian (or Jewish) names attached.

Take, by way of example, such themes as "Rend your hearts and not your garments" or the law written equally "in the heart from the greatest to the least" or the Pauline injunction to attend first to the circumcision of the heart rather than the ritual incision denoting a particular identity. By persistent extension and deepening, such themes can divest systems of authority of their justification and turn law into a matter of inward judgement and sincerity rather than external observance. Again, to make human solidarity as such the criterion of sympathy, *caritas*, and right action, in accordance with the New Testament model, is to corrode all the compulsory solidarities of particular local societies. To suppose that the universal spirit of power and wisdom can fall on hedge preachers merely because they attend to a call from within or above subverts every principle of social honor, inherent status, and necessary mediation. So, too, does the idea that "all" are priests and kings "unto God," and that anyone can understand the clear sense of Holy Scripture. The whole world becomes an open book, which "he who runs may read." A slave knows how to overhear such phrases as "You are no longer slaves but sons, and if sons then heirs. . . ."

The mere setting forth of such principles in the sphere of faith by implication secularizes the state, and one can see how a prolonged crisis of legitimation has been written into the foundation documents of Christian civilization. It is then only a matter of time and circumstance before such corrosions trickle through initially tiny conduits to undermine every structure at base. That is why the official carriers of Christianity, ensconced in seats of power, will simultaneously propagate its doctrines and restrict their implications, partly to safeguard their own position, and partly because authority, hierarchy, power, mediation, and hypocrisy of some sort are necessary ingredients of *any* kind of civilization.

Once that central paradox of social organization in relation to the Christian dynamic is understood, then it is inevitable that Christianity also embodies principles of obedience in relation to the auras of sacred authority, such as "Fear God and Honor the King," as well as subtle casuistries, and these have to be called into play by particular authorities to defend their position, and indeed by any authority to buttress stability as such. How the implications of re-formation play into the necessary stabilizations required by established power, and how these are bound to be built into the reform itself is clear, for example, from the course of the break-neck changes instituted from above and picked up from below in the short reign of Edward VI from 1547 to 1553. Even then an essential revolution was achieved through the secularization of the state and of its legitimation, which turned out in the long run to be irreversible, as the next century was to prove.[11] The immediate and apparent aim had been to emulate the Hebrew monarch Josiah through the evangelical purification of faith; the long-term consequence, however, was the autonomous Protestant and protesting individual. The fact that the Magisterial Reformation had small interest in democracy or autonomy is irrelevant.

But such ironies and paradoxes are themselves misleading and partial unless related to the complementary paradox of authority. The dynamic of Pentecostal populism, and of its partial restriction within the religious sphere, includes the paradox that autonomy depends on dependence, as equality depends on differences of power, and participation on authority. People acquire and discover their independence through mutual recognition in the assembly or community, "I" to "I," and through authoritative proclamation. They are empowered to speak collectively and individually by *being given* a new name through authoritative conferral. Observers note how vigorously authority is deployed in the Pentecostal assembly, forgetting not only that this is a standard characteristic of revolutions, even when they are restricted to the level of culture, but forgetting also just how dangerous it is to encourage everyone to speak at once. Pentecostalism invites an antinomian anarchy which can only be kept from dissolving the assembly in confusion by exercise of pastoral oversight.

Of course, that exercise of oversight is bound to echo the forms of authority to which believers were used prior to conversion, because the religious transformation is simultaneously a social transition. It has to entail old continuities in a new frame, and so observers too easily conclude that the new elder in the faith is only the old tribal elder "writ large." As already argued, all reformations re-form authority, and inevitably the old models are framed in the new forms. The important point is that these new forms are chosen rather than ineluctable and that the pastor is not bound into age-old and interlinked hierarchies of church, state, and local territorial community. Such linkages may and probably will recur. A Pentecostal leader, like Ezekiel Guti in Zimbabwe, will repudiate and manipulate the local political authorities, just as he repudiates and manipulates his useful contacts in the United States – while deploying a nationalist rhetoric of anti-colonial authenticity. After periods of conflict, excommunication, and withdrawal, rival powers renegotiate a balance of advantages and exchange favors. That is why the Spirit taking hold of those not party to this renegotiation, often the young or a denominational counter-elite, will fracture the solidarity of the religious assembly. Dissidents recognize how peace and consensus can be an ally of the established union of charisma, the powers of office, and selective patronage. The result is bound to be mutual excommunication between leaders and dissidents. Though the "mark" of the Spirit is a hard-won peace and love, its working out is bound to be breakage of fellowship. Consolidation and dissidence, pacification and excommunication follow in cycles as the young men who "dreamed dreams" become elders. Powerful dreamers develop into authoritative interpreters, and "good" and "bad" exchange masks as the dance proceeds.[12]

As with the other revolutionary principles mentioned, this invitation to join together in a shared speech, which converts the Babel of voices into the Pentecost of tongues, is both very old and very modern. It made sense in the *oekumene* of the ancient classical world before inevitable closures channeled it through restrictive forms, and it makes sense now in the "ecumenical" world of global society where you do indeed encounter "all nations, tribes, and tongues." What we see then is not simply a "legitimation crisis" in relation to the unsponsored but their own affirmation of "communicative competence." The avenue for such an affirmation is not rational exchange and competition, but the alternations and comings together of inspiration. Unavoidably, as in every possible kind of situation, rational or inspired, that too has its own potential for the expression of preponderant power, given that some are more gifted in the articulation of hope than others.

Economic Discipline and Psychic Liberation

Having touched on the *longue durée* of pneumatic lay empowerment, and its governing paradoxes, it is worth recalling that global Pentecostalism has a particular and more contingent relation to the changes in economic and social climate since the sixties. On the one hand there has been a reassertion of economic disciplines and on the other the offer of major releases and permissions. In the developed world the permissions and releases can be pursued by quite large numbers of people while ignoring the economic disciplines, at least for a quite extended period of license, but in the developing world the economic disciplines cannot be evaded. Though in the developed world you can accept disciplines in your working life and ignore them elsewhere, in the developing world your disciplines must govern your whole life, or you fall by the wayside – or fall into crime. In Pentecostalism ecstatic release actually fuels conscious discipline; release is the complement of self-control not the alternative.

Thus there is a discernible consonance between Pentecostalism and the simultaneous (indeed, related) advance of global liberal capitalism and "the expressive revolution." Pentecostals work hard and let go; they give satisfaction to the customer and sway to guitars and synthesizers. Nor is this in any way peculiar to them, since as Bernice Martin and Paul Heelas have argued, it is often the adepts of the expressive revolution who most assiduously exploit contemporary consumer culture.[13] Seeming oppositions easily become practical symbioses. Perhaps one might anticipate that as people in the developing world suffer less from exigent conditions, faith will be less a hedge against destitution and more a guarantee of satisfaction.

There is a sliding scale here of shifting validations, whereby (as suggested earlier) the poor do indeed improve their lot and find the evidence of faith in bigger and better congregations and in larger churches with shinier automobiles parked outside. A big God "has done great things for us" which it is up to the believer to emulate. Three generations, perhaps two, are sufficient for this to come about, and perhaps there may be no need at all for an initial phase of humble accumulation once mobile or already affluent people seek alleviation of stress and vacuity in charismatic fellowship. Religion offers its own kind of touching and feeling, and renews individual spiritual power in a shared spirit of collective praise.[14]

Versions of Pentecostalism not only resemble consumer culture but overlap the modes of the modern media. The overlaps began in the early years with the Pentecostal adoption of the journal and the magazine and is found now in a simulacrum of the television show. Religion is remade in the image of business with buildings more like cinemas than churches. At the same time Pentecostalism also produces its own version of an intelligentsia, picking up some of the threads of social and theological criticism. Those it has nurtured and advanced find the faith of their mothers wanting in social awareness and analytic acuity. In particular young women to whom it has offered new opportunities and fresh spaces come to feel frustrated by scant provision for their contribution at the upper levels of the pastorate and administration. As some of the older Bible Schools and institutes seek university status, for example Vanguard University in California, Pentecostalism may create its own intelligentsia and so develop a social critique. If young Pentecostal scholars seek validation from (or in) the schools of the older historic denominations, they put themselves under western tutelage and in time they emulate the style of those denominations in constituting an expert stratum of social critics and commentators. Perhaps this is the channel along which Pentecostalism donates personnel to Methodism just as Methodism has donated personnel to Anglicanism. Perhaps Pentecostal grandmothers may even find their grandsons Catholic prelates.[15]

One of the most interesting aspects of the make-over of religion in the image of the media is the remarkable hostility the secular media show to their religious counterparts. Though the former progressively exclude serious religious debate or worship, nevertheless, they criticize the religious media from a quasi-orthodox viewpoint, as if themselves practitioners of humility and poverty and opposed to egoistic aggrandizement. The moment Pentecostals deploy modern technology to orchestrate responses, or give evidence of financial or sexual impropriety, they are assured of instant negative publicity. The "Word of Life" movement in Sweden, for example, attracted much hostility from the secular media on grounds of deviation from accepted norms. Such hostility is replicated throughout the western world in the way the Sunday supplements characterize all such movements without essential discriminations, and provides a major element in the social construction of unacceptability. It takes care and insight to recognize what is coming about as the "rough beast" moves forward (though Ruskin did just that when he heard the popular preaching of Spurgeon, recognizing that one who enters the pulpit a hairdresser's assistant may leave it an inspired apostle). Elsewhere however, in West Africa or Brazil, the debate may be carried out on more equal terms, as witness the contest between the Universal Church of the Kingdom of God and the television conglomerate "Globo."

Neo-Pentecostalism? Post-modernity?

Much of the preceding argument has been concerned with the relation between Pentecostalism and modernity, supplemented by *sotto voce* hints of a relation between Neo-Pentecostalism and post-modernity. The approach throughout has been to indicate all such relationships by concrete instances and connections rather than to add to a vast literature setting out to define modernity, or debating whether or not such a condition as post-modernity even exists.

However, there are aspects of these questions worth picking up; they take off from earlier remarks about the fit of classical Pentecostalism (and early Methodism) with an initial *phase* of modernization or, indeed, looking at the contemporary scene, as just one version of modernization alongside other versions. The phase referred to is shown up in the contrast drawn by Simon Coleman between the 90,000 or so old-style Pentecostals in Sweden, who make up some 1 percent of the population, and the charismatic "Word of Life" movement based in Uppsala.[16] Whereas the "classical Pentecostals" are an accepted feature of the cultural landscape, with their own newspaper and banking facilities, the latter are – as indicated earlier – treated as a highly undesirable mutation. The Protestant Ethic has switched from the currency of virtue to a conspicuously financial currency and, as Coleman recounts it, the proper service of others has become a form of helping oneself. What was a discipline of self has become a form of self-management collectively promoted as a religious version of the "feel-good" factor. As between the old and the new there is a different mix of the disciplined and the expressive, which in the case of the "Word of Life" generates a spiritually charged aesthetic expressed in rhetoric, media consumption, and physical environment.

Such is the contrast suggested by Coleman, and it fits in very well with the observations of Bernice Martin and others about a transition from the alternation of work and release to a use of expressive modalities within the disciplines of work itself (including God's work).[17] The task may still be exacting, but it requires a mobile self and indeed a powerful persona constantly redeployed to meet constantly shifting situations and exigencies.

This fits well enough with elements identified as belonging to post-modernity: the rapid alternation of environments, and a passage across what were the conventional frontiers of cultural and ethnic identity. Charismatics who embrace this particular style are effectively laying down their own specific tracks across these shifting sands, creating their own mutually recognizable style of transnational, non-denominational identity, and expanding the self to complement an expanding globe. And, curiously, this transition is reflected below the level of classical Pentecostalism as well as above it. The mobile self may be as relevant in meeting the random buffeting of the informal economy of Rio as in contemporary Sweden. In short, though both Neo-Pentecostalism and post-modernity are shadowy and indeterminate entities, there may still be an elective affinity between them.

Global Alternatives to Pentecostalism, especially Catholicism

The advantages and disadvantages of Catholicism as an alternative option to Pentecostalism arise from its residual links to social and ecclesiastical hierarchies, to cultural continuities and folk practice. The roots of Catholicism still lie in territory, birthright membership, the organic frame, communal obligation, and peoplehood. That means that it places a sacred canopy over the average and the religiously relaxed, and lacks a defined and incisive edge. Catholicism can never be at its ease with the fissiparous dynamism of untutored religious entrepreneurship. Even when the Church monitors profound energies through its own version of charismatic Christianity, it has to retain clerical control and mark out limits and boundaries. However attractive its option for the poor may be, the Church can hardly allow the poor to captain their own barque of salvation beyond appropriate mediation or without prolonged processing through the right channels. However subtly folk practices are assimilated to mass devotion and pilgrimages to healing sanctuaries, that is not the kind of literal revelation that comes with opening the holy book, and reading it for oneself in the company of like-minded others. That is why Catholic "fundamentalism" is so unlike Protestant "fundamentalism."

The Catholic mode of entry into the modern world has been very different from the Protestant mode and, above all, different from the mode of Anglo-American voluntarism. For a long time it endeavored to conserve within a single and universal system the mutualities of an organic society *locked together* with the symmetries of ecclesiastic and political power, against the corrosions of individualism, including moral choice, and of capitalism, including consumer choice in religion. Those twin evils were focused most clearly in the Anglo-American cultural condominium. Thus in Argentina at the beginning of the twentieth century, the *revanchisme* of the Catholic Church in alliance with the military identified precisely individualism, liberalism, Protestantism, and capitalism as the enemy, and Anglo-America as the front and head of what was most opposed to a Hispanic Catholic spirit.[18] Even socialism might seem to provide more persuasive analogues to Catholic "integrism" than liberal capitalist individualism and religion offered on the open market. Socialism was, after all, a system based on mutualities like those of the medieval guild, and even trumpeted the recovery of organic relations, so that Catholic radicals could migrate to socialism or even Marxism much more easily than to the free market. The free market was more of a means than a principle, and lacked any governing idea or notion of quality beyond consumption, exchange value, and profit. That was its strength as well as its weakness.

Of course, from the 1890s on the Catholic Church began a halting movement towards modernity (or *aggiornamento*) though within a socially paternalistic frame analogous to the sacred paternalism of the Church itself. Even when the social paternalism was soft-pedaled or jettisoned the ancient linkages stayed put, not only in the public mind but in the presumptions and assumptions of the upper echelons of Catholic societies. As for holy paternalism, it could not be dropped without bringing down the whole Baroque edifice.

What happened everywhere from Hungary to Montevideo and Lima was the opening up of a fissure between Catholic conservation, more or less allied to elements of the *ancien régime*, and different kinds of liberal radical, anti-Catholic romantic nationalist, anarchist, and radical socialist; roughly in that sequence. Latin America and Latin Europe were pre-eminent cases: huge cultural blocs riven apart by social conflicts in which religion was ranged *as such* against the spirit of what the French called *laicité*. What never seriously emerged was the intermediate term of a voluntary and competitive religiosity helping forward and adapting to modernization. That was despised or rejected on all sides as spawning unsystematic accommodation to the varied sentiments of middling people like grocers and clerks, artisans and "respectable" workers. Inevitably the Catholic response was different where Catholicism was aligned with a repressed nationalism or was a minority, as in Germany or Anglo-America. Yet even in the USA, the conflict over "Americanism" acquired serious momentum. Though the "Americanists" won, it has still not been all that plausible to promote capitalism, liberalism, and Catholicism as an undivided trinity in the style of (say) Michael Novak.[19]

Eventually, however, the pressures of modernity in particular national or regional segments of the Catholic Church built up, either because, as in Latin America, conditions were appalling, or because, as in Germany, conditions were already fully modern and comfortable. The dam broke in the 1960s with the Second Vatican Council, and it did so at a time when a partial separation had occurred of ecclesiastical powers and hierarchies from their social co-equals, and the prestige and power of the Papacy had by contrast risen from its abject low point at the beginning of the nineteenth century.[20]

The post-war Catholic Church had adopted various viable strategies at the political level, as well as within its own organization. Politically it accepted democracy, abandoned alliances with organic conservatism, and attempted to promote its interests and values through Christian Democratic (or similar) parties on the Center Right, with a particular eye to combating communism. Internally it had developed a managed participation of the laity, glossed by communitarian emphases, which was worked out in ancillary organizations like Catholic Action and various youth associations, as well as in the conduct of worship. So far as worship went the strategy worked quite well, since it was only symbolic and backed up by precisely the paternalism it was supposed to mitigate, so much so that it was also propagated ecumenically by non-Catholic Churches. So far as Catholic Action and (for example) the "Christian Student Movement" were concerned, they became partly radicalized in some of the local national and regional sectors, and they were in turn followed by the movement of liberation theology, mostly incubated in Europe and the USA, but dramatically fertilized in Latin America.

Thus the openings to the Left, constantly frustrated from the 1830s on, secured a qualified validation within the Catholic Church which at least for a time made good sense in terms of ecclesiastical geopolitics. On the one hand the motivations for liberation theology were moral, faced with the material conditions and social costs of global capitalism in Latin America, Africa, and elsewhere, but on the other hand they were also rational, in that the Church needed to pre-empt the appeal of Pentecostalism or Marxism, or both together.[21] Marxism was a rival form of "integrism", and so compatible at one level, though to a quite limited extent, while Pentecostalism represented the old enemy of free-market Christianity. So far as Pentecostalism was concerned the hope was that it could be countered by the rival attractions of base communities.

The problems of the opening to the left were several, in that the initial phases of liberation theology seemingly threatened the basis of hierarchical control and even a fusion with movements like the "People's Church" in Nicaragua. However, control was in fact maintained and reinforced, especially as it became clear how dependent "base communities" were on the existence of well-disposed bishops. Of course, the global collapse of Marxism relieved the pressure so far as the Catholic hierarchies were concerned. The other side of retaining control was that Pentecostalism retained some of its key advantages, above all the autonomy of its self-made leaders and an arena of participation in which the old hierarchies held no sway. Indeed, it also seemed that Pentecostalism appealed to lower strata than those responsive to Catholic mobilization, whether these were base communities or charismatic groups within the Church.[22] More recently, of course, the Catholic Church has granted acceptability to charismatic Catholicism, especially as it may be extending its appeal downward, only providing that denominational boundaries are re-emphasized together with the Papacy and the Blessed Virgin – a reassertion of the historically effective "notes" of Catholicism.

The two most recent shifts in the global situation of the Roman Catholic Church have been a curving inward or recomposition of the radical impulse of liberationism, and a partial separating out of Catholicism from Christian Democratic Parties, as they have gone into fragmentation with the collapse of their Communist rivals. Quite what that will mean for the future of liberationism is unclear, though it was never more than a minority option even in Brazil, but the upshot is a Catholic Church following a halting course towards the status of a voluntary interest group promoting a particular moral vision.

This is not to suggest that the Catholic reflex of power-seeking has been finally relaxed. In Chile, for example, after Pinochet's departure, the Church attempted – unsuccessfully – to use the moral credit gained by its defense of human rights to turn its moral program into law.[23] Again, in Poland, the Church falsely extrapolated from the support it generated against communist repression to support in the post-communist period for the legislative enactment of Catholic principles. Of course, elite connections remain and the Church has always had an interest in elite education, but there does seem to be a new situation. The two key elements here are the decline of the Marxist threat and the way western individualism has made increasingly problematic any legal implementation of Catholic teaching by the state as, for example, on matters like abortion and divorce. Slowly even the Catholic Church acquires some of the characteristics of a denomination.

Outside the traditional areas of majority Catholicism the Catholic Church is already a denomination, and unhindered by the problems of managing a declining dominance. One says "some of the characteristics" because in certain territories previously colonized, notably in parts of Francophone Africa, it is a partner in power and can to some extent act as a political arbiter. Like other established churches it is also able to perform as a Non-Governmental Organization with a discreet influence on government, or else when conditions deteriorate to mount a critique of corruption and abuse. This it can do aided by long experience, by a high international profile, and by the deployment of international personnel. So far as expert personnel are concerned, the religious orders are a crucial asset, for example, in Korea, the Philippines, and El Salvador. In almost all the respects just canvassed the situation of the Pentecostals is different: their experience is recent, the informal contacts at the same status level are not yet fully formed, and pastors usually lack an international profile.

One consequence of the Second Vatican Council relevant here is the downgrading of those tangible and folk devotions which were associated with "fortress Catholicism" during its long war with modernity and which also had a potent affinity with local indigenous cultures. It was as if the reforming elites of the Catholic Church, with their own rational traditions, had partly compounded with the enlightened rationalism of their elite opponents to remake the Catholic Church and to ignore the way the great mass of Catholics had constructed their faith according to context. As a result the very tangible faith of Pentecostalism, with its concrete spiritual powers, moved into the vacant or over-rationalized spaces, or else segments of the Catholic Church, for example in Africa, mounted their own cultural resistance. Such consequences were ironic given that the reforming sectors of the Catholic Church both aimed to institute a modern church *and* to promote a new respect for local cultural authenticity.

What this brief overview of the Catholic Church in its encounter with modernity, and especially with pluralism, shows is the great importance of cultural factors. Even today a Catholic culture is not as a Protestant culture. In the Protestant world, especially in Anglo-America, the loosening or abolition of ties between *a* church and the state, the social hierarchy and the local community, has meant that cultural revolutions in the religious sphere can be promoted from below, whereas in the Catholic world they will be first resisted and then promoted from above. In that sense even the operations of Opus Dei in Spain represented a modernizing revolution, though at the elite level. The relative popularity of Pentecostalism compared with *basismo* in the developing world reflects just this difference between the autonomous and the managed, although the disadvantages of the former are what strike the observer from the viewpoint of the western academy. It is precisely the unsponsored populist faiths which may on occasion be tempted to collude, naively or culpably, with populist dictators, just as in the past an established Catholicism routinely colluded in defense of its vital interests with dictatorships of the right, some populist and some not.

Both Catholicism and Pentecostalism are global options, offering the two most vital versions of Christianity in the contemporary world, and it is important to emphasize the different ways in which they relate to context. Historically Catholicism attempted imposition followed by accommodation, partly because in the periods of enlightened autocracy followed by liberal nationalism it was not really in local control. In parts of the world, notably Latin America, ecclesiastical administration lacked any serious grip. The modern period, however, has seen an increase both in control and administrative grip in association with centralization in Rome. Of recent years that has meant the policy of respect for local culture already referred to, and even more recently a belated recognition that downgrading Catholic folk practice has made the Church vulnerable. In any case traditional Catholics feel that acculturation dilutes a hard-won identity. Experience teaches. What the Catholic Church cannot do as a centralized system and a global institution is to allow local believers to find out needs and meet them in the Pentecostal manner. Pentecostalism as a repertoire of themes propagated by competitive unsponsored entrepreneurs has no policy about "authentic" culture, because it responds to, and indeed *is*, the market. It is the culturally despised proffering "goods" to the culturally despised.

The other global options are really outside the scope of an initial chapter except to suggest that, to the extent that they embody the organic principle exemplified in Catholicism, they find it difficult to generate the kind of voluntaristic and competitive pluralism of Pentecostalism. Islam, because it is even more organically integrated than Catholicism, generates mass movements aiming to overthrow conservative religious elites as well as enlightened elites and westernizers, and creates a social assistance system for its radical followers in the "wild mosques." Buddhism is very different because its attitude to "the world" makes it the religion of the monk, and yet today it has been able either to graft vigorous voluntary associations on to monastic roots or generate them out of prophetic callings (as well as offering its own "enlightenment" to eastern and western elites). This is the more possible because it is less an articulated institutional system and more a cultural modality manifested in temples and monasteries. Thus the closest "functional equivalents" of Christian pluralism are in the "new religions" of Taiwan and Japan (and their overseas extensions, for example, in Brazil). Once again, the importance of cultural frames is underlined.

Niches

Thus far the argument has contrasted two simplified models: churches based on locality, birthright membership, continuity, and extended familial and communal obligations, where there is some symmetry between religious and social hierarchy, and groups based on individual choice, movement, fraternal association, and the nuclear family. The shift from the one to the other is not a simple switch of denomination but a tearing of the social fabric, since people move out of a web of embedded relationships and choose to belong to a group of fictive brothers and sisters based on a shared moral ethos. In some cases this can even mean a break with national identity and inherited culture, sometimes also involving a transition from a world of rotations to a forward-looking narrative. A new name and revised identity through second birth is therefore brought at a price, which may include a haunting to be dealt with by a discourse of delivery and exorcism.

The question of what niches may favor Pentecostalism is therefore bound up with the radical disturbance of roots, including traditional sources of authority and social control, and the accelerating compression of time and space in contemporary global society as people move about and become aware of new horizons and the options realistically open to them. They may embrace these options before they move, by way of anticipation, or after they have moved, or en route, but the key lies in a religious "movement" accompanying and facilitating the movement of people. In particular, as relations in the countryside are disrupted by agrarian reform, capitalist relations, or state action, the religious fraternity, which is to a large extent a sorority, forms a caravanserai. It transports believers in more senses than one and provides reception centers as they arrive in impersonal megacities, or else provides a depot to which they gravitate after corrosive experience of such places.

As believers acquire and reach out for this portable identity they also establish an inner compass or conscience built up by taking "readings" each from the other and by shared reading in the narrative of the pilgrim people of God. They also need and receive manuals of guidance for their new life which advise and encourage them how best to accomplish their spiritual re-vision. They are also buoyed up in their self-discipline by the discipline and discipleship of their fellow-travelers. Such a discipline is particularly important for men, as they are faced by the fragmentations and insecurities of a new world and drawn to the predatory agenda of the male peer group. Whereas women mostly fulfil their familial responsibility, men in situations such as obtain in the megacity need to acquire an inward discipline sustained by group obligations, sanctions, and respected roles. Street and home are rival pulls, and the voluntary group, with its standards imposed equally on women and men, is a hedge against chaos and a pledge of mutual support.

This is the paradigmatic transition where one may locate "classical" Pentecostalism today, for example, the Assemblies of God, a body which in many places makes up about one in three of the Pentecostal family. The Assemblies of God and similar bodies like the Methodist Pentecostal Church in Chile are rafts for the respectable poor. The poor hold on tight to the rules of the raft and to their barely achieved gains, as they move towards relatively safe collective havens, and maybe into the lower middle class.

However, there are also many for whom such bodies are too centrally controlled. These are people in the informal economy who create an equally informal economy of faith made up of a myriad micro-enterprises, some of them run just by husband and wife. Most Pentecostal churches are of this kind, and they abound everywhere from Lagos to Seoul and Santiago, honeycombing the poorer sectors. They operate under a thousand names in the interstices between the stable frontages of the larger churches. These are the "little people" running their own show, often at the margin of viability, and sometimes they will make up (say) one in five of the Pentecostal family.

Such micro-enterprises contrast sharply with the megachurches, which are communities often offering a wide range of services, some mainly for the very poor but some for middle-class clienteles. The Universal Church of the Kingdom of God in Brazil, and its rival, God is Love, constitute one kind of megachurch with an extensive constituency among the poor, and especially the black poor. One might characterize them as main-street, cut-price emporia, in which popular religion is repackaged in the Pentecostal format: the repudiated ghosts of the past *sotto voce* reassembled and controlled under the presidency of the Holy Spirit. Their buildings often look like cinemas or hangars, opening all day on to busy thoroughfares. Here tumultuous religious business is transacted, sometimes resembling the traffic of Catholic side altars but without a dim religious light to suggest ritual or piety. The main religious "entertainments," complete with comperes and ushers, often resemble lively soap operas, but their message nevertheless is psychic liberation. They operate in the random world of the big cities turning the inexplicable rotations of mundane luck into the donations of Providence.

The churches just mentioned happen to be distinctly controversial examples from Latin America, but the megachurch is found all over the developing world (as well as in the United States, where indeed it originated). Some of the largest are in Seoul, Korea and, as in Brazil, some of them repackage popular shamanistic practice in Christian form. On the one hand their members have the sense of making up a multitude which cannot be ignored, and on the other their more intimate requirements are met in a myriad cell-structures.

In the middle-class variants, megachurches cater for new professional and business people, or for potential elites (or counter-elites) with university backgrounds. Some of these churches will be formed *de novo* in a style appropriate to the clientele, and others will gravitate upwards away from the stricter disciplines of an older Pentecostalism. Professional and educational cadres may meet in comfortable living-rooms, where they find a friendly environment, a gentle participatory style, and an atmosphere supporting the integration of the family. The business equivalent, such as the Full Gospel Business Men's Fellowship, may emerge in the same way, attracting successful members of Pentecostal churches and then becoming the effective core of their devotional life and social activity. In some places, for example Argentina or parts of East Africa, these fellowships and charismatic enterprises will smudge the older denominational boundaries or simply proclaim themselves "Christians." Those involved in their running, and indeed many who belong to them, will entertain transnational vistas and relate to others of like mind in other countries, including the USA and diasporas in Europe or South East Asia. Many of those belonging to the Chinese business class in diaspora are attracted to such groupings. This is a fluid milieu where people recognize each other by spiritual affinities and where "executives may cry," and it often includes historic churches "in renewal."

On the whole charismatic fellowships and new-life churches do not extend above the emergent middle classes but there are a few places, such as Guatemala, where elite cadres feel at home in a warm evangelical discourse supporting their aspirations and buoying up their increasing confidence in an expansive future. Here influential people gather in well-appointed and even plush venues, sharing common concerns and anxieties in an atmosphere of pious animation. They will absorb a literature of advice on how to handle ethical and personal problems, and how to deepen their inner life. Whether you are of Catholic or Evangelical background may not be all that salient.

Pentecostalism (and associated charismatic movements) find a quite different kind of niche deep in the interior of major civilizations or at the margin among ethnic groups which seek differentiation from the wider whole, and want to exchange inferior status for modernity. Perhaps suppressed for centuries, as in Latin America and the Philippines, and knowing that their culture is dismissed in stereotypical terms as backward, they find in Pentecostalism a chance to leap over their immediate environment to a wider world. Whereas previously viewed as dissolute or as colorful exhibits for the benefit of the tourist gaze, they dramatically "better themselves" and modernize, so overturning the stereotype. Of course, there may also be losses here in overall communal solidarity, of the kind documented by anthropologists. But it is difficult to see how or why such groups are to be sealed off, or how comprehensive change, including modern medicine, can be held at bay. Even a nationalistic reassertion and recreation of "traditional" culture such as may be seen in parts of Mexico (or in the Mari El Republic of Russia where the intelligentsia promotes paganism) is a characteristically "western" import.

Where conversion is to Evangelicalism it by no means depends on missionaries. Once people acquire extended horizons through their own mobility or the media, new messages do not need messengers. Whether one considers people on the Papuan border in Irian Jaya, or in the Tibeto-Burmese valleys of Nepal, or gypsies in Eastern Europe, they review themselves in global perspective. Sometimes that review affects a whole people, or an outer segment, or one particular local genealogy rather than another. Moreover, they do not swallow Christianity as a package but creatively appropriate it, sometimes turning the message back against those who brought it. If Mrs. Baker Eddy of Boston mingled the Bible with what she believed were contemporary notions of science and health, so too do many Africans.

What one perceives with regard to contemporary global Christianity is a spectrum of appropriations selected according to circumstance, with Pentecostalism appealing most to those who have quite recently detached themselves from local practices, obligations, and authorities, and are most anxious to find their footing in the modern world. They wish to draw a line under so recent a past. That is why in the African context in particular, but not only there, they can both incorporate previous practices and demonize them, or create a new version of a traditional witchcraft eradication movement. A previous culture functions in a new format. It is in Africa too that modern communications technology makes possible large "imagined communities" of Pentecostals beyond the local memberships, so that Pentecostalism not only relates to local context but occupies and adapts to a much more extensive social space. That social space is mostly not defined by a homogeneous global character but, as David Maxwell points out in the African context, a distinct transnational regional identity.[24]

One final element in this religious recombinant genesis includes fresh appropriations of the Old Testament (as well as a philo-Semitic tradition of Christian Zionism derived from readings of prophecy concerning the Jewish role in the end-times). The Old Testament narrative, with its emphasis on the origins of a people, can be transferred in such a way as actually to create new peoples, with or without territory. The Mormons, for example, are simultaneously scattered round the world and concentrated in a territory, while the Witnesses are aliens in all nations, often to their cost. One of the more dramatic cases of Judaizing is found in The Light of the World church, which is in diaspora over much of Mexico and the USA, but also has a temple and a Vatican City (or New Jerusalem) of its own in Guadalajara in the state of Jalisco. If one wants evidence of the creative appropriation of a fundamental biblical narrative and its relation to local cultural contexts one need look no further.

CHAPTER TWO

north america and europe: contrasts in receptivity

The Framework and Some Themes

The problem surveyed here is the variable distribution of Pentecostalism, Evangelicalism, and free-ranging charismatic movements throughout "northern" Christianity from California to the Caucasus. A key element in that concerns why Pentecostalism proper plays a relatively minor role in northern Christianity compared to the major role it plays in "southern" Christianity. Of course, northern and southern are not strictly geographical expressions because the "south" begins at the Mexican border and the Caribbean – and parts of West Africa.

The framework utilized for gaining some understanding in these matters rests on a continuum of "cases" running from the USA to Britain, proceeding then to northern "Protestant" Europe and southern Catholic (or Latin) Europe before concluding with those countries of Central and Eastern Europe, whether Catholic or Orthodox, absorbed by communism from 1947 to 1989. Travelling along this continuum one observes a steadily decreasing receptivity to Pentecostalism or Evangelicalism, but there are also two significant breaks or caesuras. The first is the break between the USA with its nearly 300 million people and all the rest of the northern Christian world, comprising some 600 million. The second is the break between all Protestant cultures and the Catholic or Orthodox traditions of Southern, Central, and Eastern Europe. One notable feature of the continuum is the ambiguous condition of Britain, making it a kind of axis, sometimes bracketed with the USA, sometimes with Europe.

Mostly this approach follows what I originally devised in *A General Theory of Secularisation* (1978) (as well as in certain chapters of *Tongues of Fire*), except that the analytic tools of social differentiation and increasing pluralism are relegated to the status of background assumptions. The focus here is on differences as these are channeled by historic filters and contingencies and these cannot properly be understood by appealing to general and abstract processes.

One needs to pay particular attention to the two breaks in the continuum because they are related to massive sociological and historical questions with reference to which I can only make sketches and suggestions. The first, between the USA and "the Rest" (i.e. Britain and Europe), has been labeled by Peter Berger the question of "European Exceptionalism." What is at stake here is which of these two broadly contrasted patterns, the American and the European, is to be regarded as exemplifying the standard process of secularization. Is the USA peculiar in its religiosity (even allowing maybe for such factors as a late urbanization) or is European secularity, genuine if exaggerated, due to various special and maybe temporary factors?

If such an issue seems odd by implying the existence of standard paths as compared with deviant ones, then one needs to recollect that secularization, as observed process and as explanation (both rooted in European experience and thinking), was regarded as an unchallengeable norm until the mid-sixties. In 1965, however, I initiated a critique, the first of a number by people like Glasner, Greeley, Stark, and others, each from varied premises, and these critiques at least had the effect of rendering the European experience problematic. José Casanova's account in *Public Religions in the Modern World* set the issue of secularization in a magisterial context, emphasizing differentiation as its viable core by comparison with rationalization and privatization, and further challenging the normative character of the European model.

One of the evident problems was a lack of attention to those historical filters discussed in my *A General Theory of Secularisation* which inflect such processes as differentiation (and associated pluralism) and are required to make sense (say) of the dramatic difference between lively religiosity in a pluralistic USA and apathetic religiosity in a collapsing monopoly such as the Church in Sweden. Among these neglected historical filters were the differences between the French and Italian Enlightenment, the German Enlightenment, and the Anglo-American Enlightenment, exemplifying hostility in the first two cases and a degree of co-operation elsewhere. Thus Peter Berger's formulation of "European Exceptionalism" takes off from critiques of the supposed norm and dramatizes an alternative approach at least worth trying heuristically to see what it yields.

The second break in the continuum is that between all Protestant cultures and all Catholic or Orthodox cultures. The key markers on either side of this second break will be suggested in due course, but at this point it is only necessary to underline the historical confrontation between militant Catholicism and militant secularity beginning with "the"

Enlightenment, each seeking monopolistic powers, with no intermediate space for the kind of pluralism found in voluntaristic and competitive Evangelical Protestantism. It follows that, with one or two significant exceptions, Southern, Central, and Eastern Europe are decidedly unfruitful fields for Evangelical and Pentecostal sowing.

Inevitably, that broaches another feature of Europe's postulated "exceptionalism," which is the difference between the lack of receptivity in Southern Catholic Europe and the extraordinary receptivity evident in southern Catholic "Latin America." So there is a further complication in the analytic task because not only do we have to explore variations in northern Christianity between the USA and "the Rest," and the variations as between Protestant and Catholic cultures, but the difference within Catholicism between "southern" Latin Europe and southern Latin America. Analysis has to face in several directions.

Before sketching how that analysis might be pursued there has to be a brief thematic index as to which factors might be especially relevant as sources of difference and variation, alerting readers to what they should look for. One theme has to do with effects of earlier religious mobilizations, more particularly in the northern Protestant world and beginning with German Pietism and the Anglo-American Evangelical Revivals and Awakenings. Clearly familiarity with Evangelical revivals not only prepares the way but also blunts the edge of novelty and pre-empts a space. Moreover, if religious mobilizations successively travel, if in a very jagged fashion, down the social scale, as suggested in *Tongues of Fire*, then by the time poor whites, poor blacks, and poor women are reached, the provenance of Pentecostalism is restricted to a particular social niche, and even there other alternatives already exist. By contrast, in European Catholic societies mobilizations either take place within the Catholic format, or largely outside the religious arena altogether, while in Latin America the relative absence of previous mobilizations, in spite of resistances and millenarian movements in a culture still spiritually animated, means that vast masses are vulnerable to conversion. Indeed, as has been often suggested, it may be that in the Protestant cases successive downward mobilizations involved a rough parallelism between salvation and the extension of citizen rights, whereas in Latin America the domination of masses by elites, with citizenship too often a formal category, means that a large-scale mobilization takes place in religious form. At any rate, the contrast is clear between a steady effusion of charismatic motifs in Protestant cultures, inside or outside historic churches, and a vast volcanic eruption in Catholic Latin America.

A closely related theme is the contrast between the operations of secularizing elites in Protestant cultures and of secular*ist* elites in Catholic ones. In European Catholic societies these elites can attempt to monopolize cultural reproduction on the Catholic model (especially in France, a major distributor of influences) whereas in Latin American societies these levers are broken or only partially available, except in a semi-European society like Uruguay. In Protestant cultures one observes (to this or that degree) undramatic shifts from mild sympathy towards religion to mild antipathy. In the key areas of welfare, media, and education, sometimes nominally under ecclesiastical aegis, rationalization and professionalization are associated with pre-emptive strikes in favor of secularity by personnel on the ground, sometimes cued from above. One factor affecting how this operates is the degree of effective centralization compared with federalism and an associated dispersal of cultural power. Another way to express this is to suggest that in the federal structure of the USA the secular intelligentsia lacks the power or status to inhibit the reproduction of religious sub-cultures, in spite of the grip of a sub-intelligentsia on the media, whereas in France the political class and intelligentsia have both the status and the power to inhibit religion, as witness the recent law to rein in religious dissidence. In this, as in so much else, Britain is an intermediate instance: federal in its religious sub-cultures but centralized (until recently) in such institutions as the BBC.

If the above themes are linked, so are the two which follow. These have to do with the relation between religion and nation-building, particularly liberal nation-building, and between religion and liberal economic individualism. Taking each in turn, it can be suggested that whereas in the USA there is an alignment between adjustable competitive religion and the creation of the nation and its economic ethos, in Europe there is what I label "a misalignment of discourses." Britain, in between, is a complex case, moving backwards and forwards between the US and European models, though with periods when nation, economic ethos, and religion were closely allied.

Taking nation-building first, religion in Protestant societies has generally been positively involved, at least to begin with, in part because of the (lengthy) philo-Semitic tradition which links new nation with new Israel: Ulster, Holland, Britain, and America are obvious instances. In the long run this can leave Protestantism trapped in an identification with state and nation that becomes seriously problematic with increasing ethnic and religious diversification. However, in the USA that problem is precisely the starting-point for the creation of the new nation, and a secular or Deist constitution separating church and state can actually allow the enlightened structures to rest on the base provided by piety, most of it initially Protestant, but gradually extending its range without too much disruption.

As I suggested in *Tongues of Fire* there is also a positive relation between Protestant piety and "peripheral" regional consciousness, whether in Scotland, Wales, or Ulster or in the post-bellum American South, or in Western Canada, and indeed there has been a sympathetic exchange between these cultures. However, there is a very significant difference between a vast periphery like the American South and the defensive enclave of regional piety pressured by "the center" in Britain (e.g. North Wales) or in Scandinavia (e.g. Jutland). In that context the appearance of Neo-Pentecostal movements in metropolitan areas like Helsinki may be a portent. The older rural revival is very different from the urban megachurch.

With regard to Catholicism there has been a tension between nation-building and the Church, especially in France and Italy – and also in Germany, though for different reasons – which was too often linked to alliances between the Church and threatened hierarchical structures. That has reinforced conflict between ecclesiastical and secularist "state-bearing" elites, as well as generating an anti-liberal Catholic critique capable of being radicalized once old social alliances with land or military have atrophied or been jettisoned. As for regional consciousness, "peripheral" micro-nationalism, or repressed nationalism, Catholicism has frequently been allied to these, because they are so often under pressure from the secular centre, e.g. in Ireland, Poland, Brittany, and Croatia. One would not have expected these impacted solidarities to be at all sympathetic to religious pluralism and evangelical or Pentecostal incursion.

As for the relation between religion and a liberal economic ethos, there is the usual continuum between "the Continent" and the USA, with Britain moving uncertainly in between, but it may be worth suggesting that the discernible architectural unity of Europe, including Britain, from Monreale in Sicily to Durham in England, and Trondheim in Norway, is also replicated – with perhaps Calvinist exceptions – in a Catholic residue present throughout the whole region. Such a residue is conspicuously absent in the USA. Catholic approaches, rooted in the *longue durée* of Europe, favor organicist or at any rate communitarian solutions over liberal individualistic ones. This is one of the problems about providing "a soul" for a capitalist Europe and it leads to intermittent tensions between ecclesiastical and secular elites which can be also considered part of what I call "misalignment of discourses." (Who is right, of course, is a different matter.) In the USA such a critique of liberalism tends to be confined to the Catholic and Protestant clerical directorates.

This, then, is a governing frame supplemented by a thematic index for examining in turn three main civilizational complexes along a continuum: the northern Protestant or post-Protestant world from Vancouver to Leipzig, the Catholic world of Southern Europe (counterposed in addition to Catholic Latin America) and the world of Central and Eastern Europe overprinted by communism 1947–89. Taking northern Protestantism first, one begins in the west with the USA and travels east to Germany, thus working back along the historical trail of mobilizations which stepped westward from Wittenberg and Halle in Germany to Britain and finally to the American East and the Far West of Los Angeles.

In the following analysis, the USA is taken first as the extreme end of the Protestant continuum, and perhaps, taking into account its original template, the only Protestant nation in the world. But that apart, the USA was a major matrix of Pentecostalism, and its contemporary role at the center of global communication make it a major distributor of Pentecostal messages and messengers, for example through Filipinos who came, picked up the messages, and took them home. None of this is to be taken as some refurbishment of the discredited notion that Pentecostalism is somehow the religious arm of American hegemony. The real situation is ambiguous and paradoxical: what has so many American connections is also capable of rapid indigenization in which the ex-empires strike back.

The sequence of discussion then describes the transfer of power from the old global capital in Britain to the new capital in the USA, then takes up the theme of the USA as a potent transnational center of messages, until it finally surveys the key issue as to why there is decreasing receptivity moving eastward from Atlanta to Leipzig, and why Pentecostalism plays a relatively minor role throughout, compared with its expansiveness elsewhere. (I should add that the intellectual debts here are too multifarious to footnote, but they conspicuously include Grace Davie, Steve Bruce, Bryan Wilson, Rodney Stark, James Hunter, Penny Marler, Robert Wuthnow, Wade Clark Roof, Robin Gill, Roger O'Toole, Reginald Bibby, José Casanova, Karel Dobbelaere, Roberto Cipriani, Seymour Martin Lipset, George Rawlyk, Hugh McLeod, Jon Butler, Mark Noll, and Andrew Walker – as well as, in slightly different contexts, Jonathan Clark, Adrian Hastings, Anthony Smith, John Walsh, Linda Colley, David Hempton, René Rémond, and Felipe Fernandez-Armesto.)

The North Atlantic Fulcrum

Today the fulcrum of the North Atlantic (and indeed the Oceanic) axis turns on the USA, with a major penumbra of other societies – Australia, Canada, New Zealand, the Caribbean – also linked historically with Britain and (partly in consequence) sharing many cultural characteristics with respect to law, language, polity, religion, federal organization, and common historical, philosophical, and literary reference.

Any contemporary analysis has to begin with the USA, whereas at an earlier period, perhaps a century or a century and a half ago in 1851, at the time of the first Great Exhibition, it might have begun with Britain. The USA has become, like any other empire of the past, the center of global radiation, religiously, culturally, and economically. Today the four centuries of interchange and mutual religious investment between North America and the island littoral of Europe in Britain has reached a point where Britain receives much more than it gives out. There was a major shift in the last quarter of the nineteenth century, and then further shifts as Britain was weakened by the two world wars and essentially bowed out in 1956 at Suez.[1] As late as 1914 the secular radicals of Latin America looked to the whole North Atlantic tier of the USA, Britain, and Germany, as the lead societies, where progress and Protestantism went together. It was these countries which were encouraged to send their Protestant migrants to Latin America: the Scots and Welsh, the Germans, and (after 1865) Americans from the defeated South. The railways of the continent testify to the British role, as do many minor markers, such as Liverpool in Guatemala and a station in Santiago named after Cochran, who was instrumental in creating the Chilean navy.

What then can be said about the USA as the global capital of Protestantism and capitalism? Too much can be said, and too little. Too much can be made of the export of the American "power of the Spirit" if you see the process as consciously planned, as would be the case in France, or if you stress the impact of hundreds of organizations sending out thousands of missionaries (especially after the post-war expulsions from China). Like the earlier British empire to which it is lineal successor, the American imperium exports itself "in a fit of absence of mind." As for the missionary, neither he nor she is the critical agent, or remotely necessary, since all sorts and conditions are now traversing the globe carrying messages in their own persons. Every traveler is a messenger, and the trail runs above all along personal networks.

On the other hand too little can be made of American influence if you neglect the attraction of the myth of America, as land of liberty and opportunity, for peoples with little enough of either. America is much more popular with the great mass in Latin America, for example, than is Europe. Though the guardians of sophisticated national cultures and the elites of emergent nations may advertise the dangers of American goods (while ensuring adequate access to them on their own account), the poor, the unfree, and the ethnic minorities threatened by local majorities seek them out. After all, the wall below San Diego keeps eager entrants out where the Berlin Wall kept desperate fugitives in. President Clinton is wildly welcomed in West Africa and a similitude of the Statue of Liberty was paraded in Tianenmen Square, Peking.

Of course, television is a major exporter of myth and image. Just as millions of people carry messages everywhere, so millions of messages reach people everywhere. People desire the goods of every kind which these messages advertise, and it is a poor Central American pastor who has not visited the USA, and a very poor slum dweller in South America who has never watched Elvis Presley – or a televangelist, local or American. What is physically seen by those on the move is visualized by those still at home. If anybody it is the evangelicals who speak warily of the American goods displayed on television because they conspicuously include the evils of moral chaos, family break-up, and consumer hedonism.

In an argument focused on global developments, more particularly in the developing world, it would take too long to recapitulate the vast literature on American Protestantism in general and Evangelicalism in particular. The crucial points are in any case simple. Whatever the eventual size of its Catholic minority or even the postulated arrival of a "Catholic Moment," the template laid down over four centuries has made America the first and only Protestant nation on earth. North America brought to explicit fruition what was elsewhere implicit potential cancelled by unpropitious circumstance: the individual inwardness of Luther, the godly city of Calvin, as well as the combination of church–state separation, pluralism, voluntarism, and Puritan asceticism trundling in the wake of England's aborted republican revolution 1642–60. The English appeal in 1642–7 and again in 1688–9 was to ancient rights, lately denied, and to constitutional liberties hardly won. That became in 1776 a rather different appeal, which was not only to "the free system of English laws" (in the words of the Declaration of Independence) but to self-evident, universal, enlightened principles.

In a similar manner the English sense of nationhood, based on a unique unity of language, territory, law, and polity, forged in the protected space of an island fortress, became the American sense of new nationhood, picking up and developing that unity in the protected space of a vast island continent. England, the first self-conscious nation, defined with messianic overtones in a declaration of independence from Rome, gave birth to the yet more expansive messianism and a first new nationhood eloquently framed in a declaration of independence from the British monarch. Ideas could be freely nurtured and implemented in vast open spaces, and an ethnic hegemony enjoyed beyond reach of any serious enemy once the Anglo-Americans had defeated the French in 1763. The protected experiments of an island became the protected experiments of a continent, far from the rancorous territorial rivalries of Europe.

So, as the Protestant foundation of British North America became by evolution and revolution the United States, the increasingly populist mobilizations of Evangelicalism converted the country into a power-house of missionary impulses rivaling Britain and Germany.[2] Power in one kind is power in other kinds. Cultural radiation follows geopolitical eminence, and that is specially the case where empires justify them-selves, or increasingly have to justify themselves, in terms of ideas and their own boasted principles. Gandhi and Luther King were fired by principles only half-implemented, and in Gandhi's case they were the principles of J. S. Mill "On Liberty."

The "goods" exported by the expansive empires of Britain and Amer-ica not only included the writings of Paine, Mill, Locke, Franklin, and Jefferson, but innumerable pedlars of divinity, beginning with Wesley, Coke, and Whitefield.[3] The enlightened writers and the pedlars of divin-ity had their own internal difference but a voluntaristic piety provided a stable base for a social world in rapid motion. Paine, after all, not only came out of a partly Quaker background, with a genealogy leading back to the initial revolution in England, but also had a period as a Methodist preacher. And Paine was a guardian spirit for both the American and French revolutions, however much ignored later in America, and pushed aside in France. Of course, Wesley and Paine would not have got along any better than Wesley and Beau Nash, but Wesley's "enthusiasm" cer-tainly did not exclude rational discourse or radical innovation. There was room for creative co-existence here such as hardly existed in France, Spain, or Italy.[4]

Religion, Migration, the USA, and Transnational Contacts

Globalization means emigration and immigration, and among the trails around the globe the USA provides a nodal point of entrance or exit, temporary visitation or permanent settlement. In fact, in today's world the difference between settlement and visit is increasingly blurred, since ease of travel allows frequent contact between the new domicile and the home base. It follows that cultural deposits are moved rapidly back and forth. People are always poised between recollection and novelty, taking novelty back and carrying recollection forward. And the way-station you create may be from pampas to Buenos Aires or Seoul to Vancouver: the point is that you are seeing yourself in company with the brethren, not in passive receipt of a service such as the Catholic Church or the state may provide. That is the crucial difference to keep in mind.

If the USA with its Protestant culture is a nodal point of global move-ment, so Evangelicals and Pentecostals wherever situated are likely to be on the move more than their immediate peers. They have, after all, made a specific and active choice, which defines them as on the look-out for new possibilities even before conversion, and often the faith they choose is one with transnational connections. In the new environment they have come upon a culture with global and American affiliations; they make contacts that include Americans; and they are exposed to English as the global metropolitan tongue. All that makes the idea and the reality of travel or migration more readily accessible. Alternatively those who set out on the international trails become aware of the religious support bases already set up, and either when traveling or on arrival find them familiar and welcoming, as well as a haven of stability in a strange land. There are many ways in which conservative Evangelical or Pentecostal churches may expand further through the services of assistance as well as worship they offer to people on the move.

Precisely how this works out depends on the nature of the home base, Korean, Hispanic, Caribbean, Ghanaian, or whatever. In the case of English-speaking Caribbeans, for example, a shift has already occurred in the islands from established to Pentecostal churches and this means there may even be some erosion of commitment on moving to the USA. Erosion certainly occurs when Caribbeans come to secular Britain, even though there is still a shift towards Pentecostal churches as warm places with a welcome from people of their own kind. In the case of Hispanics moving to the USA, they are (like the Caribbeans) poor, but the proportion of Protestants is perhaps not much higher than in the home country (6 percent in Mexico, 23 percent in Guatemala, for example). There is therefore quite likely to be a rise in the Protestant proportion after arrival in the American environment. America is, after all, more "religious" than Mexico according to most standard measures of religiosity and the "reception centers" provided by Evangelical churches are very evident, especially in the poorer sectors of American cities.[5] The briefest examination of the yellow pages of a city directory provides dramatic evidence of this, so that in Boston, for example, one finds not just the standard Spanish or English "Assemblies of God" but groups like the Zion Fire-Baptized Holiness Church of God, the Gladtidings Assembly, the Rehoboth Bethel Church Apostolic Inc., the New Cornerstone Exodus Church, the Iglesia de Dios Arca de Refugio, the Ministério Associado Iglesia El Mesias, the Ministério Dios con Nosotros, and Jesu Cristo La Unica Esperansa. Whatever else these people do or don't know they have scoured the Bible from cover to cover to discover a name and a title defining who they are.

What happens in Boston and New York happens also in London (and Coimbra, Portugal, and Lourenço Marques, Mozambique). The trails go everywhere, so that the activist and proselytizing Universal Church of the Kingdom of God from Brazil is in the USA, Britain, Portugal, and Mozambique. La Luz del Mundo, which has built its vast temple in

Guadalajara, has its forward bases in Dallas, Texas, Los Angeles, and Sydney, Australia. Its messengers call themselves the new *conquistadores* in order to show the empire can strike back armed with faith not a sword.

Things may be rather different among the Koreans, who have after all been in contact with Evangelical religion for over a century, and whose advanced educational system owes much to American Presbyterian initiatives. It follows that those who make the transition to the USA are often already well-equipped and highly motivated to enter professions and higher education. Indeed, they may want more in measurable returns than American public schools are happy or able to deliver. Some of them, on reaching university level, may encounter liberal or liberation theology (of which Minjung theology in Korea is a variant) and Pentecostals in particular might find themselves disoriented by liberal American seminaries, and their commitments undermined. Certainly, there are deposits of Korean culture in the many clusters of Korean settlement, including the churches, such as the Bible treated as a Confucian text or characteristic Korean hierarchies and masculine authority persisting inside apparent adjustments to the American way. There are many piquant problems inherent in all such transitions, for example, how far one may continue with non-Christian rites embedded deep in communal and familial relations and obligations such as funeral practices. Presbyterian theology is not particularly accommodating to "Chinese rites," although in common with other denominations Presbyterian Koreans are clearly involved in shamanism *sub rosa*.

The megachurches and fellowships (like the Vineyard Fellowship or the Full Gospel Business Men's Fellowship) are also way-stations on transnational trails, with important nodal points in the USA. Megachurches are mostly independent enterprises but they foster far-flung networks among the like-minded. Often organized on the Korean or American model, they exist all over the world from Seoul to Lagos and Bogotá to Manila. In the huge black-led Cathedral of the Holy Spirit in Atlanta, for example, you have a virtual community almost medieval in the enveloping environment it offers, yet at the same time there will be constant coming and going between its staff and, let us say, Nigeria.[6] Not all such churches are independent of outside help, of course. The Baptist megachurch in Oradea, Romania, is a case of one which arose independently, but for its recent ambitious buildings it needed American and other help, as well as teachers from abroad to assist in its new college. On the other hand to go to Guatemala City is to encounter several megachurches, some like "Verbo" with important American origins and links, but servicing confident and comfortably off clienteles well able to look after themselves.

Not only is the USA a major nodal point for transnational trails but the largest junction for the networks of evangelical leaders and an entrepot of agencies for sending out personnel. To take only agencies, these include denominational headquarters such as that of the Assemblies of God at Springfield, Missouri. It is not that this headquarters directs the world-wide denomination, since after all its Brazilian counterpart serves a much larger constituency and zealously guards its independence. It does, however, provide a point of reference and it is a place where leaders may come and go in their "grand tour" of North America, just like any professional or academic association. The same would be true of the Wycliffe Bible Translators center or the Christ of the Nations Institute, both in Dallas, though these might well be more directive than the Assemblies of God headquarters.[7]

A major evangelical agency in the USA is World Vision, overseeing global development projects in much the same way as Christian Aid, Adveniat, Diakonia, or Caritas.[8] Inevitably, transnational organizations of this kind offer models of administration from India to Zimbabwe, whether or not run locally by local personnel.

Such cultural radiation from the American superpower and the mutual exchange of cultures is, of course, also characteristic of Catholicism and of Catholic radicalism. Maryknoll in the USA was a notable entrepot of liberation theology, sending out messages and messengers to Latin America. The ubiquitous devotion of Our Lady of Guadelupe provides a way-station for Mexican Catholics, and devotion to the Lord of the Miracles re-establishes itself among Peruvians in Chicago.[9] Para-Christian groups such as Witnesses and Mormons are equally nodes of import and export, and Witnesses in Mexico or Mormons in Chile will be decidedly North American in orientation, much more so than Pentecostals, and that will be part of their distinctive appeal to certain kinds of people. The superior and very modern facilities of (say) the Witnesses in San José, Costa Rica, or of the Mormons in Santiago, Chile, will exude an aura of efficient modernity, and it is suggested that in spite of their special resources of missionary labor the Mormons pay out more per dollar than others for every convert gained.

None of this documents in any straightforward way the suggestion that the American Gospel is exported as part of a sinister geopolitical plan, which trails in its wake destructive consequences for local cultural integrity and capacity to resist oppression.[10] At the same time it remains true that the transnational and multicultural dynamic exacts its costs and that some American emissaries, or their co-adjutants in societies like Korea or Argentina, are indifferent to or culpably ignorant of local exploitation and oppression. The world of mass rallies and five-star hotels in which such people quite often foregather (on the universally appealing grounds that laborers in the vineyard are "worthy of their hire") is not always directly adjacent to the world of immiserated hovels, though these are rarely far away. It is easier to spend time with local bosses soothing away such scruples as they may discover about novel faiths than in visiting the impoverished. Overworlds often find underworlds invisible, which is one reason why so few journalists or academics even know that the Pentecostals are there.

As for preachers like Swaggart, Bonnke, or Cerullo, they must live and die by publicity and with all that means in terms of automatic accusations of graft or charlatanry. Sex and money are universal bedevilments and eros is uncomfortably close to agape. When a Swaggart falls many other personal disintegrations follow, and his work with "Swaggart scholarships" counts for nothing.[11] If the local beneficiaries of assistance sometimes channel it to their own advantage that, too, is a universal problem. At the same time wherever there is a plague, earthquake, or just the needs, sorrows, and adversities of poverty there will be North American personnel and assistance to hand, much of it evangelical in inspiration. The earthquake in Guatemala in 1976 released a torrent of assistance, personal and financial, with a discernible effect on the expansion of non-Catholic churches.

Evangelical Pre-eminence in the USA and North Atlantic

The issue to be addressed here is why throughout the Anglo-Saxon world Evangelicalism should be so strong, not only in relation to its Reformed predecessor, but also to its Pentecostal successor and offshoot. It is understandable enough that evangelical populist enthusiasms aroused on an advancing frontier could erode the staid establishments of the American north-east, or that something similar could happen in industrial northern England and Wales between 1790 and 1850. But one might have expected that erosion to happen in turn to Evangelicalism once Pentecostalism took fire in Kansas and California. To have staked out the ground first is rarely in itself enough to prevent landslides, and perhaps it was simply that frequent revivals within the Evangelical camp were sufficient to prevent Pentecostalism taking over. Persistent mobilizations further and further down the social scale could be carried, for the most part, by revival movements, whereas among the teeming populations of the developing world the natural carrier came to be Pentecostalism.

In any case in due course many evangelicals in the USA sought control as much as release and pursued an intellectual defence of Scripture which rejected signs, wonders, and gifts. There was, so to speak, a stabilization which in the Evangelical South circled the waggons in gestures of cultural defense against the north-east. So whereas in the Caribbean, Pentecostalism did indeed gradually undermine the Evangelical establishment, in Texas or Georgia it did not, though paradoxically the Caribbean islands on the margin of the English-speaking world had been fed historically by the multiple marginalities of the black revivalist South.

The point can be put rather differently. Evangelicalism is able to entertain charismatic effervescence but need not and often does not do so. By contrast effervescence and charismata are of the essence of Pentecostalism, and that essence resonates with the ethos of Hispanic and African cultures, or mixtures of them both, as in Brazil. Above all a fissiparous Pentecostal faith offers seductive opportunity to set up on your own and run your own show.

In a prosperous and settled North America it is perfectly possible for charismatic gifts to be experienced in all kinds of social milieux in the historic churches, including the Episcopal Church and the Catholic Church. Many well-educated or comfortably-off people might prefer to join a charismatic network among those of their own kind and denomination than to join one of the stricter Pentecostal churches with a very different social constituency. As with everything else, churches gather adherents by a religious variant of assortative mating: feeling at home makes all the difference. Certainly that seems to be the case among charismatics in the emergent middle classes of South Africa or South-East Asia. Such people either seek out networks within historic churches or else are attracted by new bodies, many of them founded by Americans, but otherwise simply created by themselves. It seems that the older labels are too restrictive for those feeling expansive.

At this juncture it is worth noting what Donald Miller has called the reinvention of American Protestantism or Henry P. van Duren a "new reformation."[12] The argument is that while Christianity remains potent in the USA, the main sources of contemporary potency are in such movements outside the mainline as the Calvary Chapel, Hope Chapel, and the Vineyard. Founded in the late sixties and early seventies, these churches are non-hierarchical and non-liturgical, putting Bible before doctrine and emotional experience before rational argument. There are nearly 1,400 such congregations made up in particular of baby-boomers born after 1945 with the expected values of individualism and the search for therapy. At the same time, they object to the narcissism of the therapeutic style, stressing personal responsibility and obedience to biblical injunction. Their individualism is tempered by an emphasis on community which lifts up the bounded community of the local congregation as a protection against the anonymity and isolation of secular culture. The analogues with Pentecostalism are obvious.

When it comes to politics, however, alliances need not be based on meetings of like with like, but on an overlap of values and interests. Pentecostals and Evangelicals have co-operated in the New Christian Right, but then so also have Mormons. This kind of political pressure group based on alliances between conservatives of different stripes is not really replicated in the developing world, even in Brazil and some of the African countries where one finds some apparent similarities.[13] What happens in the USA is just what you would expect in an advanced sophisticated society where your voice is not heard unless you lobby, combine, and recombine according to well-understood cultural cleavages, especially cleavages between conservatives and liberals, locals and cosmopolitans, religious people and a culturally influential secular elite. Such a situation leads to a certain fuzziness of perceived denominational identity among public figures like Robertson and Buchanan on the New Christian Right – an entity in some trouble and often more problematic than helpful to the Republican Party. In Europe, the emergence of evangelical parties, more particularly in Scandinavia, may indeed represent protest from the pietist margins against cosmopolitan values, with Västerbottenland or Jutland substituting for Des Moines, but somehow the bartering in the political market is not quite the same. It so happens that the votes of North American Pentecostals (as distinct from the attitudes of pastors towards the standard moral demarcations of American society) mostly go to the Democrats, whereas the votes of Episcopalians, as distinct from the politics of priests, mostly go to the Republicans.

The same relative dominance of Evangelicalism is found throughout the religious universe of the North Atlantic and Oceania. Whether in New Zealand or old Zealand, New England or old England, Nova Scotia or Scotland, New South Wales or Wales, the evangelical groupings are the liveliest single sector in the Protestant churches, and though Pentecostals expand they do so as more recent, junior partners and from a smaller base. This is not to say that Pentecostalism in Britain, Scandinavia, or Oceania is all that recent, but it does follow on in territories already "burned over." The new fire travels where old fire has traveled many times before: the sight of the evangelical preacher in the Bristol street is not quite as surprising as it was (till quite recently) in Santiago – or Tallinn.[14] Methodism inoculates in the North Atlantic where it facilitates in the South Atlantic.

Britain, Canada, Australia, New Zealand

Moving from the American center of cultural radiation to the English-speaking penumbra we have a group of societies with shared linguistic, legal, cultural, religious, and democratic traditions, though with roots in colonialism and expropriation. There are fainter shadows of this influence in the English-speaking Caribbean, and in South, East, and West Africa, particularly Ghana and Nigeria, places where slavery as well as empire was a major means of entry into "New Worlds." The common element in religious terms, following from British influence, is a culturally influential Protestantism, the presence of a sizeable Catholic minority, a degree of multicultural pluralism and federalism, and a major evangelical sector with Pentecostal and charismatic offshoots. How these varied elements combine under the controlling influence of the way in which voluntarism relates to establishment, sets the parameters for secularization in the limited sense of the progress of social differentiation. Together they filter social differentiation. Thus in the USA, where voluntarism has been almost total for two to three centuries, the cultural power of religion is most evident, and evangelicalism very much part of it, while in Britain an establishment has remained in place which (however much weakened) has set certain limits and created an overall religious tone also affecting the voluntary sector. The limits and the tone together link the British situation to the Scandinavian.

It could also be that the apogee of British influence and of a confident Evangelicalism went together, as they do now in the contemporary USA, and that the decline of Britain finds a mirror in indifference towards the faith which animated a time of confidence and progress. If there is anything to this then it is interesting that since the 1960s Britain's sister societies in the "old" Commonwealth have followed a British rather than an American trajectory with respect to secularization.[15] At the same time in each of these sister societies the decline of their "shadow establishments" (Anglican, Methodist, Presbyterian, United, Uniting Church) has gone along with a relative vitality in the evangelical sector and some modest Pentecostal expansion.[16] As in the USA this relative vitality indicates a resistance to the kind of internal secularization found in mainstream bodies through the firming up of boundaries and creation of warm, close-knit networks better able to retain young people. So far as Pentecostalism is concerned, Evangelicalism has already pre-empted the available space, helping to inhibit the kind of Pentecostal take-off evident in Nigeria, Ghana, or the Caribbean (notably Jamaica).[17]

The underlying trend affecting the sister societies of Britain (rather than their American cousin) is one it shares with Western Europe as a whole. Established religion gently collapses as the supports provided by ecclesiastical control of welfare, education, media, and so on finally give way. The continuing process of social differentiation not only places these spheres to a great extent under state and/or professional aegis, but separates ethnic belonging from religious identity, distances social from ecclesiastical hierarchies, and to some extent shifts the location of religion from local community and social control (with all that implies for clerical status and role) to the creation of a portable identity. There are also breaks in generational continuity, in particular the interposition of a youth culture which since the sixties has replaced personal discipline by consumer hedonism. Of course, the power of a faith with territorial roots, and the influence of life-cycle events, and religiously toned communal and national identities never entirely disappears. In certain circumstances the bedrock of religious and national identity can be very resistant.

In one respect all the societies of the British penumbra and Western Europe share one characteristic: a degree of centralization and so of elite control which inhibits lively voluntary sub-cultures, including religious ones. Though societies with a British inheritance are federal and voluntaristic compared to Western Europe, they still share with Europe a tendency to expect the state to oversee welfare, sustain community and promote social capital. By contrast religious institutions in the USA know it is their special business to promote social capital and are vigorous in doing so.[18]

Rather than review all the evidence for the sister societies it should be enough to indicate the situation in Britain (more particularly in England) and in Canada.[19] In Canada the decline in the influence of mainstream religion began in the traditional Protestant bodies in the 1950s, before appearing in the Roman Catholic Church a decade or so later, most dramatically in Québec. Significantly this sequence in Canada was very similar to the sequence in Holland, a country with a similar proportion of Catholics, who were likewise concentrated territorially and (until 1960) distanced from the traditions and mythic self-presentation of the country. In Holland the 1970s saw the same process affect the strict Protestant minority.

In the decade 1981–91 those in Canada not identifying with Christianity rose from 7.4 percent to 12.5 percent, and of those who did identify themselves as Christian, about one in seven were Evangelical (including Pentecostals), though Catholic Québec clearly contains a smaller proportion compared with English-speaking Canada. This Evangelical minority has been expansive enough to fuel speculation about Evangelicals eventually displacing mainstream Protestants. Apart from ethnic churches fed by migration, the area of growth has been in the category "Pentecostal (and Other)," and those in this category now number about a million, or 3 percent of the population. Some of this Pentecostal growth has occurred in Québec following the replacement of religion by language as the bond of identity, and this provides a contrast with the two societies cognate with Québec: (southern) Ireland and (southern) Holland. All three societies were enclaves left by the successive

Anglo-Dutch and Anglo-American victories over the French as champions of Catholicism. In Ireland, where the fusion of subordinate national consciousness with religion was especially strong, the fall-out in power and practice has been much slower than in Québec and Holland, and any recourse to Evangelicalism is precluded by its association with Northern Ireland. Instead, charismatic movements emerged inside the Catholic Church itself. In Holland the organization of the country into religio-cultural parallel columns meant that a Catholic fall-out was unlikely to include recourse to the rival column of the conservative Protestants. Québec, therefore, remained the sole instance, even if the movement is not all that striking, and it also appears that sectors of the Inuit in Québec have adopted Pentecostalism. Rather like the gypsies of Europe they reversed the stereotype of themselves as dissipated and irresponsible.

An illustration of migration and transplantation in the Canadian context, paralleling that cited for the USA, is provided by Hispanic missionaries who came to Québec to found French-speaking churches. As reported by Luis Fontalvo, the arrival later of fresh waves of Hispanic immigrants stimulated these churches into acting as a linguistic and cultural bridge and language school, as well as a focus of business and friendship networks. After that some English speakers joined, and gradually the congregations included a dozen or so ethnic groups – Italians, West Africans, Caribbeans, Central Americans, and so on. Then missionaries were dispatched to metropolitan France.[20]

In Britain the situation is similar to that in Canada though overall levels of belief and practice are considerably lower. Within the established Anglican Church, for example, conservative Evangelical churches experience relative growth, at least in urban and suburban areas, particularly where a charismatic element is present. Nearly half of the 14–21-year-olds in contact with the Anglican Church are in Evangelical local churches, and this chimes in with a general observation as to the outreach of those conservative Evangelical churches which operate outside the ecclesiastical mainstream.[21] The retrenchment of historic Liberal Protestant denominations, notably the Methodists, has been matched by an expansion of Mormons and Witnesses as well as Pentecostals, though this by no means balances out overall decline. As Methodism has shifted upward socially and southward geographically one sees the chapels of its old northern heartlands turned to secular or Pentecostal use, or spick and span new churches set up by Mormons as well as the discreet Kingdom Halls of Jehovah's Witnesses.

Classical Pentecostalism has been long established in Britain and (leaving aside the effects of migration) is not all that expansive, so that the charismatic impulse either affects the Anglican (or Catholic) Church, often through ancillary networks, or else takes new initiatives, such as the House Churches, New Frontiers, or the Vineyard Fellowship. The House Church movement was the first new denomination in Britain for some time and until recently had quite an appeal, especially in middle-class groups. Clearly there is a search among some business people and professionals for an expressive tactile faith offering networks of personal support, a moral discipline, and a hedge against chaos. One has the sense that the atmosphere in these networks overlaps the style of Anglican, Free Church, and Catholic charismatics (as well, one may add, as those in Ulster and the Republic). Such networks can be international, and relatively indifferent to ethnic constituencies. Charismata leap over ethnicity.

So far as migration into Britain is concerned, it is a minor version of the migration into America, except that there are relatively so many more from the Indian sub-continent, mainly Hindu and Muslim. The Caribbean migration to Britain is like the Hispanic migration to the USA, except that the religious shift is mainly from evangelical or Anglican faith towards Pentecostalism, both in the sending and the receiving culture. What Pentecostalism offers to Caribbean women is security and respectability, while its rival in Rastafarianism has appealed more to men seeking a patois of defiance, African identity, and difference.

Just how Pentecostal churches serve Caribbean migrants, especially women, has recently been analyzed by Nicola Toulis.[22] Her study of the black New Testament Church of God in Birmingham, England, shows how it provides a source of identity and memory for Jamaican women, especially through their dress and familiar presidency at table. Whatever the injurious estimates of the world outside, all the sisters and brothers share a common citizenship in heaven which rises above ethnic categorization. Their life and comportment, and their cleanliness and godliness, give them a "respectability" too often invisible to the white community. They believe God honors and rewards honest work with blessings, provided that these do not become worldly seductions.

Not only have Caribbeans found the religion of established denominations cold and unwelcoming but they have encountered problems where they might have expected an easier passage, for example among Seventh Day Adventists where rising proportions of blacks produced white flight. At the same time there was a very different migration from English-speaking West Africa, in particular Nigeria, made up mainly of students and professionals. Such groups came together in their own sizeable charismatic or evangelical churches, while some other West Africans became involved in vibrant churches with a more distinctively African accent, such as the Aladura or Cherubim and Seraphim.

Northern Protestant Europe

In Northern Protestant Europe, especially Scandinavia, the voluntarism of the English-speaking world is much less prevalent. The equivalent movements of pietism or "personal Christianity" or revivalism have worked more inside the churches, and the number of denominational schisms has been restricted. However, Scandinavia is very like Britain in the retirement of the older pietist spirit to the provinces and margins, the highlands and islands. Just as in Britain there is a resistant piety in Ulster, North Wales, and the Scottish highlands and islands, so in Scandinavia there are pietistic enclaves in northern Denmark, northern Sweden, rural Finland, and south-western Norway around Bergen. Variants of dissent or piety lodge in adjacent niches, in one place the prayer house, in other places low-church Lutheranism, or one of the free churches.[23]

Yet, however local and enclosed these peaceable enclaves may seem, there was in all likelihood just the same differential migration as noted elsewhere. As in Scotland and Ulster so, too, in Scandinavia, motivated and energetic believers have sought more open spaces, socially and geographically, in the USA. Indeed, Swedish Baptists were once harried in their homeland; and it was Swedes experiencing conversion on arrival in the USA who founded the first Pentecostal church of Brazil.

But back in the "base camp," as it were, Pentecostalism has been only the latest of many revival movements, and Scandinavia as a whole has been thoroughly secularized under Social Democratic aegis, leaving the Church a nostalgic shell, ignored by a confirmed but non-practising majority. In Scandinavia people belong more than they believe (as in England they believe more than they belong) and established Christianity feels the gentle hint of approaching dissolution. Perhaps the ground has been harvested once too often.

Peter Berger has suggested (in a personal communication) that new life is likely to emerge in just that milieu where the sweet smell of decay is so especially evident, and there is an example of that in the industrial district of the cathedral and university city of Uppsala. Today one might see Uppsala's magnificent hospital as the most prominent house of consolation, but there is also a flourishing megachurch and Bible School called "Word of Life." This church is on the American model, validating prosperity and fostering close relationships among a prosperous clientele. Helsinki too supports a lively charismatic community but within the Lutheran Church, and focused on the healing which streams from the "golden hands" of its pastor.[24]

Southern Latin Europe

Latin Europe is for the most part unresponsive to Pentecostalism, in large measure because the historic confrontation of a single dominant church with radicals has created a distinctive secularist and anti-clerical tradition. Perhaps the situation is best illustrated by an anecdote from George Borrow where he relates how Spaniards met evangelical missionaries with the comment that if they did not even believe in the one true Church they could hardly be attracted to Protestant alternatives.

However, there are exceptions, including a thin sprinkling of free-ranging charismatic groups, mass conversion among the depressed and itinerant minority of the gypsies, and certain modest inundations at the geographical margins, notably in Portugal and in Italy south of Ancona, where conditions resemble those in Latin America. In the case of the gypsies this is yet another instance of a minority passing through an effervescent reformation whereby they revise their lives and reverse a stereotype of themselves as lazy, unclean, and thieving. Whereas once gypsies intermittently conformed to the rites of whatever was the local faith, they now gather from time to time in selected towns in France and Spain to proclaim and celebrate their reformed character.

With regard to Portugal, the seeds of new faiths have arrived from its ex-colony in Brazil, as earlier they arrived in Britain from the USA. Yet again the empire strikes back, and in the case of the Universal Church of the Kingdom of God has found a constituency rather more middle-class than in Brazil. As in Brazil this church, now the second largest in the country, also has political representatives.

Southern Italy has been for some time moderately vulnerable to conversion, not only to Pentecostals but also to Witnesses. One of the best studies of Pentecostals anywhere has been made by Salvatore Cucchiari, and he traces the socio-psychological transformations brought about by them in Sicily.[25]

Cucchiari begins by pointing out that early Pentecostalism was broadcast to virtually every corner of the globe, including Italy as early as 1908. The broadcasting was *not* carried out by professional missionaries but by returning migrant workers who had been converted in the urban industrial centers of the USA. Once again, the primary role of migration has been brought out. Italian Pentecostals were, of course, repressed and oppressed for several generations and characterized "more as beasts than men."[26] Nowadays they operate freely, and number from a quarter to a third of a million, with some concentration in the Italian south. In Sicily, Pentecostalism strenuously opposes traditional Sicilian religion, that is, the whole family of visually powerful religious structures, from high Catholicism to the cult of saints and shamanistic healing and sorcery.

Instead it offers the austerity of the preached Word and an imminent eschatological future, and with that a sense of direct personal power, available here and now. Above all else, Pentecostalism is both a radical departure from folk-Catholicism and a continuation of it, which in part accounts for its transformative potential.

Interestingly enough, in the particular sector of Palermo selected by Cucchiari, the Pentecostal community was socially fairly diverse, though skewed to the less fortunate. The community was equally diverse politically, with Christian Democrats roughly equal to the Socialists and Communists. It also consisted disproportionately of incomplete families, a fact which led to domestic tension rather than domestic stability. Furthermore, it contained more long-term than recent migrants from the countryside. In other words, the standard theories have a very modest "fit" for this material.

Before leaving this analysis, with its references to rapid global dissemination, it is worth extending the story. For example, an Italian Waldensian Protestant, Waldemar Francescon, made his way to Chicago, associating there with Presbyterians before switching to Pentecostalism and creating his own church. Contacts with Brazil followed, helping to create what was then an Italian-speaking Pentecostal Church, and today the trail includes Italian Pentecostals in Australia. Although Italy is a Catholic country, the experience of migration can breed a transmigration of souls, finding in Pentecostalism a portable identity. When it comes to religious choice, global air "makes free."[27]

Why is Latin America so Different?

The remarkable contrast between the two vast Catholic regions is clearly related to the issue of "European Exceptionalism." At one time Latin America seemed to be traveling a Latin European path, with France as a major model, and a prospect of major communist parties such as grew up in both France and Italy. However, and perhaps in part for reasons due to phasing, the minatory history of the Soviet Union and the gravitational pull of an American model, Latin America left the Latin European path and became a hybrid, incorporating an Anglo-Saxon type of trajectory, with Pentecostalism emerging as the vehicle of a major mobilization of the poor. The question relates to the factors which "like switch-men" turned the trajectories of Latin America and Latin Europe in such different directions.

One massive and obvious difference between the two Latin civilizations is the sheer extent of immiseration and urban chaos in contemporary Latin America, as vast masses pour into the megacities. The sequence of such changes is accelerated by comparison with Latin Europe and the phases are superimposed, leading to disjunctions with educational and political developments. Certainly, so far as political development is concerned, the elites have mostly remained corrupt custodians of the state maintaining their power by clienteles, which so far as maybe have included the Catholic Church, even in recent decades. That alliance with the Church has gone through vicissitudes, for example under Peron in Argentina and in the history of Mexico, but it has generally been renewed.[28]

At the same time the hopeless contemplate an indifferent opulence literally next door (if they possess a door) and that either breeds desperate remedies through violence or a religious search for a different solution, especially on the part of women. (When thinking about Pentecostalism one must always remember that women prefer peaceable, stable homes to itinerant male violence.)

Yet some at least of these conditions have existed in the European past, and even today there are steady northward migrations in train without myriads of small churches springing up in Switzerland or northern Italy, though there are a few. Perhaps a clue must be sought in the successful propagation downward to the people at large found in the French model of secularization. In France a confrontation between secularist elites and ecclesiastics polarized a society from top to bottom over religion *as such*. In Latin America, apart from Uruguay, which is strikingly European in the origins of its population,[29] the same confrontation certainly takes place, and is consciously emulated by Francophile intelligentsias, but it is not successfully propagated downward. Though the social system may be highly centralized it is also poorly articulated. Indeed, the structure of the Catholic Church is poorly articulated in just the same way, so people go their own way religiously and otherwise. In any case, they do not form an urban proletariat on the European model. The radical elites inflict huge damage on the ramshackle institutional Church in Guatemala, Mexico, or Brazil, without destroying this inchoate popular religiosity, which in the end they have to take into account, as they did in Mexico in the 1890s and 1930s. Popular religion takes its own course as it has for centuries, at times redeploying Christianity against Hispanic conquerors or assimilating its symbols to other purposes, or breaking out into millenarian expectation, or following eccentric and dissident Catholic leaders like Padre Cicero.[30] Throughout it all the inspirited world-view remains intact and eventually vulnerable to a religious appeal which picks up "the power of the spirit" and actively mobilizes the poor for their own betterment.

The contrast with France is evident, since the French upper-middle-class radicals did not need to compromise to that extent with popular religiosity, and things had gone too far to reinstate a useful collusion with the Church. Though there were resistant pieties in Brittany or Alsace (under German control after 1870 during the anti-clerical Third Republic) they were not comparable to the exuberant popular faiths of Brazil or parts of Mexico. As a result charismatic religion has restricted impact in contemporary France, picking up the personal needs of the comfortable in well-appointed fellowships. Spain and Italy were less extreme cases than France. The drive to create a universal secular consciousness was less thoroughgoing and the administrative instruments available were less effective and comprehensive.

Before making some general comments about post-Protestant and (maybe) post-Catholic Europe it may help to revert briefly to Northern Europe with its less radical enlightenments and frequent mingling of enlightened elites and ecclesiastics. Clerics were educated in universities alongside other professions and had no universal and embarrassing Roman view to transmit. Sometimes, as in late nineteenth-century Germany, an enlightened upper middle class would take a hostile stance to religion, but there could usually be some accommodation, some mixing of pietist and enlightened motifs, even though that might emasculate evangelical power among the people.[31] In due course, the centralized powers of the state previously available to established religion, for example through education and media, came into the hands of religiously apathetic or Laodicean administrators. Then, in the wake of the sixties, these were deployed by professionals hostile to religious solidarities and traditional continuities. In particular, educational and welfare professionals, trained according to state-sponsored norms, propagated pre-emptive capitulations to secularity, even when working in organizations retaining religious charters. Such pre-emptive capitulations might even be condoned or countenanced by liberal ecclesiastical elites, leading to dismay among laity and pressure for religious schools or schools with a religious and disciplined tone. In these ways the borders of religious belonging were firmed up, a process which was consonant with the reinforced boundaries created by conservative Evangelicalism. As for Pentecostals, they were one of the few groups capable of creating welfare organizations based on their own religious norms; in Norway, for example, the state professionals were certainly not sympathetic but Pentecostal achievements were acknowledged.[32] Their drug-addiction programs demonstrated the potency of religiously inspired transformations, though it is clear that a religious approach can hardly provide a universal panacea.

What this means for a post-Protestant, post-Catholic Europe remains problematic. The restriction of Pentecostal penetration to Catholic regions approximating Latin American conditions in some degree is evident enough, as is the inoculation created by familiarity within northern

Protestantism. Throughout the continent all religion suffers from the wide dissemination of simple notions of conflict between science and religion, as well as from the propagation in the media of the Left-libertarian modes mandatory since the sixties. As neo-liberalism has conquered in the economic realm, so existential libertarianism has colonized the personal realm, and neither are entirely grateful to Christian norms. "Enrichez-Vous" is not a gospel injunction, whatever prosperity teaching suggests. What may, however, be in train, if there is anything substantial to the notion of post-modernity, is an openness which includes religion and a loosening of the hegemonic prestige and control of a restrictive and abstracted rationality. As for a rediscovery of moral disciplines, in conditions of prosperity, life's lessons have a way of being learned too late. Youthful permissions may persist into middle age, in spite of familial and career obligations.

European Exceptionalism: a Misalignment of Discourses

In now approaching directly the key issue of European exceptionalism there are, of course, certain broad features related to the general process of social differentiation and pluralism. One such is the tendency to firm up boundaries between explicit Christian commitment and the apathetic mass, which in Evangelical churches is an insistence on discipline and commitment and in liturgical churches a shift to eucharistic participation as marker of "membership." Thus overall practice drops as eucharistic participation increases. Another feature is the way churches to some extent become voluntary associations or "faith communities" acting as critical pressure groups rather than semi-detached blocs of class or regional resistance capable of delivering votes to particular parties. Such associations cannot expect their views to govern secular legal regulation, for example, of divorce. In Europe, as in North America, the effects of differentiation are evident in the separation of church from state and law, from local communal solidarity, and from welfare, education, and media.

However (as argued in my *A General Theory of Secularisation* (1978)), just how this works itself out in concrete instances, and how far and how fast it goes, depends on historical filters. Contingency modifies process, and when specific combinations operate, contingencies can profoundly redirect or even cancel it. If we are not to explain European secularity by grand narratives of secularization which require North America and not Europe to be designated as exceptional, then we need briefly to specify contingencies and sketch their cumulative impact. Brevity and sketchiness are inevitable, because though this issue is generated by the variable impact of Pentecostalism, and by the challenge which its rise poses for secularization theory, it is not the principal focus of the overall argument. One does not have to write a long book about Europe or even a long book about Europe and North America, in order to write one about global Pentecostalism. (Hard-line proponents of secularization theory need feel no pressure even to sketch an answer since it is all entirely self-evident apart from such incidental and no doubt exaggerated oddity as may exist in the United States.)

In exploring contingent circumstances, the two world wars are obvious candidates, and they are all too rarely built into sociological accounts of secularization. It was the first world war which deepened to the point of near-disaster the struggle between passionate political dogmatisms, and so reinforced Catholic proclivities to side with the organicist right wherever the Church was part of established order. It was the second world war and its cold-war aftermath which pushed the Catholic Church into an uneasy alliance with liberal-conservative reconstruction and enabled it to act as a psychic bastion of Western resistance to totalitarian enlightenment. That was very much the project of Adenauer, Monnet, and Schuman. For just long enough the Catholic peripheries from Bavaria to southern Italy could help shore up with votes and sentiments the ability of Christian Democracy to preside over the liberal-conservative centre and European revival. Catholicism also helped hold at bay the large communist parties of France and Italy. And all this was in the context of a long-term struggle of faith and enlightenment, partly on the French model, lasting from 1789 to 1989. Indeed, in the last phase of the struggle, from 1945 to 1989, authoritarian church and authoritarian enlightenment gained weight by counter-definition so that when communism collapsed in Italy, as also in Poland, the embedded alliances of Catholicism likewise began to fray and fragment. Today the Communists cannot even hold their heartland in Bologna and the Catholic collusion with Democrazia Cristiana is no more.[33]

The history of the Catholic Church throughout the onset of modernity began with disentanglement from the grip of enlightened autocracy, and then went through two phases: alliance with the forces of the *ancien régime* against radical secularism, and then alliance with the center against atheistic communism. In the first phase there was a partial consonance between ecclesiastical and conservative paternalism and organicism, while in the second phase there was a partial consonance between ecclesiastical doctrines of mutuality and a centrist concern for welfare, so that John XXIII was even dubbed the Keynesian Pope.

Throughout this period of nearly two centuries, the Catholic Church moved from a low point when the enlightened autocrat Napoleon made the Church his footstool, and even proposed moving the Papacy from Rome to Paris, to a position of qualified independence as the voice of an international faith community. In a way the Church was assisted by the rise of totalitarian communism, because in principle it increased the viability of alliance with the liberal center even though initially it had accentuated the attraction of concordats with fascism.

There were two crises, one of maximum danger for the Church, and one which played to its advantage. The first crisis came with a shift in attitudes towards communism after Russia was forced by Nazi attack on to the Allied side in 1941. Up to that point the tactics of communist parties had been opportunistic, apart from subservience to Russian interests, and had played into the hands of the extreme right,[34] but in the period after 1941, which was also the time of communist participation in the Italian and French resistance, communism appeared in a benign light. In the immediate post-war period the West might have been endangered had not the ruthlessness and autocratic brutality of the Soviet Union and its surrogates united a broad band of opinion from center left to center right in opposition to the totalitarian threat. The crisis of apparent communist virtue passed and the Church was able to take position as a central column holding up Western Europe, as well as the symbolic reference point of national autonomy in Eastern Europe. Practice stayed stable for a whole generation, and it is worth remembering that four-fifths of active Christian participation in Europe was (and still is) Roman Catholic. To that extent the long-standing schism in European culture between faith and enlightenment in its radical liberal rather than its Marxist form was ameliorated.

However, at the same time, the Church was now in a current of ideas pushing towards modernity and *aggiornamento*, which came to a focus in 1962 with the Second Vatican Council. From the nineteen sixties onwards, modernization included (as already pointed out) economic liberalism and libertarian consumer hedonism, in intermittent conflict but also in more profound alliance. After a brief quietist moment in the immediate post-war years, the Church was once more in serious disalignment, and this time with the whole European project.[35] Though that project included some serious Catholic concepts, such as subsidiarity and mutuality, the thrust of its dynamic, in the wake of American economic hegemony and example, was in a neo-liberal direction. In such circumstances the Catholic Church could not provide, as Delors hoped, "A soul for Europe": with its roots in "solidarity" it lay athwart that project.

On the other side of the political spectrum, the release of the Catholic Church from intimate relations with power and hierarchy in countries where it was established, meant that some Catholic sectors could explore a consonance between Catholic and socialist organicism, especially in France and (later) Latin America, the former feeding the latter, for example via Louvain.

However, the strains which a socialist liberationism imposed on the hierarchical structure of the Church itself led to inhibition from Rome until the whole project became implicated in the fall of communism and major revisions of social democracy. The Church now stood in the neutral public square of civil society, but with the resonance of its voice restricted by the tally of disalignment and misalignment over the past two centuries, since the low point when Napoleon forced the Pope across the Alps to marry him and Josephine in Notre Dame. Its voice is at last independent of ancient entanglements, but compromised by recent history.

All this was in marked contrast to the USA, where an unequivocal Protestant template was consolidated in economic liberalism and legitimated by the prayerful invocation of God and America in happy conjunction. Where in Europe the collapse of religious frames of consensus and power was often violent, revolutionary, and projected by an enlightened upper middle class, in the USA religion included a popular base and proceeded by a combination of evolution and revolution which mixed principles with pragmatics.

The center holds, and religion is part of its sure foundation. Whatever the ferocity of culture wars taking place in the upper air, and the scraps over religion by the battalions of the New Christian Right and American Civil Liberties Union, the heart of the national project stays sound.[36] Liberal clergy may criticize the implementation of that project while their congregations applaud it, but they are all members incorporate in adjacent elites. They all invoke "America" as liberally as any populist politician or journalist. The French may and do invoke "La France," and with almost equal fervor, but there is no united nation "under God" since precisely that has been in contention for all of two centuries.

Of course, there have been major divisions in American society and the clashes of traditional Christians with metropolitan liberals have been persistent, as have clashes between economic liberals and social radicals, for example, in the 1890s and 1960s. But the explosion of idealistic radicalism in the 1960s (mutating rapidly into consumer hedonism) had very different consequences for religion in America compared with Europe. In Europe the division of the generations and of styles left religion once again disaligned, and practice fell steadily in the following decades. In America the tremors were palpable, but buoyancy reasserted itself even if the religious quests were more experimental than in the period of the mid-century and less emphatic about church attendance.[37]

The world wars which destroyed European confidence and induced moods of cynical faithlessness, in America confirmed a natural confidence in the "last best hope" of humankind. Furthermore, the absence in America of the tie between ethno-religion and territory has meant that religion suffers relatively little discredit as the seeming hinge of ferocious struggles over space, and as a motive for ethnic cleansing.

At this point this analysis needs brief restatement, more especially with respect to what distinguishes the USA from its closest cultural affiliate in Britain, since what applies in Britain (especially England) applies a fortiori in continental Europe. In the United States (and long before it became such), the crucial ties of religion with an ethnic identity rooted in a distinctive territory and linked to a social hierarchy and the state were broken, and broken early at roughly the same time. Religion, with or without an ethnic constituency, was thus released to expand, adjust, and experiment in open social space, vigorously vulgarizing as it did so and actively supplying the necessary forms of social capital between state and family and neighborhood. A self-reliant religious entrepreneurship complemented and expressed the economic liberalism animating the whole society, just as the pullulating variety of religion complemented a federal constitution in which secular elites did not control centralized institutions in such a way as to reduce the capacity of religious sub-cultures to reproduce themselves. To put it another way, secular elites do not matter *that* much in the USA compared even with Britain, let alone with countries like France.

This means that an increasing emphasis on individual spirituality, with all that implies in the mixing and matching of religious flotsam and jetsam, largely proceeds in the USA within religious institutions, thereby retaining some reference to historic Christian paradigms. In Britain and Europe flotsam and jetsam simply drift on the surface, and where the religious institution is still largely in place, as in Italy, you can observe and document the mix and the match going on inside, as indeed it has done for centuries. The big difference is that Americans with their historical *tabula rasa* in the big open social (and geographical) space know they must actively embody their faiths in competitive institutions, whereas Europeans with their statist traditions and historical givens wait for what religious institutions may provide on the model of provision by public utilities.

The above argument with its suggested contingencies does not cancel out long-term processes going back as far as the late nineteenth century or further. Hugh McLeod has given a magisterial account of them as they work through historical filters, for example in New York, London, and Berlin, and my own *A General Theory of Secularisation* was focused in just the same way.[38] At the same time, as I have argued with specific reference to Unitarianism, sociologists have not adequately integrated processes with contingent events and intellectual history.[39] Crucial outcomes depend on combinations of all these, and it is notorious that deaths are due to multiple diseases: factor A has a very different consequence mixed with this combination rather than that.

After all, in Russia, one of the most dramatic instances of a national project in disarray and of the disalignment of religion, the contingent events involved military defeat, the availability of ruthless cadres armed with a militant ideology, a civil war with no assured outcome, a Stalin, and so on, all combined with processes of modernization and concomitant disalignment of religion (with partial realignments in 1942 and 1990). The historical world is contingent.

Multiple Misalignments: Catholic and Post-Protestant

In reviewing the disalignments which had adversely affected the viability and vitality of European religion, it is useful to begin with the Catholic instances since they are more dramatic, selecting France as exemplifying trends in extreme form.

If one goes back only so far as the period following defeat by Germany in 1870 one finds the French Church blaming the Republic for moral and military disaster and the Republic trying to destroy the power of the Church to reproduce itself by an attack on monasteries and schools.[40] Again, after the 1914–18 war, in spite of a unity forged in the conflict, divisions were rife over Action Française on the right and the Popular Front on the left, and there was widespread defeatism.[41] When France fell in 1940 the Catholic Church was implicated in the Vichy régime which followed. In 1958 the Gaullist call for an autonomous France reviving its grandeur as light of nations, trailed part of the Church in its wake while other sectors constructed a radical political critique.[42] Thus throughout the whole period, and stretching back to 1789, France had oscillated violently between being eldest daughter of the Church and first beacon of enlightenment. The secular Parisian center pressed hard against the pious peripheries of Brittany or the Massif Centrale, and in the end the center largely succeeded. But struggle over the national project is endemic not only with respect to religion, but over a socialist or a neo-liberal future, as the contentious years following the early eighties demonstrate. The chief *causes célèbres* involving religion were the mass protest at the attempt fully to integrate Catholic schools into the national system and the attempted banning in school of Muslim female head-dress.[43] Anyone preaching a religious message in France awakens all these contradictory echoes, along with sophisticated disaffection with the very idea of religion.

Spain is perhaps marginally less schizophrenic, though the oscillation of Catholic and Republican Spain has been just as violent, as has the clash of the Castilian center with peripheries like Galicia, the Basque country, and Catalonia. The Church was fiercely attacked in the civil war and in its turn complicit in the dictatorship which followed. Rather like Pinochet in Chile, Franco set about a technocratic modernization, in part through the religious agency of Opus Dei. In the 1960s, however, the Church provided a space for change. All the same, a younger generation entering Europe for the most part with a government of the left (ousted in 2000) could hardly feel much continuity with a past dominated by the Franquist version of the crusades. Throughout the thirty years and more of the dictatorship, a combination of *raison d'état* and *raison d'église* had inhibited the emergence of a neutral civility. That, in combination with the secular impulses emanating from the European Community (and tourism), led to disillusion with religion as such, and a sharp decline in vocations and in practice – apart from pilgrimages and folk festivals.[44] Religion, from having been quasi-normative, is now almost as "disaligned" as in France.

Italy is the least secularized of the three Latin countries, partly perhaps because of its proximity to the Vatican, even though the Papacy was a major obstacle to Italian national unification. In the 1920s the Church came to a useful arrangement with fascism, and in the war failed to take a moral position over the holocaust, motivated perhaps by hope of Soviet defeat. After the war the internal communist threat and vigorous American pressure led to a prolonged Christian Democratic dominance with implicit Catholic support, which became increasingly corrupt, especially in its southern redoubts.[45] Indeed, the country was divided into rival patronage systems as well as into north and south. There were attempts to mobilize Catholic youth in organizations like "Communione e Liberazione," and these had some impact, but against a background of some cynicism and much variety in everyday belief.[46] After the war the tone of public life became overtly secular, and in 1975 Italians voted for the legalization of divorce in the face of Church opposition. Practice remained fairly high and yet the Pope's critique of "The Culture of Death" and "Narcissism" has some difficulty in finding its mark.

These three key countries of Latin Europe display classic features: the clash of enlightenment with Catholicism, of radical secular elites with ecclesiastics, of republicans with more organicist or traditional types of regime. In other Catholic countries the fissures are somewhat different: in Belgium a linguistic divide is crossed with a religio-political divide, and in Austria there is a divide between a Catholic Upper Austria and a Social Democratic Vienna. Ireland is an interesting case because there the Church was as closely aligned with nationalism as in Poland and practice remains the highest in Europe. So it would be reasonable to argue that the partial secularization now evident is the consequence of social differentiation and economic development in a society where public norms have been subject to ecclesiastical veto from a Church with an effective monopoly. In Ireland the power of monopoly had the usual consequences in terms of corruption, legal coercion of morals, and complacency, and the Catholic Church now pays the price of de facto establishment.

In post-Protestant Europe, practice is low everywhere apart from Ulster. In Scandinavia the Lutheran monopoly seems to have been replaced by a Social Democratic monopoly for which the Church is another welfare station for recourse in emergency. Holland and Germany are countries split down the middle by religion, with the national myth Protestant rather than Catholic. Holland was organized into a system of separate sectors. There were established "pillars" rather than established churches, and their collapse in the sixties extended secularization from the Dutch Reformed to the Catholics, then to the strict Protestants, and resulted in a sector of explicit non-Christians which is the highest in Europe. In Germany the immediate pressure of the border with communism, and the arrival of millions of refugees, consolidated religious identity in a country where division had given considerable advantages to the Catholic Church. The alliance of Christian Democracy with the Bavarian Catholic Christian Social Union became the most powerful force in German politics and presided over reconstruction. However, from the sixties on there was less interest in a discourse of forgiveness and reconciliation, and practice dropped, and the Protestant theological faculties were enthused by the widespread student radicalism. The Catholic Church for its part began a discreet withdrawal from the profane dynamism of German politics, though the extent of corruption and graft only emerged at the end of the century. For the younger generation churches appeared as service stations acting as the staid bulwarks of declining establishments, with compromising shadows from the past: the "German Christians," the Catholic Church's absorption in its own institutional survival. To the south of Germany in Switzerland, now with a slight Catholic majority, the country was as divided in religion and language as it was united in the national myth.[47] As in most of the Alpine region, religion was fairly stable, uneventful, involved in gentle decline and growing similarities between confessions.

England (rather than Britain) exemplifies multiple disalignments in religion combined with a partial recovery of its neo-liberal traditions. England, with Ulster, its peripheries in Scotland, and the thirteen colonies, was after all the country of the Evangelical Awakening (or Revival) and the expansive course of that revival continued in England as in the USA from 1790 to 1860, or indeed later. As in the USA, evangelicals envisaged a christianization of the country, but in England they ran into decline from the late nineteenth century onward.[48] After two stabilizations following the wars, all the churches, Catholics included, went into a continuous decline from the 1960s onward, with evangelical (and Pentecostal) sectors gaining in relative prominence. Not christianization but dechristianization looked possible.[49]

The Established Church, though weak, sets a tone with respect to all religion which links English with Scandinavian apathy. It is "disaligned" in several senses. Whereas in the nineteenth century there was some consonance between the Anglican God and "Great" Britain,[50] that became distasteful to the Church, and the more recent lower-class chauvinism has become even more so. Again, Anglicanism has strong links with the global English-speaking world, especially in evangelical circles, but there is also a sense of (erring?) sisterhood with continental Catholic Churches, especially in France, which appeals to Anglo-Catholics. Politically the Church has tended towards the liberal–conservative post-war consensus on welfare, and maintained that through the neo-liberal revival under Thatcher,[51] even constituting a kind of unofficial opposition. The Church is happier with Blair, who is stylistically evangelical but with an interest in Catholic social doctrine, and mostly chooses not to notice the continuing pursuit of a (modified) neo-liberal agenda.

More space has been given to the English situation because of the historic relation to Evangelicalism and because it illustrates what multiple disalignment means. In particular the situation in England underlines the difficulty which all European churches have in devising an approach to neo-liberal economic doctrine, and its awkward relation in libertarian hedonism. England has managed a partial return to its traditional neo-liberalism, health service apart, and under Thatcher that project resonated with the evangelical and Jewish constituencies, and their preference for prosperity and moral discipline, but the drift of European Christianity is not in the neo-liberal direction. No doubt in the USA these reservations about the utilitarian calculus are shared by denominational leaderships, but not by their memberships. There is neither disalignment with respect to the nexus of culture, morality, and economic ethos, nor with respect to the idea of "the nation."

The Catholic Church throughout Europe, whatever its vigorous anti-Marxism, has stayed with the post-war consensus, which it shares with sizeable sectors of the constituent nations of Europe, at least so far as welfare arrangements go, though not with respect to moral discipline. That shapes its response to current events, though clearly the response varies from country to country. However, within all those countries its earlier alignments still weigh on the minds of the living, and restrict the resonance which a Catholic voice might have following its release (or expulsion) from substantial social power. Moreover, the areas of its maximum influence are in the peripheries, such as Bavaria within Germany, or southern Italy, or Ireland, and in the older segments of social structure, and these are hardly platforms for a Catholic assault on the European center.

One interesting theoretical issue attaches to the Irish case. In Catholic Ireland under British rule the Catholic Church, however reluctantly, became aligned with Irish national aspirations, and on independence in 1922 succeeded in imposing itself to a degree unparalleled anywhere else. What we see now, therefore, are the effects there of social differentiation in pure form, plus whatever margin of impact has to be attributed to rationalization. The disalignment in Ireland is the result of monopoly and established power, fueled by recent prosperity in the context of European Union membership.

That theoretical point can be related to the implications of the Canadian and Australian situations. Both in Canada and Australia there are problems with national identity, some but not all of them connected with huge Catholic minorities, respectively Quebeçois and Irish. So there is a modest disalignment of religion and nation in these countries, as well as a much moderated attachment to economic liberalism compared with the USA. Since Canada and Australia have entered on a British rather than an American trajectory of secularization since the sixties, it follows that they provide another relatively pure instance. The prime significant difference between them and the USA is the persistence of shadow establishments along (maybe) with a comparatively less abundant pluralism.

Eastern Europe: Impacted Ethno-religion

In Eastern Europe one has a situation heavily marked by communist overprinting, so that forcible secularization by autocratic enlightened elites at the state level (or takeover of the upper echelons of the Church) has resulted in a potent alignment of faith with nation,[52] and even of faith with aspirations to liberty and public truth. Such an alignment was forged in Poland but it existed in varied degrees in Croatia, Serbia, Lithuania, Slovakia, and Romania, and even in Prague. The implications for any extension of pluralism are obvious, even after the fall of communism created an ideological vacuum. Thus in Poland evangelicals number no more than 0.15 percent – and overt pressure against Pentecostals is apparently present in Catholic Lithuania. In Greece, historically lying at the border with Communism and Islam, contemporary Orthodoxy visibly improves its position in the context of ethnic solidarity, and voluntaristic minorities (as distinct from ethnic ones) are minuscule. The impact of this union of faith and ethnicity over against a defined and powerful enemy is also clear in the Hungarian diaspora just outside its official borders: practice is high in Romania and Serbia (Voyvodina) which are Orthodox, low in Slovakia which is, like Hungary, mostly Catholic.[53] It follows that as the enemy collapses your own solidarity declines, as it has done in Poland. As already mentioned, the union of faith and nation does not imply reinstatement of ecclesiastical norms either in law or personal behavior.

However, this potent fusion is not universal, since there were countries where religion was on the wrong foot for resisting state-sponsored secularization. In these countries an incipient pluralism is inhibited by the erasure of the spiritual premise, as is evidently the case in the former East Germany and the Czech Republic. It may be best to begin with these negative instances, before surveying other situations where, whatever the fusion of faith and nation, circumstances may offer greater opportunities for religious pluralism.

Beginning with the former German Democratic Republic we have all the conditions operating over a long period for maximum secularization and the creation of a spiritual desert – but not a vacuum. Historically the Protestant Church was a state-sponsored monopoly fusing two churches by decree, and it gave rise to a pietist dissidence, for example in the poorer parts of Berlin.[54] At the same time, industrialization and urban conditions undermined active participation in the state church, and an "enlightened" upper middle class was alienated by court control and patronage. After the febrile experimentation of the Weimar Republic, the Nazi regime found co-operators in the German Church who had their stronghold in the Berlin Cathedral. With communist control yet more co-operators were available to promote state socialism, and the Church, in common with every other institution, was infiltrated by the STASI. Yet it was this Church, largely confined to welfare and reduced to perhaps 2 percent regular participation, which first opened up debate and then provided the principal space for opposition, especially in Leipzig, where public demonstrations materially helped bring down the regime. However, once the fervor of revolt was over the channel of the Church again ran dry. The one alignment available to the Church was the historic link of German culture in Bach, Handel, Herder, and Luther. Evangelicals are few, though there is a small Methodist Church.

The situation in the Czech Republic was only marginally better given that the Czechs (as distinct from the Slovaks) had a historic liberal tradition linked to a national myth forged in Protestantism and opposed to the reimposition of a Counter-Reformation Catholicism under foreign auspices. That made Catholic participation in cultural resistance less important than elsewhere, though Catholics were involved in Charter 77 and had a presence in the demonstrations of 1989. Catholics appealed to ancient traditions, but religious practice and belief declined in the communist period without the conspicuous return which began in Hungary in the late seventies. Pentecostals number no more than 10,000.

Romania is a special case because although there is a fusion of faith and Romanian nationhood forged under the Turks and second only to Poland, there have been openings for pluralism more particularly on the western border of the Banat and Transylvania. In Romania there was ecclesiastical collusion between national Orthodox faith and national communism, and some subversion of church by state, particularly at the top. Yet, by a kind of agreement over national symbols, religious motifs continued to be cherished in the population and surfaced very strongly in the overthrow of the Ceausescu family dictatorship in December 1989.[55] Memorials at Sibiu and Timisoara to those gunned down by the Securitate are in the form of crosses, whereas most of the earlier ones to the liberal nationalist heroes are not. The revolution was initially sparked off by a Hungarian Reformed pastor in Timisoara speaking for the oppressed Hungarian minority, but the Hungarians were joined in demonstrations by Romanians demanding "bread and warmth" and waving flags with the communist emblem removed.

In Romania there is some vulnerability to Baptist and Pentecostal preaching throughout the country, and Witnesses have also made an impact in particular areas. But the main region open to religious change is Transylvania and in particular the province of Bihar, bordering Hungary. Historically this region has been westernized and developed under the Hapsburg empire and has a long-standing tradition of religious tolerance and pluralism as between Hungarian Catholics and Reformed Protestants (including Unitarians), German Lutherans, Jews, and Romanian Uniates and Orthodox. The city center of Oradea has virtually all these, including a large disused synagogue half hidden by a vast icon dedicated to Coca Cola. Oradea has also been the centre for a fervent Baptist movement, founded by Germans over a century ago among Hungarians, which expanded in the seventies under charismatic leadership. It now has a megachurch and an associated Bible Institute. Baptist churches can be seen in many neighboring villages, serving Romanian or Hungarian congregations, and the megachurch both sends out emissaries all over Eastern Europe and draws students from far afield as, for example, Moldova and Siberia. Baptists, like the equally active Pentecostals, successfully cross ethnic lines, even though tensions remain, and Baptist leaders are careful to stress their Romanian loyalty. This is also wise given the pressure exercised by the Orthodox hierarchy and some local priests with respect to the unity of Orthodox faith and ethnicity.

In the main church in Oradea different layers are plainly visible: those brought in off the land, often forcibly, and marked by stolid peasant endurance but responding to a new personal mode of address, and the younger generation, often their children, with mobile faces and body language, alert for new opportunities and knowledge, especially through the Bible Institute. There they are taught by local people with experience of western education as well as by British and North Americans from (say) Aberdeen or Wheaton.

There are dangers here analogous to those noted everywhere else. On the one hand there is a conscious attempt at the formation of a Christian intelligentsia, backed up by the attempted creation of a Protestant faculty in the University of Timisoara, and on the other a wariness about whether the importation of Derrida (along with other ambiguous western goods) is what struggling people most need at the moment for their advancement. At the same time the alert and sophisticated Pentecostal looking after local evangelical radio suggests other paths as well as that leading to absorption in the contemplations of culture. Pentecostals are more interested in the pragmatics of communication than the cultivation of the schools. Their forte and preference has always been useful skills to promote messages.

Romania is also remarkable for two other channels of transformation. One has to do with the gypsies, already mentioned in relation to their conversion in France and Spain. As elsewhere, members of an oppressed and despised group reverse the stereotype of themselves as thieving, disreputable, dirty, and dissipated. The other is the "Lord's Army," a group within Orthodoxy originating between the wars and persecuted both by the Orthodox hierarchy (infiltrated by the government no doubt) and the communist leadership. Charismatic outbreaks are relatively rare in Orthodoxy, though they occur, for example, in the contemporary Coptic churches of Egypt and Ethiopia, but in Eastern Europe the Lord's Army is an exception. Every year there is the equivalent of a mass Pentecostal rally, for example at Sibiu (Hermannstadt) in central Romania, led by an Orthodox priest of impressive bearing and eloquence. There are even minor analogues of this kind of intensification of religious feeling leading to public rallies and demonstrations among younger members of the Hungarian Reformed Church. The leadership of the Reformed is as uncertain how to view this as the leadership of Orthodoxy is with respect to the Lord's Army.

Looking beyond Eastern Europe to the Ukraine and the Russian Federation, the first presents an analogue of the situation in Transylvania. Like Transylvania the western Ukraine is border country where currents of East and West have mingled over centuries, often through conquest and reconquest as between Catholic and Orthodox – and Islamic – powers, and there are Catholic, Uniate, Russian, and Ukrainian communities, as well as active remnants of the Jewish communities. There is the same plurality of alternative communal faiths historically present in Transylvania interspersed with western voluntarism, creating communities of choice and seeking inward conversion. There is here the same sequence of Baptist conversions followed by Pentecostal conversions, neither of them novel faiths imported since the collapse of communism, but able now to pursue new opportunities, alarming to Uniates and to Ukrainian Orthodox – and to their rivals, the Russian Orthodox. At the same time, there are new arrivals even more alarming to guardians of ancient cultural deposits than Baptists or Pentecostals. Ecclesiastical politics and geopolitics commingle and this fusion persists in Russia itself. There Orthodox and communist ultra-nationalists seek legal remedies to reinforce cultural and national boundaries.

Though regular religious practice in Russia is perhaps only 6–7 percent, ethnicity and religious identity are still bound together in the Slavic imagination, and the West in whatever form, as democracy or individualism or religion, is dangerous.[56] If western emissaries are American and Protestant the danger is clear and present. In Bulgaria, for example, in the immediate post-war period, some Bulgarian Protestant pastors were imprisoned for twenty years on charges of spying. It does not matter whether the context is Eastern Europe or Latin America, left or right, atheist or orthodox, all can agree on the menace of transnational religion. Historic domains are inviolate, and in Russia pluralism is a pollution of a soil defined by onion domes and deep bass sonorities. Noisy and extrovert electronic music (like jazz in the Soviet period) intrudes. Religion is a national cultural resource and a marker, though mostly uncalled for, or called on for support by corrupt and opportunistic governments and legislatures, local or national.

Things may vary a little or a lot in the territories once occupied by the Soviets, depending on ecclesiastical tradition, national culture, and history. Georgia is different to ex-Soviet Russia, for example, in the support given by the old communists to Baptists under pressure from powerful elements in the Georgian Orthodox Church which promote an ultra-nationalist and even messianic agenda. The reason is presumably that communists have historically been allied with Russian influence, linguistic and political, against aspirations to national autonomy which could appeal to roots in Georgian Orthodoxy.[57] Certainly Zviad Ghamsakurdia, the leader who came to power in the immediate post-war period, was armed with a passionate and poetic Orthodox messianism, and he succeeded in fuelling all the rival allegiances of the nation until he was defeated in a nasty civil war. The difficulties and fragmentations of these first years were made worse by conflicts with minorities in Abhazia and South Ossetia, which were fomented further by interested Russian interventions on their behalf, until Georgians felt it politic to return to some partial dependence on Russia. For that matter the Christian nations of the Caucasus have always felt pressure to accept Russian protection given that they are next door to Muslim nations, above all to

Turkey, and may currently face pan-Islamic aspirations fed from Chechnya and elsewhere.

Clearly this is not the kind of situation where Orthodoxy feels relaxed about its territory, and the Baptists in particular tread cautiously, emphasizing how Georgian they are. Indeed, those Baptists who speak Russian (and look back to an earlier foundation in 1878) are somewhat scandalized by such sensitive "inculturation," which includes feasting and moderate drinking and the adoption of Georgian architectural styles. Baptists have made considerable progress since the end of the civil war in 1992, and a few Pentecostals have emerged. It seems prosperity teachings make little impact, being seen as un-Georgian (but not un-Armenian). As in Romania the Baptists feel confident behind their reasonably well-educated leaders. They understand their situation, maintain sensible contacts with local governors and prove their independence by rejecting Southern Baptist money requiring them to accept American missionaries. However, European Baptist money offered without strings and designed to help an impoverished people build facilities is another matter. Congregations are now emerging in the semi-dechristianized countryside, just as they have done in Bihar province, Transylvania. The main church in Tiblisi has a congregation of about four hundred, much smaller than the Oradea church, but quite impressive all the same and, as is usual, nearly two in three are women.

Estonia, to the far north-west of European Russia, is very different, particularly since migration, some of it forced, had created a huge minority of Russians by comparison with the smallish minority in Georgia. The Lutheran Church there is the culturally established body with fine buildings and choirs, and historic German and Scandinavian connections. Indeed, connections with Lutheran Finland have been revived on the basis of a pan-Baltic (or Hanseatic) concept of the future, but the dechristianization of the Soviet period was at least as thorough-going as in East Germany. Religious recovery has been confined to the very young or old, and that includes the small Methodist Church and enthusiastic non-denominational evangelicals just calling themselves "Christians."

What these territories in Eastern Europe lack is a confident middle class seeking personal fulfillment complementary to their impersonal professional avocations, such as have offered fertile ground to the Word of Life (or "Faith" Church) in Uppsala, Sweden. These will emerge with prosperity, and the first indication so far is, as one would expect, in Budapest in Central Europe, where prosperity was already en route even in the later and more lax stages of communist rule. The Faith Church in Budapest is now the fourth largest religious grouping in the country (paralleling the "Universal Church" in Portugal). It commends prosperity, has neo-liberal links with politics and, as is often the case, has a Zionist element, shown in its special interest in the fate of Jews in Hungary in 1944–5, when the Germans took over. Its trademark is technical sophistication and, as might be expected, it arouses considerable journalistic animus.

Restatement

The whole tenor of this analysis suggests that classical Pentecostalism is unlikely to be a major power in the developed world because it represents the mobilization of a minority of people at the varied margins of that world, whereas in the developing world it represents the mobilization of large masses. Insofar as a comparable phenomenon exists in the North Atlantic religious universe, it takes the more stable form of Conservative Evangelicalism or works through the cultivation of charismata within the historic churches, including the Roman Catholic Church, as well as through newly created bodies and churches which combine evangelical and Pentecostal elements, like the Calvary Chapel. There is no pressing need to walk out of the established denominations in order to enter an explicitly Pentecostal denomination, given that the Pentecostal style, and social status, are viewed as embarrassing.

At the same time, the overall Evangelical movement, with its minor Pentecostal affiliates, makes up the liveliest sector of contemporary church life, by its warmth and its sense of boundaries and of moral order. This distinguishes it from Liberal Protestants, however massive that constituency, and is part of the reason "why conservative churches are growing" at least in their ability to retain their young. Just how large the Evangelical sector is depends on the historical context of different countries. In the USA, which is the one country with an unequivocal Protestant cultural template and a pluralism and voluntarism likely to generate active and competitive religious bodies, the Evangelical sector is very large. Indeed, as the one contemporary superpower the USA is the capital equally of Liberal Protestantism, Conservative Evangelicalism, and Pentecostalism. Conservative Evangelicalism is itself concentrated most massively in the "sub-dominant" culture of the USA, which is in the South and Texas, though it has growing outposts elsewhere. The global radiation of Evangelical Christianity occurs in tandem with the myth of America, and in particular comes out of major organizational centers in the South and Texas.

Elsewhere in the North Atlantic universe, Conservative Evangelicalism, and perhaps a vigorous Christianity more generally, varies inversely with how far there is an established and/or state-supported religion. Even in the USA there remains an established liberalized Protestantism, but in Canada, Australia, and New Zealand there have been genuine shadow establishments of different kinds of Protestantism, mostly made up of Anglicans, Presbyterians, or Methodists, often in combination or in "United" Churches. In Britain there are two weak legal establishments with voluntary sectors, in Holland disintegrating yet still segmented cultural establishments, and in Scandinavia there remain established shells, with "personal Christianity" partly within and partly without. Whatever the situation all the way from the pluralistic USA to monopolistic Sweden, and from Presbyterian Dunedin in New Zealand to the United Church constituency in Ontario, (English) Canada, the evangelical sector is active, and Pentecostalism energetic. Even in secular Britain, for example, the Baptist denomination has been the least liberalized of the historic Protestant churches and has retained its membership more effectively, though with charismatic breakaways. At the same time as Pentecostal churches experience some growth, there is a fraying at the edge of Conservative Evangelicalism, for example in England and in the Re-Reformed tradition of Holland. That is most clear in the Free University of Amsterdam which has deserted its founding charter and followed the liberalizing trajectory of comparable bodies in the United States, such as the sometime Methodist universities, and even maybe some of the "conservative" colleges.

Throughout post-Protestant Northern Europe the establishments, official or unofficial, are gently collapsing, and the people at large have been inoculated against the latest waves of Evangelicalism by earlier ones, such as the Revivalist traditions of Finland, Evangelicalism in England, and the Pietism of Norway and Germany. Insofar as Pentecostalism finds a niche it does so in migrant populations from the third world, but in practice this means the Caribbean migration to England, since otherwise migrants are for the most part defined ethno-religiously through Islam, Hinduism, Catholicism, or Orthodoxy. So the primary impact of the current wave on the "home" populations is either through charismatic movements in historic churches, parallel to those in America, which often create para-ecclesiastical networks, or independent variants and house churches. Nor would one expect these to be confined to post-Protestant Europe since at the margin they may emerge in post-Catholic Europe in, as one occasionally observes, parts of France. The most successful "free enterprise" of this kind is the Word of Life megachurch in Uppsala (and affiliates elsewhere) with its strong tincture of community spirit and prosperity teaching. All these initiatives emphasize spirituality, setting up strong emotional and moral bonds, and offering the opportunity for personal expression. In those respects they are cognate with similar groups in the emergent middle classes of Nigeria, Buenos Aires, Singapore, or wherever.

"Latin" Western Europe is somewhat different, since only France is "post-Catholic" and there have hitherto been only very minor waves of Evangelicalism. So the analytic task becomes focused on what distinguishes Latin Europe from Latin America, which may be that in Latin Europe the secularist anti-clerical elites, for whom *all* religion was politically dangerous, possessed the administrative and educational instruments required to transmit their world-view downward, as well as a mass ready and receptive in an industrial proletariat. (So, too, did the secular elites of Protestant Europe, but there enlightened and religious motifs commingled in the upper strata, including the clergy, with the result that education and welfare simply tipped over time, and under state aegis, in a secular direction.) The French model was exported to Italy and Spain, and for that matter Latin America, where the capitals and intelligentsias often emulated Paris. But the conditions were different. Neither in Spain nor Italy were the masses secularized, and both countries experienced a fascist corporatism with which the Church colluded in return for an opportunity to socialize the population in Catholicism. The eventual outcomes of these reactions were, however, different. The democratic opening up in Spain in association with the European Community led to a consumerist secularism combined with the sense that religion as such was compromised and archaic. In Italy an increasingly corrupt Christian Democratic dominance collapsed with the collapse of its communist counterweight. As a result Spain became secular much more extensively than Italy, with the corollary that conditions in the south of Italy remain even today closer to those in Latin America, and so hospitable to Pentecostalism. Portugal is an intermediate case. It is a country at the margin of Europe, with a secular south, and the Church suffers from implication in the Salazar dictatorship. However, the northern areas were not secularized from above when after 1910 metropolitan liberals persecuted both Catholics and radicals, and there is clearly some vulnerability to Pentecostal imports from Brazil.

In Eastern Europe the imposition of communism encountered very different situations: yielding in the German Democratic Republic and Czech lands, massively resistant in Poland, depending on how positively related religion was to the national tradition and how compromised religion had been historically. In Albania, for example, where the nation was split between several religious traditions, the governing intelligentsia tried to erase religion altogether. Where nation and faith were fused, in Poland (or Greece), pluralism was unlikely to make headway. Nevertheless, when the fall of communism left a vacuum there were regions of vulnerability in interstitial areas, such as Transylvania and the western Ukraine. Throughout the whole of Eastern Europe there are different layers of Protestantism, the oldest and most historic having an ancient ethnic base, for example German Lutheranism in Hungary and Romania, and Hungarian Calvinism inside and outside the Hungarian border. These embers can be revived by evangelical sparks, but not seriously inflamed.

Then there is a layer of denominational Protestantism, often Baptist, quite strong in Russia and in one or two other Orthodox countries, which had been tolerated for its temperance and moral disciplines and also persecuted as western (or American). This kind of Evangelicalism can be revivified, as it was in Transylvania (and in Romania more generally) in the later years of the dictatorship, and as it is now in Georgia after the civil war. Pentecostalism was an extension of this tradition throughout the whole area, but subject to more persecution as somehow more awkwardly virulent and sometimes pacifist. At any rate, Pentecostals now make considerable progress in Romania and the Ukraine, and in Romania may be twice as numerous as the Baptists. At the other end of the spectrum in Budapest, a "Faith Church" with prosperity teachings makes an impact comparable to the Word of Life Church in Uppsala.

CHAPTER THREE

latin america:
a template?

In turning to Latin America where the first explosion of Pentecostalism (and Evangelical Protestantism) took place in the sixties and even earlier, we need first a recapitulation of themes. The "Third Force" of "Third Person" Christianity has been expanding in Latin America since the mid-century, invigorating large masses by a combination of participation and flexibility. It takes those marooned and confined in the secular reality by fate and fortune, and offers them a protected enclave in which to explore the gifts of the Spirit, such as perseverance, peaceableness, discipline, trustworthiness, and mutual acceptance among the brethren and in the family. Real and fictive fraternity are mutually supportive. The believers, nearly two-thirds of them women, link themselves together in chains of mutual encouragement. They sing and pray by the hour because that sacred time tells of their discovery of themselves as of infinite value, not in the eye of the law, but in the eye of the Author of all law.

We are in a new phase of global capitalism in which culture is increasingly recognized as a key variable, including such attributes as responsibility, discipline, and trust. The point has been argued by Fukuyama and Harrison, but even those on the left, alert for the economic skeleton beneath the cultural skin, acknowledge that culture and economy are intertwined.[1] The type of capitalism emerging in the culture of Eastern Europe is a case in point.

Two points are crucial. First, there is a consumer (or, if you prefer, post-modern) capitalism with a transnational dynamic drawing "first"- and "third"-world societies into a single cultural and economic system, so that all societies have "first-world" segments clustered around multinationals in the megacities, with a smaller or larger underclass on the periphery.[2] Second, cultural representations are consumed globally, so that the culture industries, whether concerned with tourism, information, or leisure, increasingly play a key role in economic life.[3]

Religious entrepreneurship depends on the arrival of the open religious economy, pluralism, and choice. The late twentieth century has seen the collapse of overarching and all-embracing systems, notably fascism and communism, and to a lesser extent Catholicism. This is not to predict the imminent decline and fall of Rome but to note the final arrival of pluralism and the slow disengagement of all the historic churches, Catholicism included, from their organic relation to state, nation, and local community. People are no longer and forever consigned by baptism into a religious identity which is also a national identity. Rather they are exposed to options and alternatives. In the initial stages of this process the historic churches remain embedded in the total social system, and are often rejected for their apparent implication in its corruption and structures of preponderant power. They reap the disadvantages of a precarious monopoly in terminal decline. The new evangelical groups by contrast reap, for a while at least, the advantages of a new start and a clean break. Many of the evangelical believers see the past as "dirty" and their induction into a new future as a form of cleansing. In this way two potent shifts come together. One is the rigours of competition on an open and decentralized religious market. The other is the promise of a transition from darkness and dirt of implication in society as a whole to the light and cleanliness of a second birth in the society of the brethren.

The difficulty for Catholicism resides in its subtle combination of sacred and secular, as in the festival of Mardi Gras or in the way the baroque dome harbors a pullulating syncretism. By contrast the clean break offered through Pentecostalism and through other evangelical groups cuts the ties with the carnival, with the fiesta, and with godparenthood, as well as with the politico-economic system of clientage, though the tentacles of that all too easily grow again. This in turn means cutting free from the world of alcohol, of deals in bars, and of football and the weekend male spree. As Andrew Chesnut has recently suggested, Evangelicalism is a faith of the household poised against the seductions of the street.[4] In this titanic contest it requires every resource of discipline, and of a mutual support continually renewed. The contrast of "faith" with "world" needs persistent reinforcement. Again the theme of cleanliness comes to the fore, for example, in the decoration of churches. Instead of the Assumption or the miracles of the saints there emerge images of peace and purification: the rose of Sharon, the lily of the valley, still waters and cleansing waterfalls. The human body itself has to be reclothed in modesty, marking out a safe distance from male pride and female vanity. In short the dynamic dualism of primitive Christianity, so criticized in the western theological academy, has been restored. That was precisely the element indicated by the term "walk-out" in *Tongues of Fire*.

If all these features are brought together, we find an analogy of a new man and a new woman in a new society. The context is that of religious entrepreneurship in a competitive religious economy and of enthusiastic participation on the part of all the believers; the inner transformation is that of honest dealing, trustworthiness, peaceableness, hard work, independence, self help, mutual assistance, and the ability to be articulate and fluent in the presence of others. Clearly all this has implications for the world of work as well as for the kind of work preferred. With respect to work as such Pentecostals are not swept up in the Weberian notion of vocation, but they do believe that they should give a proper return for their wages and should be trustworthy. That, for example, is one reason why many Catholic women seek out evangelical women as domestic helps. With regard to the kind of work preferred there is a complicated dialectic between being already in occupations which allow a chink of independent vision and seeking out occupations where such chinks exist. Evangelicals are part of a psychic mutation towards personal independence and individual initiative dramatized in their sense of "personal salvation."

It is clear that in the contemporary situation initiative and independence are required even for mere survival and, after all, a large number of evangelicals are struggling for precisely that in the informal economy. Survival is made more likely by their priorities in terms of expenditure, and by their religiously-founded hope that they will not descend into the abyss of social chaos. And many do better than survive. As and when chances turn up they are amongst the people most likely to seize them. Within a generation they may have put a foot on the ladder of small business or of educational advance.

And one must add that in slowly climbing out of the maladies of poverty they are pragmatic, canny, and apt for a bargain. They know how and when to help a miracle happen. There is no pursuit of pie-in-the-sky to the denigration of their circumstances in the present. "In the world you will have tribulation" – but you have been given ways and means to meet tribulation. As one Methodist Pentecostal pastor in Chile put it: "I would like technological university for my people so that they could gain skills . . . it is time we Hispanics caught up with the Japanese, the Americans and the Germans." Part of these changes has to do with that matter of catching up, and as such it can have economic implications.

What is the staying power of this dramatic mutation? There is always the problem of the revolving door and the obvious difficulty of holding young people, especially males, when confronted by the seductions of the adolescent and young adult life-style. Yet as John Burdick has argued, the appeal of Pentecostalism and Evangelicalism is precisely to a large number of young men and women who do not wish to be embroiled and sullied by the street life of the contemporary city.[5] Peaceable young adults find a haven in the church and in each other where they can set about making something worthwhile and lasting. The abandoned young woman finds a husband among the brethren and together they can bring the children under control.

With regard to the long-term sustainability of the movement there is also, of course, the bureaucratization of churches as they become large-scale enterprises, and the relativization of perspective which arrives as the next generation acquires education. These processes have tamed the organizational thrust of earlier movements like Methodism and damp-ened the ardor of believers. And it is true that some of the larger churches have ameliorated the participatory fervor of their origins and sought to quench the disruptive power of prophecy. When these changes take place ecstasy becomes routine and the church settles down into yet another denomination of largely lower-middle-class members who have become secure in their respectability. David Lehmann has given a minatory account of the degree of bureaucratization in the Brazilian Assemblies of God.[6]

Yet this is where the fragmentation, fission, and flexibility of Pente-costalism offer advantages. As one church becomes a standard denom-ination others emerge, offering vents to the flow of molten lava. The lay spirit helps to ensure that the pastorate does not graduate too rapidly from Bible Institute to seminary, and so convert the Christian ministry into a subordinate arm of the western intelligentsia. Independent charis-matic churches emerge in the new middle classes helping their members to deal with problems of job and marital insecurity and the drug culture, which run parallel to the older churches now "in renewal." The ethos of these even mingles with that of similar movements in the Catholic Church. Thus in the more affluent suburbs of the new middle class one may encounter a Catholic house group, an evangelical group coming together in a basement to sing, share experiences, and meditate on the Bible, and yet another group meeting in a large and well-appointed "Baptist Church in Renewal." In Chile the Anglican Church offers a warm, supportive atmosphere which "gets to" the new middle classes with their work and family problems.

All of these groupings involve what in eighteenth century Britain was called a "Reformation of Manners." If one believes that cultural change is more than an epiphenomenon then such a reformation has implica-tions for development. Curiously enough such implications are (in terms of their economic ethos and moral temper) not light years away from what was proposed in documents like *Rerum Novarum* in the eighteen nineties. It is as if the possibilities projected by Catholicism have in part been realized outside its boundaries, and necessarily so, given its centuries-long entanglement as the carrier of Hispanic civilization. This helps explain how it could be that the Catholic bishops of Chile found their views on moral disorder most closely shared by those belonging to the Evangelical churches.

Such a profile of the Protestant movement makes it clear that radically new social and cultural capital is being created at the level of the person as well as at the level of church and communal life within the protected enclaves of the believers. Persons, women as well as men, are individualized in a culturally novel way which carries a sense of unique worth and spiritually driven empowerment while at the same time grounding the individual in a network of mutual responsibilities and obligations, within the family crucially, but also within the wider believing community. This contrasts sharply with the traditional license afforded to the male – freedom without responsibility – especially in what John Burdick with elegant euphemism calls "the male prestige arena,"[7] that is the street, bar, brothel, football stadium, and drug culture, and which Elisabeth Brusco encompasses with the Brazilian epithet *machista*.[8] The restoration of the family as a viable moral, cultural, and economic household, largely through the reformation of the male and the elimination of the double standard of morality for the two sexes, is the pivotal transformation wrought by conversion. From it can follow all the other forms of betterment – in health (many spiritual/physical healings arise on account of the excesses of the *machista* life), in work, in giving priority to feeding, clothing, disciplining, and educating the children, and oneself, in discovering a potential for leadership and initiative within the life of the church.

The new Protestantism is more than a passive adaptation to the massive economic changes which have swept Latin America since the 1960s; it is a creative and active response, a seizing of opportunities and not merely a spiritual consolation for the hapless victims of social change. John Burdick makes a case for considering Pentecostalism a "cult of affliction" in Victor Turner's sense, in that it appeals directly and explicitly to those who are suffering, particularly poor and often chronically misused women.[9] Yet the term is also misleading because the new Protestantism, notably in its majority form of Pentecostalism, has strong reservations about the European Christian approach to suffering as exemplary. It draws on indigenous Amerindian and black spiritual currents which have always flowed strongly beneath the surface of a colonial Catholicism and which regard suffering as something to be overcome. This indigenous spiritual tradition assumes no great distinction between spiritual, physical, and material well-being. Salvation consists in reintegrating these three dimensions and returning human life to the properly benign state which God intended. Virtuoso asceticism is not so much valued as a spiritual good in itself as a means for spreading the gospel – as for instance in the case of the elderly Brazilian Assemblies of God pastor who boasted of the privations he had endured in planting seventy churches in his adult lifetime – or as a divine test of the believer's faithfulness under tribulation. Pentecostalism, more particularly some of the groups like the Brazilian Divine Cure movement which grew most strongly in the economic hard times of the eighties, has called

on women to leave passivity and fatalism behind and demand the reform
of their menfolk.

It has also grown a wing promoting a prosperity gospel which, while
owing something to the North American Bible Belt, also draws on African
and Amerindian spiritual traditions. These were for centuries preserved,
half-hidden, in the semi-autonomous black brotherhoods and in the
syncretism of folk cults only recently banished from the Catholic Church
by the new broom of the Second Vatican Council. Miraculous physical
healings and spectacular reversals of material misfortune are legitimate
expectations within a world-view that regards them as the proper complements of spiritual restoration rather than as materialist contradictions
of sovereign "spiritual" values. In these respects Latin American Pentecostalism strongly resembles the "third force" Christianity of contemporary central and southern Africa.

As argued earlier, Pentecostalism re-creates the thoroughgoing dualism of Primitive Christianity, a view which may seem to contradict the
argument just presented. The point is that this is primarily a moral
dualism, not a dualism of body and soul. It sharply marks the boundary
between the corrupt outside world and the redeemed enclave of the
believing community. It sets up absolute moral rules for the governance
of the community in particular to establish sexual and marital discipline,
but it does not elevate the spiritual above the embodied. Burdick's findings
indicate a culture which, while struggling hard against it, can tolerate a
common poverty, but which does not accept immiseration as the Lord's
will for believers. It is a culture which positively celebrates material and
physical goods as the Lord's blessings, especially the healed bodies and
full tables which everywhere signal domestic comfort in place of *machista*
chaos and waste. As one Chilean ex-alcoholic put it: "We believers may
have given up manly drink (alcohol) for the drink of young girls (cola
and orange juice) but in the women's kitchen we eat better."

Satisfied bodies and full pockets are not in themselves evil or worldly.
There is, however, a pervasive suspicion of great wealth, both through
the suspicion of corruption and because riches may be a test from God,
since material blessings also bring the obligation to use them for the
Lord's work and not just for personal pleasure and aggrandizement.
What is rejected is excess of all kinds, particularly sexual promiscuity
and the unrestrained hedonism typical of *machista* culture – and of popular
commercial culture.

It is here that Pentecostalism finds itself in serious tension with a
central thrust of consumer capitalism. The movement has no reservations about new technology as such: indeed it hastens to exploit every
new form of communication for the work of evangelism. What it deeply
mistrusts is the "corrupt communications" that technology habitually

carries – its messages of sexual permissiveness, moral relativism, and self-indulgent hedonism. Thus religious movements which seek access to radio and TV networks, the Internet and the rest, also forbid their members to tune in to anything except the gospel and, sometimes, the profane news. It is unbridled Desire as muse of the post-modern market place which the new Protestants fear and avoid even as they rejoice in the material and bodily well-being of the believers.

They promote marital faithfulness not celibacy, and moderation and responsibility rather than a monastic renunciation of wealth. The new Latin American Protestants may be disciplined and, mostly, poor but they are not world-denying and they have by no means set their faces against wealth creation. Indeed, one might almost argue that they have recognized exactly those dystopic dimensions of a secular ultra-individualism to reconsider whether it might be economically as well as socially advantageous to restore cultural guarantees of mutual trust, self-discipline, and social cohesion.

Global Capitalism

There is no doubt a striking coincidence between the rise of Protestant-ism in Latin America and the development of the latest stage of global capitalism there. In the 1960s and 1970s the states of the region progres-sively opened up their economies to world trade and inward invest-ment. The various military regimes of the seventies were particularly instrumental in this, welcoming multinational companies and dismant-ling the apparatus of protection for the local import-substitution indus-tries erected by earlier, often leftist, governments. The megacities swelled to vast proportions in the boom years of the seventies and even much of traditional agriculture was transformed into agribusiness. At the same time as opening up their economies, the seventies governments began to apply policies of privatization and deregulation such as were being fol-lowed in North America and Europe, creating by installments "flexible" labor markets in place of the corporatist and clientist systems of the past.

By the time the colonels gave way to civilian democracy the debt crisis of the early eighties made it impossible to reverse the integra-tion of Latin America in the global economy. The international financial institutions which managed the debt imposed further applications of neo-liberal economic policy as a condition of debt rescheduling and of assistance with development projects. The net effect was to fix Latin America irrevocably inside the new global patterns of distribution of capital and labor, and to integrate its economy into that of the post-modern West, particularly the individualistic capitalism of its powerful northern neighbor, the USA.

This history falls into the two broad phases. The period from the 1960s up to the debt crisis is one of immense population movements from rural to urban areas and of considerable net upward occupational mobility as rural migrants were transformed into workers in the post-industrial labor markets of the cities. The new Protestants were not factory fodder like the early English Methodists, because the factory was not the definitive institution of this latest economic revolution.

Alan Gilbert notes that up to the end of the seventies it was the better educated and more ambitious who went to the cities and that even the city poor were better off than their rural relations.[10] He says that despite the decline of the "Fordist" manufacturing sector in the import substitution industries which no longer enjoyed tariff protection, there were very low levels of unemployment in the formal economy and of reliance on the informal labor market; that by the end of the seventies the urban workforce was typically 40 percent white-collar, a sector which had grown so fast that first generation rural migrants had had to supply the deficit which the existing urban middle classes could not meet; that in addition up to 30 percent of the urban workforce comprised domestic servants who were largely female and worked in ones and twos for the new urban middle-class professionals. This is the period of real Protestant take-off.

The decade after the debt crisis was one of recession and economic hardship, especially for the poorest, as the benevolent processes of mass upward mobility were interrupted, unemployment rates rocketed, and the informal sector was proportionately swelled alike, though to different degrees, in successful economies such as Chile and problematic ones like Brazil; manufacturing industry shrank (by 25 percent in Mexico City, for instance); wage rates plummeted and women and children were driven on to the informal economy; family break-up, already accelerated by the population mobility of the boom years, became endemic, not least because male bread-winners who found they could not afford to support a family were tempted to abandon their responsibilities altogether; "street children" came to be seen as a major social and public-order problem (and one much exaggerated). None of this slowed down the rate of Protestant advance. Indeed, new movements like the Brazilian Cura Divina flourished mightily under these harsh conditions.

Although in some sense Protestantism was a response to the conditions created by this social and economic upheaval, one cannot see it as primarily or intentionally an answer to economic or social problems. It was and is a movement of spiritual renewal with economic and social implications. Moreover, it is a response which gives a powerful new sense of agency to individuals and groups in spite of the limiting circumstances within which they are able to exercise it. Both in the boom time and in recession one of the most important aspects of Protestantism has been its ability to create enclaves of order and social capital within the unplanned and chaotic sprawl of the megacities. In such places the invasion of common or undeveloped land has been the most usual form of urban settlement for migrants: services like roads, street lighting, and electricity come later, if at all, through the exercise of political pressure and ruthless bargaining. Analysts of the post-modern city have referred without much exaggeration to the "impacted ghettoes" and "ungovernable spaces" of megacities. It is within such urban spaces that the majority of the new Protestants have been found, and it is in such areas that the ratio of Protestants to practising Catholics is highest, sometimes one to one or more. This is where the domestic order and cleanliness of the Protestant, the secure family, and the church support systems create social capital out of nothing.

Though there are continuities between the "Reformation of Manners" on which this social capital is founded and the classic Protestant ethic there are also differences. The crucial difference lies in the economic context. The new urbanites have to make their way in the deregulated, flexible labor markets of the post-industrial, service-based economy. The new Protestants are not typically part of a manufacturing "proletariat" but workers in the service sector, frequently in the informal economy, within a high-tech, information-based global capitalism. In such a world the ability to be punctual, regimented, and obedient, so crucial in the (Fordist) factory system, is less relevant than the capacity to be self-motivating, to control the work process without direct supervision, to be reflective and self-monitoring, and to manage interpersonal encounters skillfully. Honesty and trustworthiness remain essential, but the context of their performance is radically altered. These post-industrial virtues call for increments of feminization in the worker. Pentecostalism supplies just these personal qualities. Moreover they are as vital for the street salesman, the hotel waiter, the self-appointed tourist-guide-cum-beggar, or the domestic servant (the ubiquitous nanny-housekeeper working unsupervised in the home of her new middle-class employers) as they are for the software engineer, the media professional, or the social worker. This new labor market calls not for deference and hierarchy but for independence, initiative, high-octane energy, a willingness to ride the time and work rhythms of the twenty-four-hour economy and above all, a refusal to accept failure.

If anything, all this is even truer of the informal than of the formal economy. Furthermore, the *faute de mieux* "survival entrepreneurship" of the informal labor market, especially in the lean years of the eighties, has needed every boost from the Holy Spirit just to keep the effort from faltering. The energizing impact of Pentecostal worship, and the self-confidence which comes from the certainty that God is on your side in your "spiritual war", are powerful resources with which to face such an economy. The framework of moral controls set by the strict rules of the believing congregation and the need to render individual accounts to God and to the brethren together enable the believer to internalize a self-control which can survive the buffeting of the corrupt world in which he or she has to earn a living, often outside corporate structures altogether. A number of believers changed their employment to escape secular pressures – for example a banker who became a self-employed financial consultant to extricate himself from the endemic bribery and corruption in his head office; a security guard who found the violence of his work incompatible with his Christian beliefs and so opened a corner-shop butchers; and a brewery worker who gave up his well-paid laboratory work to become a street seller of wholesome sweets. These cases are instances of a more general tendency among Protestants to opt for independent work whenever possible rather than to work for or among non-believers, though there are also many who have taken the war to the enemy and endured decades of *machista* ridicule and worse on building sites, farms, and urban streets.

Since the late 1970s a number of groups have emerged on the fissile Pentecostal scene which both address and mirror cultural strains of post-modern capitalism. From the wrong side of the tracks or from the criminal underbelly of the megacities, "consumer" capitalism must sometimes look more like "casino" capitalism, with fortunes to be won and lost in an instant – a feature strongly echoed in the prosperity gospel of these newer groups. Churches like the Brazilian Universal Church of the Kingdom of God and Renascer both reflect and harness the expectations and style of this febrile world. Such churches foster an aggressively entrepreneurial spirit in their evangelistic enterprises as well as in the secular avocations of their members. In their different social milieux both have been notably successful in recruiting among the casualties of hedonistic excess, notably from the drug culture and the culture industries. While the Universal Church attracts the underworld sector of the underclass – a senior pastor at the Church's Rio headquarters suggested that up to half the young pastorate has been drawn out of the lower reaches of narcocapitalism – Renascer's appeal is to the educated professional classes, not least the media, entertainment, and communications sectors of the new middle class who may have drunk too deeply of the worldly pleasures of the night-time economy. Both these churches have incorporated many of the cultural traits of post-modern city life from which they save their members in order to turn them into holy hustlers, wheelers and dealers for God. They reject the key destructive indulgences – alcohol, tobacco, drugs, promiscuity – but retain much of the style. Their dress, body language, music, and rhetorical appeal are thoroughly contemporary and set them apart from the old-fashioned and distinctively lower-class style of respectability enforced in the older established evangelical culture. They are the newest breed of post-modern Pentecostals.

Today Protestants are found in critical mass at almost every economic and social level. The majority are still the respectable poor whose virtues enable them to make the best of what little they have. Yet even in the most unpromising economic circumstances there are striking instances of economic initiative conceived in the spirit of doing the Lord's work. This includes the landless casual laborers on the margins of Chilean agribusiness whose chances of economic improvement are slender but who collectively strive to afford the truck which will do joint service as mass transport to distant harvest sites and means of mobile mission; the street traders, self-employed collectors of waste materials and all the myriad creators of their own work in the informal economy who combine work and evangelism and seize every entrepreneurial chance that comes their way; the pastors who instruct their flock in the need to take two or three jobs or teach them skills ranging from building and driving to keeping household accounts. The Protestant poor are not typically passive.

The established evangelical denominations like the Methodist Pentecostals and the Assemblies of God have produced at least one generation of educated young professionals, some of whom eventually leave the parent body to found house churches, but who carry the evangelical culture into the heart of the new professional world as teachers, office workers, welfare professionals, and media executives. There is also an addition to their numbers from converts like those of Renascer who seek limits and disciplines to protect them from the disorienting potential of affluence and unlimited cultural possibility.

Protestantism has a first-generation business class too. The boom years of the seventies were a time when the informal economy was able to produce capital accumulation, particularly perhaps in the construction industry and associated trades. Examples of such self-made businessmen indicate that they are forming a continent-wide set of organizations which engage in charitable work, evangelism, and economic networking in roughly equal proportions. There are even signs that such organizations have had some influence on non-evangelical business culture.

Among the forty to fifty million Evangelical Protestants in Latin America a powerful new culture is incubating. It is a culture which has enabled many to survive who would otherwise have sunk into abject immiseration, and has aided many to ride the sea of economic change with some success. It has created social capital where none existed and has motivated and sustained a labor force which shifted from being

pre-modern to post-industrial often in one traumatic step.[11] Without the
Pentecostal movement the transition might have been less successful
and involved far more violent social disruption. The much-debated contribution of Methodism to the lack of violent revolution in Britain could
have a second lease of life in Latin America.[12]

CHAPTER FOUR

latin america: ambiguity in different cultural sectors

In some ways the studies now discussed bring up-to-date the review undertaken in my *Tongues of Fire* though there is no attempt to be exhaustive. The broad intention is to bring out the potent ambiguity of Pentecostalism (and of contiguous movements) in relation to economic ethic, politics, and the family, before turning to such issues as healing, apostasy, development agencies, and para-Protestant groups such as La Luz del Mundo and the Witnesses in Mexico, and the Mormons in Chile. The ambiguity is summed up at the end of the chapter by noting disagreement as to whether or not Pentecostalism shares a family likeness with liberationism.

I begin with Daniel Míguez's study *Spiritual Bonfire in Argentina*, partly because he picks up the theme of the ambiguity of Pentecostalism, but also because Argentina is distinctive in its history, cultural mix, and level of development. Pentecostalism expanded there relatively late and has been more than usually prone to doctrines of Spiritual Warfare. I then turn to complementary studies of the economic ethic of Evangelicalism by Henri Gooren and Bernice Martin, and a group of studies which though fairly general in their scope touch in particular on political culture: John Burdick and Rowan Ireland on Brazil, Roger Lancaster on Nicaragua, Frans Kamsteeg on Chile, and David Smilde on Venezuela. Venezuela parallels Argentina with regard to the late expansion of Pentecostalism, and Smilde's work includes a discussion of the Pentecostal "gender paradox" which leads naturally enough to the discussion of the family.

Daniel Míguez's study is primarily ethnographic, but it includes the wider context of late twentieth-century Argentina.[1] He indicates the social controls and governmental repression operating until the early eighties, and one infers that these have had something to do with the relatively tardy expansion of Pentecostalism. Maybe the particular cultural mix of Argentina also has something to do with it, as well as a relatively early urbanization in which energies were absorbed in the ambiguously democratic mobilizations of Peronism. At any rate, Pentecostalism expanded very rapidly from 1985 onwards, running parallel with the economic "lost decade"; and it showed a greater tendency towards doctrines of health, prosperity, and "Spiritual Warfare" than most other countries. As others have pointed out, the historic evangelical churches, including classical Pentecostals, felt undermined by these doctrines or else half-adopted them on their own account by way of pre-empting their appeal. Many of the groups and ministries of mass evangelism which sprang up at this time had a strong stake in media, deployed "personalities," some of them very dynamic, and sat loose to denominational distinctions and conventional church buildings, somewhat in the recent North American style of charismatic Evangelicalism. Another feature of Argentinian society, unexplored by Míguez but clearly relevant to the spread of ministries of healing and exorcism, is the unique popular dissemination of psychoanalysis. There is, after all, more than one way (or one language) in which to deal with "demons." People may even eclectically combine them as when a taxi driver gave testimony of the benefits of conversion to a friend of mine in psychoanalytic terms.

At any rate, whatever the precise elements at work, the proportion of evangelicals in Argentina had by 1990 risen to about one in ten, and in the poor urban area called Villa Eulalia studied by Míguez active evangelicals ran active Catholics quite close. Míguez focused his attention on the main Pentecostal church of the area and in particular he set out to analyze the life-world inhabited by believers, two thirds of whom were migrants even though their conversion had only come after a decade of urban residence. He stresses how in Argentina early urbanization meant an early acquisition of the "industrious virtues," which again leads one to speculate whether that has anything to do with a relatively greater emphasis on psychic turbulence and inner warfare within Pentecostal culture. Of course, warfare of the spirit is a standard feature of the long-term historical origins of Pentecostalism in Methodism and Pietism, but its remarkable effervescence in Argentina still needs some further analysis.

The core of Míguez's analysis eschews purely structural or actor-centered approaches to which he rather fancifully consigns earlier researchers, and concentrates on the ambiguity of Pentecostalism in the experience of those attracted to it. He even compares the ambiguity of Pentecostalism with that of Peronism, a religious and a political populism respectively. Modern and "traditional" elements are mingled, for example, in relation to healing, so that demonic powers may be involved, but secular medicine will not be rejected. Again, education is an object of suspicion and yet the Pentecostal church hosts an adult school. Political activity is suspected and yet the evangelicals have a small political party. Such combinations are pragmatic. Míguez points out that "People find emotional strength by resorting to spiritual forces to deal with the economic insecurity which working in the informal sector entails" (p. 163). He also underlines, as have many others, the multi-faceted character of Pentecostalism enabling it to adjust to many contexts. For him its potentials are in the religious realm, reconfiguring antecedent beliefs in spiritual powers and molding new identities. Catholicism in certain respects and for many of the poor has not "delivered the goods" (though no mention is made of the rather direct involvement of sectors of the Catholic Church in the repression). From the interviews quoted it seems likely that illness is a major precipitating element in a search for wholeness. That certainly is the case in my own interview material and is consistent with the pioneering work of Andrew Chesnut on that aspect of conversion.[2]

Economic Ethic

Henri Gooren's study of Pentecostal (and Mormon) growth in Guatemala and its relation to economic ethos is very much in line with what was argued in *Tongues of Fire*.[3] The situation in Guatemala has been a familiar one in much of Latin America but, if anything, worse in that country when it comes to violence, warring factions, extremes of wealth and poverty, and a history of external exploitation and subversion. The backyards of the great powers are rarely advertisements for their better principles, as the histories of Ireland, Armenia, and Poland illustrate.

Gooren's study was carried out in a low-income neighborhood of Guatemala City, honeycombed with Pentecostal churches and micro-enterprises. Such has been the deterioration of the social fabric as people have streamed into the megacity under conditions of land starvation and violence that key social units have been reduced to a basic level of family, micro-enterprise – and church. The context here is male irresponsibility, generated initially in a history of child "labor," then reinforced by the machismo of the male work group, and working itself out in alcoholism, dissipation of resources, sexual depredation, violence, and family deterioration. Home and work are undermined by the culture of the street and the bar, symbolized in the weekend soccer spree. At some point, however, a minority of men contemplate the dreary future ahead of them and are ready for the change many of their womenfolk most ardently desire: a new social network in the church that breaks with the street, cherishes the home, and promotes thrift, discipline, mutual respect among spouses, trust, honesty, self-confidence, hard work, and sobriety. Sobriety on its own makes a vast difference to most budgets, but the other qualities referred to are crucial to entrepreneurship in the informal economy, however small, and of course, such qualities are now supported in a network of believers. In this network there are opportunities for participation, the exercise of social skills and of responsibility which expand a sense of being able to take charge of one's own life.

It is a simple story, told by the participants themselves, with no need of a Weberian concept of a calling but simply illustrating the old adage that honesty is the best policy even if it does mean certain short-term costs in terms of fair dealing, paying taxes, and church tithes. The story has varying emphases from church to church, and the Mormons are somewhat more inclined than Pentecostals to offer direct teaching about prosperity and to have explicit concerns with techniques of entrepreneurship (such as budgeting) – as well as being socially somewhat better placed. Pentecostals focus simultaneously on the moral sources of impoverishment and on the dangers of pursuing prosperity for its own sake. The particular group studied by Gooren belongs to a branch of a megachurch, Rains of Mercy, which has put down roots among the fairly poor, and has quite a strong other-worldly emphasis. The local congregation is not typical of megachurches in Guatemala (Verbo, Bethania, El Shaddai) which have a middle-class corporate image and some connections with the political elites.

The problem for the Catholic Church has not been the apathy of its leaders, since it has expanded its organization and revived many of its parishes, some of them through the adoption of a charismatic style. It is rather a history of disorganization, dating back to ferocious anti-clerical legislation in the 1870s, so that even today most priests are foreigners and very much concentrated in the megacity area. Obviously dependence on the priesthood as a channel of mediation hampers Catholic efforts. The result is that active Catholics are a small minority and the proportion of active Catholics to active Protestants is 1:4. However, the great expansion of evangelical Christianity seems to be over and a ceiling reached. The expansion accelerated after the earthquake of 1976, especially in response to assistance offered by Protestant organizations and NGOs, but seems to have leveled off with partial returns to relative stability in the 1990s. Curiously the parallel leveling off in Korea has been attributed to the economic downturn, so perhaps expansion in both countries has encountered an upper limit.

In Bernice Martin's account many parallel features appear.[4] Indeed, one of the research sites is a very similar area in Santiago called La Pintana, marked by chronic alcoholism and violence and visited only by social workers, the police, and evangelicals. The evangelicals are of very many kinds, from dozens of tiny micro-enterprises made up of a family and friends in the faith to sizeable firms like the Methodist Pentecostals. The prime sites seem to be at street corners where you can combine your spiritual and material "transactions" in adjacent chapels and businesses. About one person in three here is evangelical, and the titles of their enterprises speak of their aspirations: "Prince of Peace," "Voice in the Desert." The other research sites were mostly in urban areas of south-west Brazil, in particular Campinas, Sâo Paulo.

Bernice Martin's study of the ethos of evangelicals, more particularly in Chile and Brazil, and its consonance with global capitalism and consumer culture, again stresses ambiguity. In her view the consonance is partial and the consumerism selective. She begins by stressing the relevance of culture and of non-economic institutions, including religion, to the working of the economy, and in this her argument agrees with (for example) Lawrence Harrison in *Who Prospers?* and *The Pan-American Dream*.[5] So far as Latin America is concerned, the shift towards democracy in the late 1970s or early 1980s came when the economy had been so integrated into global capitalism that the option of a return to protectionism no longer existed. Rural economies had, in some cases, become post-modern service economies with barely a manufacturing economy in between. The peasant became the worker for agribusiness or joined the trek to the cities to work in a deregulated world of sales, domestic employment, and the office. As reported in Míguez's study, the informal sector swelled, with many workers eking out existence as "penny capitalists" and women and children often abandoned in the struggle for survival.

Obviously, for the poor, swept along on the torrent of economic change, evangelical discipline, and especially the reintegration of the family, not only assists survival but imposes sense on random calamity. Male restraint is highly advantageous, and the enclave of the church hedges the male about with group surveillance and an alternative expenditure of time. It follows that adolescents, particularly males, within the churches, feel the call of the street, the cinema, and the fiesta, and often fall "out of the Way" for a period, until dissipation brings some of them back. However, the self-discipline and group-discipline are far from being dour, but they rather subserve celebration. The "fruits of the spirit" are reckoned as joy and healing, and Providence generates self-confidence and energy where the gods of fate and fortune would grind people down into apathy and despair. Employers appreciate this discipline and trustworthiness, which has obvious advantages, for example, in domestic service where workers are active in ones and twos and effectively run households while parents are away. Ancillary workers in catering do not need training in how to smile and give exact weight. Pentecostals are holy hustlers, for God and for that matter for their own survival, and fellow believers or pastors often see it as part of their role to help with instability in employment and the insecurities of ill-health.

At the same time the combination of consumer advertising, modest success, and the spread of Pentecostalism (or free-range charismatic groups) in the white-collar and business sectors leads towards an easing of rigor and an acceptance of prosperity along with health as blessings properly associated with salvation. Social improvement can increasingly be seen as faith's validation. From recognizing the potential dangers of wealth some believers find in it the God-given rewards of faithfulness. The Lord, after all, is good, and one is thankful for bounty and perhaps proud to have worked one's way out of the murk of poverty. The bargain with God has turned out well, and spiritual investment has returned a hundred-fold.

Moreover at a certain level the dangers one faces are as much inward as external: corruption, drugs, colleagues who lead one into conspicuous consumption. Thus in the Universal Church of the Kingdom of God the style is that of salespeople promoting spiritual assurance and converting the skills of the illicit economy to licit advantage. A liturgy of exorcism and celebration assists the gamble of faith with the land of promise, overcoming risk with hope and set-backs with constant supplies of energy. In Argentina (as has been pointed out earlier) this is dramatized as "spiritual warfare" against the demons that undermine self-possession, and in this world the demonic is ever-present. Nevertheless, through most of the middle-class charismatic world the tension of unalloyed consumerism with evangelical disciplines remains, though if one looks (say) at Dallas evangelicals the tension can certainly be kept within manageable limits.

Political Culture

An appropriate entry into this complex and highly ambiguous area is offered by John Burdick's much-quoted study, *Looking for God in Brazil*, the main focus of which was an enquiry into the Catholic base communities.

John Burdick is one of the most insightful observers of Pentecostalism in Brazil and he takes off from the view that Pentecostalism is a conservative force, teaching submission to authority, eroding lower-class solidarity, and undercutting justifications for collective action. However, a growing number of researchers, above all those who have lived among ordinary *crentes* (believers), have begun to complicate this picture.[6]

He argues that one needs to untie the paradox that on the one hand their new sense of self and personal value provides a strong sense of rights and citizenship, while on the other hand they do not often constitute a major presence in social movements. It is true that the religious logic of their faith includes sources of empowerment that promote participation in social movements, and even a "highly critical social consciousness" *and* it is also true that Pentecostal meetings do not mix religion and politics. It is important to add here that attitudes to politics emphatically cannot be read off from the statements of the pastors.

Take the fact that believers are not much involved in neighborhood associations. This is certainly not due to indifference to material things like cleanliness, good water, stable tenure, electricity, and so on, or any supposition that these are laid on by prayer rather than human activity. But it is connected with the way such associations are run by closely knit cliques of local notables, often the lay leadership of the local Catholic Church and by local merchants who promise to deliver votes to local politicians in return for improvements and who also carry on their activities around factions forged in the streets and the bars. Believers naturally balk at being drawn into corrupt dealings carried out in a raw and raucous machismo atmosphere, by people who do not respect their opinion or consider their religious schedule. However, where associations are more fluid in the newer barrios, believers do participate, and become leaders trusted in particular for their honesty. In other words, they will step into spaces that do not draw them into either the corrupt atmosphere of male wheeling and dealing or the paternalism of the Catholic Church's relation to social movements.

With respect to labor unions, it is first of all important to recognize that in the state-controlled unions few people of any religion participate because there is room only for the clients of the managers. But that apart, it is true that believers have a longer fuse in responding to crises such as unstable employment. The crucial point is that while Pentecostals accept poverty, they reject unemployment and misery and, for that matter, the arrogant life-style of the rich. As among Franciscans, there is an aureole around the poor; below that beggary is sometimes seen as a consequence of disobedience to God while riches are signs of hypocrisy and "vanity." Usually it is not that the believer is poor on account of sin, because believers are perfectly capable of identifying the economic conditions – and employers – afflicting them, and of recognizing that amelioration requires action. Since they believe so heartily in the biblical injunction to work, they resent being denied the opportunity to do so.

So what of their supposed lower rates of participation? In the first place, in many industries most workers, irrespective of religion, do not participate in labor activism. Because Pentecostals are identifiable in the first instance and remain outside the union networks of drinking and wheeling and dealing, they can easily be tagged as responsible for low levels of support. But when believers do participate they can be relied upon: they lend legitimacy to complaints and make violence much less likely, which is significant where they form up to about a tenth of the workforce. Believers have a particular dislike of confusion and disorder and random violence; they also share the widespread perception that the employers have the cards stacked in their favor.

In view of the perception that believers voted disproportionately for the conservative or government parties, particularly in the 1982 election, it is intriguing that about one in ten of the Workers Party in the area studied belonged to the Assemblies of God. This is partly because the record of the Workers Party had been unstained by corruption whereas the military had grown corrupt. Burdick even goes so far as to say that evangelicals involved in the Workers Party are more combative than the militant Catholics, because these are always restrained by priestly authority, the social etiquette of the Church, and a visceral preference for conciliation rather than confrontation. Catholics are, after all, Christians and, like evangelicals they find the religious imperatives of brotherhood, love, caring, peaceableness, and forgiveness incompatible with warfare. They concentrate, therefore, on issues connected with the infrastructure of the neighborhood. While the Church leadership champions the rights of the landless to legal title, it does so in accordance with an ideal of small proprietorship and strict observance of the law. By contrast, engaged believers are able to see their opponents as a tool of the Devil and so fit the confrontation into the duality of Christ and the "World." The association with the "Enemy of Mankind" is reinforced for them by middle-class and business associations with Umbanda and with Kardecism.

Burdick concludes that the last word has not been heard on the political understandings of believers, and adds that the militancy of the CEBs (Base Communities) is constrained within overall Catholic policy in a way Pentecostal militancy is not. This analysis is entirely compatible with extensive research by William Hewitt on base communities in the progressive diocese of São Paulo.[7] Hewitt points out that the base communities are essentially religious and composed (like the Pentecostals) to a large extent of devout women. Only about a third are politically involved and that involvement tends to be over local issues of infrastructure, which benefit specific areas, and once solved leave militancy nowhere particular to go. This is not in any way to denigrate the base communities, but rather to ameliorate the standard contrast between them and Pentecostals and to provide a slipway to viewing the two kinds of development as having crucial characteristics in common. The idea that they should be viewed both as complementary *and* as alternative is supported by such distinguished investigators as Rowan Ireland and Daniel Levine.

There is a further point, to be developed later, which is of the widest possible significance. Ideals of brotherhood and peaceableness which generate respect for persons are in constant tension with ideas of warfare and secular victory over evil. Organizations which faithfully fulfil the imperatives of love, brotherhood, peace, and universal respect tend to throw the conflict with evil up on to the transcendental plane, and find their mission confused once the militants attack secular manifestations of evil. There is, in fact, an inherent though partial division of social labor between religion and politics. There is a parallel paradox over work: believers work honestly and dislike go-slows or going behind the system to get their own cut, but they also dislike the dishonesty and corruption of those who have risen on the backs of the system and at the expense of the poor. The morality of honest work and due reward cuts in several directions. If these complex logics are not understood, the role of Pentecostals is not understood either, and they are merely subject to dismissal on the basis of intellectual checklists of political rectitude. These are not matters of philosophical attitude to be changed by a better attitude, but of unavoidable socio-moral logic. Such ambiguities occur in the literature on Evangelicalism over centuries.

Some of them are clearly implicit in the patient, credible, and irenic research of Rowan Ireland, a political liberal and a Catholic. In his *Kingdoms Come*, Ireland asks his readers to broaden their categories of political action, to deconstruct institutions, to listen to people at the grass roots, and, above all, to suspend "taxonomic skills that become all too easily a trained inability to see the shapes of political economies in the making at the grass roots."[8]

Ireland's study of north-east Brazil compares three basic cultures of contemporary Brazil: activist Catholicism, Pentecostalism, and Spiritism. The core of his argument comes out in an eloquent plea to those who would encase material and comprehensively tag it with terminology. He asks them to consider

> that the millions of Brazilian Pentecostals are acting politically, when they assert, celebrate and argue about their images of legitimate authority and righteousness, and when they organise this vida passageira [life of passage] for the Kingdom the Lord will bring. Similarly, I ask the reader to consider, when the million or more Catholics engaged in their church's base communities proclaim and plan the future they are called to by their Christ the Liberator, that they too are acting politically (probably more consciously than the Pentecostals but usually not with any intent to be "politically engaged" in any narrow formal sense). Again, when Afro-Brazilian spiritists call their spirits down to earth, I invite the reader to consider that they might be reconstituting patronage politics or, alternatively, acting politically as they reveal to one another that Brazil in which the poor teach, heal and empower one another, as they contest the Brazil of the cultura alta [high culture] of the professionals and the experts.[9]

Several things have first to be understood. In *no* church are most believers engaged in directly political discourse. Those who do only rarely challenge the system in any direct way, and most of those they inspirit and animate to challenge expropriation find the costs are too high, and retire hurt. There is a pervasive cynicism about the political sphere which reappears in Pentecostal understanding as the moral recalcitrance of "the World" compared to the Kingdom. Nevertheless, claims Ireland, each faith was able to tell a story contrary to the narrative of official Brazil, and that in itself was to be accounted valor.

Ireland singles out the new priest and the new Pentecostals as protagonists of this different story. The priest is enabled to criticize the status quo because formed in the protected enclave of the seminary. The Pentecostals can reject the all-enveloping reality by reinventing themselves in the protected enclave of their church. The priest is a positive presence, upheld by the prestige of his ancient role, but on that account imprisoned by strict expectations. The Pentecostals are an eloquent absence from everything the culture entails: the corruption, indignity, and the frivolous idolatry of the fiesta. They have walked out. Priest and Pentecostal both want to clean up, the former the town, the latter themselves. Their churches are as bright and bare and clean as each other.

The priest's reforming presence at the fiesta disturbs the town more than the Pentecostal's reforming absence. As a result his fiesta is no longer the comprehensive jamboree of the whole town. Music symbolizes the situation. The priest chooses traditional folk music for the fiesta, but the new organizers broadcast pop, and the fraternity passes by on the other side tooting its ancient brass. As for the Pentecostals, they have their own concerts, bathed in holy enthusiasm: solos by old and young, male and female, young people's groups, instrumental ensembles, amateur choirs.

Ireland underlines two points. One is that the Assemblies of God can acquire a churchiness of its own, through the private meaning assigned to suffering, through an increasingly professionalized pastorate, and "the intense desire for respectability to ensure the triumph of the church in the institutional market place." This is not to say that there does not remain a tension between passive acquiescence and "critical address to local wrongs." There remains an ambiguous repertoire of myth, symbol, and practice, and a moral sense that may motivate denunciation of unjust patron or compromised bureaucrat.

The analysis of Pentecostal consciousness in Brazil by Rowan Ireland took place against the background of an oppressive national security state; the analysis of Pentecostal consciousness in Nicaragua by Roger Lancaster took place against the background of an oppressive Marxist state. In both contexts, Pentecostals saw themselves biblically enjoined to respect "the powers that be." Lancaster is a Marxist, which makes the candor of his analysis all the more remarkable, though his is not the only instance of fair assessment from a Marxist.[10] Blanca Muratorio is equally candid and illuminating on evangelicalism among the Quechua.[11]

Lancaster emphasizes features of the Sandinista movement which grate on western academics and spur them on to constant lamentations about "betrayal." Consider the following: if some observers have seen Pentecostalism as corporatism *redivivus*, and as traditional faith recast, then Roger Lancaster has a similar view of the Sandinistas. Of course, the official definition of the Sandinista state is modern and secular. Nevertheless, it "erects the irrational and magic as a high bulwark against capitalist rationality," and its corporatist traits represent so many "safe-guards against exploitation."[12] (In speaking of the Sandinistas, it is appropriate to retain the present tense: they still control much of the apparatus, and are part of the multiple linkages binding together the elites, whatever their political line.)

At the same time, the "Popular Church" which provides a social base for the Sandinistas is bound to be opposed to the Pentecostals and evangelicals. Why so? It is, in the first place, much weaker than they because faith and activism are already incorporated in "mass political organizations." The Popular Church is solidary and communal, and to that extent traditional. That implies considerable difficulty in tolerating whatever is out of line. This is a religion of clear consensus and inimical to personal conscience. Hence, the evangelical objections to the ideological *corvée* put them and the Sandinistas on a collision course. So, too, did the Sandinista attempt forcibly to incorporate and mobilize the traditionally evangelical and non-Hispanic east-coast population into an Hispanic consensus: the first time they were violated in this particular way.

The main clash, however, is between a religion assimilated to a political and nationalistic mass movement, and providing it with a language and an idiom, and an individual and personal faith. In other words, the Popular Church tries to reconstitute a Durkheimian "conscience collective," and in so doing throws into relief the cultural politics of Pentecostal religion. This cultural politics does not so much appear as direct opposition, but as inherent, ineradicable difference. What Lancaster goes on to argue is that this difference and a parallel doctrinal difference is compatible with very similar effects, especially with regard to moral conservatism. Pentecostals and the followers of the Popular Church are alike moral conservatives. The point could be illustrated anywhere in Latin America, provided one is clear what the moral conservatism is primarily about.

When the Sandinistas took over, evangelicals probably accounted for no more than 5 percent of the population. By 1990 the proportion was more like 15–20 percent. There was, of course, an attempt to manipulate them against the government, in particular by North American television evangelists, and a number of local evangelical clergy obliged. This is precisely the kind of manipulation against which David Stoll's work provides a warning. At the same time, Lancaster unequivocally considers "evangelical practice as a popular phenomenon." In the "very poorest barrios, the religion that competes with liberation theology for the status of 'religion of the poor' is neither the traditional popular religion, nor the clerical religion of the official hierarchy, but rather evangelical Protestantism."[13] Moreover, the key witness to the power of Protestant conversion is *the example of evangelical deeds* (my italics). In the middle-class professional neighborhoods, there is support for the official church. There is similar support in the better-off working-class areas and the better-off peasantry in combination with adherence to traditional popular Catholicism and the Popular Church. These sectors are, maybe, only 5 percent evangelical.

In the poorest and newest barrios, however, there exists a very general anti-clerical sentiment, and active religion is split half and half between liberation theology and Protestant evangelicalism. Both movements are opposed to a debased, idolatrous Christ (which offers yet another comparison, this time with the situation described by Rowan Ireland in Brazil). Both movements renounce formalism, embrace practice, and seek salvation not religion. Both movements denounce drugs, crime, poverty, *and social disorganization*. Though Protestantism "represents the harder break with tradition . . . each movement tries to reclaim and re-establish the conservative or normative social milieu lost with urbanisation and lumpen development."[14] Both sides of Lancaster's comment need taking into account: the break and the re-establishment.

The evangelicals in these poor areas neither rob nor fight. Among them there is a disproportionate number of female-headed households or households with other economic disadvantages such as recent or persistent illness. Many evangelicals are vendors in the large, decentralized informal economy. They encounter two kinds of Catholic response. One is a tolerance and readiness to give them a hearing related to their disabilities. They "set a good example. . . ." They don't drink, they work hard, they believe in education for their children. It is also recognized that they are essential for keeping order in the barrios where they live, and for inculcating moral responsibility. On the other hand, Catholic workers not suffering from economic marginality insult them and use the difference in status to ridicule their faith as "the religion of beggars." Some of the better-off members of the base communities dismiss them in standard stereotypical terms as anti-Sandinista.

Lancaster concludes that the affinity between evangelicalism and political (as distinct from moral) conservatism has been overstated. Indeed, this may well be borne out by the fact that studies of the February 1990 electorate did not single out evangelicals as a distinctive voting bloc, a conclusion with interesting parallels in studies of the electorate in Guatemala. The point about the usefulness of "order" is important, because in non-Marxist contexts their orderliness is not accounted virtuous. Indeed, when E. P. Thompson described their work-discipline in the course of the Industrial Revolution it was not intended to be complimentary.[15] Lancaster concludes that "on balance the evangelical sects have accelerated, not impeded the revolutionary process." Where liberation theology has provided the ideological element, Pentecostalism has provided a cultural component. For people engulfed by anomie, "a religion of renunciation and despair opens up a space of order in the midst of disorder, morality in an immoral world, and a defined hope in a prevailing social terrain of hopelessness. It ultimately combats the culture of despair by causing the poor to lead more exemplary lives."[16] The despair is, therefore, "creative despair" and makes possible participation in reconstruction and productivity, not "lumpen delinquency."

Lancaster's conclusions on conversion are worth quoting. Having elsewhere noted that Pentecostalist conversion often involves a special individual trauma followed by the conversion of the entire family, Lancaster writes,

> The conscious preoccupations that lie behind Pentecostal conversion are not so different from those of Popular Church activism. Each religion emphasises as its nemesis the characteristic social traits associated with urban poverty and lumpen-development, each cites the threat and the reality of social disorganisation. If prostitution and drug addiction are the master metaphors of liberation theology in the barrios, the themes that preoccupy the evangelicals are perhaps only slightly more familial in keeping with the more personalising approach of Pentecostalism: drinking, wife-beating, stealing. . . . If distinct at all, these preoccupations are continuous with liberation theology's, and more frequently entirely interchangeable. In essence, each movement tries to reclaim and re-establish the conservative or normative social milieu lost with urbanisation and lumpen-development.[17]

One of the most controversial issues of Pentecostal involvement in (or withdrawal from) politics is the particular stance adopted by the Council of Pastors in 1975 with regard to the Pinochet regime in Chile, symbolized in the offer of a *Te Deum* to Pinochet as head of state in the Methodist "cathedral." Among a large number of accounts, the recent study by Frans Kamsteeg represents a balanced view. He begins by saying that Pentecostals over the twenty-five years since 1975 have shifted away from withdrawal and hostility to "the world," which was particularly pronounced in Chile, and have shown "divergent political tendencies" pointing up "the complexity and ambiguity" of Latin American religion.[18] After 1975 these two tendencies were represented by one group – the Council of Pastors – who were willing to offer the regime legitimacy in return for the illusory hope of public and legal recognition, and another which developed a sense of social commitment and political consciousness. This latter group, the Christian Church Fraternity (CCI) eventually went so far in the mid-eighties as to protest about injustice, the situation of the poor, and human-rights violations, and laid the blame at the door of the state. However, ordinary Pentecostals were committed to neither of these tendencies, and their voting behavior seems throughout to have been much the same as their socio-economic peers. As in Argentina and Brazil, so in Chile extreme positions have been mostly abandoned in an atmosphere of increasing political pluralism and surveys undertaken in 1991 by Fontaine showed that Chilean evangelicals had clearly democratic attitudes and scant sympathy for military rule.[19] They did, however, tend to prefer independent candidates, showing their strong suspicion of the whole political process, though that suspicion is as a matter of fact widely shared among all those below the level of the political classes. As ever, evangelical faith tends to be more in personal transformation than state action. What remains of the old stance of withdrawal is a certain tendency to accept that the powers that be, whatever their political color, are "ordained of God."

David Smilde's study of Pentecostal mobilization in Venezuela is noteworthy as dealing with a culture which like that of Argentina experienced Pentecostal expansion later than elsewhere,[20] and it seems as though some of the same elements were operative, in particular a prior urbanization which in the case of Venezuela was under the aegis of oil-supported populism. In this period a state-dominated economy and clientist political parties together created a culture where material and consumer expectations were at least in part satisfied. However, structural adjustments under the aegis of the IMF following the drop in oil prices brought about widespread impoverishment and a crisis of political legitimacy. A cycle of protest focused on corruption and crime followed, as well as new social movements seeking spaces outside the complex of state and party and programmatic political rationality. These movements, including environmental action groups and neighborhood associations, might not be all that large but they acquired symbolic salience. One notable example was the evangelical El Clamor por Venezuela, organized by an evangelical radio station and supported by the Federation of Pentecostal Evangelical Churches of Caracas. Smilde underlines how Pentecostals in Venezuela have recently made inroads in to the Venezuelan middle class, but have usually been most effective in creating spaces among the poor for personal reorientation in an atmosphere of renewed primary social ties. However, in the case of El Clamor this kind of mute reorganization of life by the poor and voiceless of Venezuela has acquired a public presence.

Smilde analyzes this public presence in terms of a "collective action frame" based on perceived injustice, a feeling of identity in terms of "we" who suffer confronting a corrupt "they," and a sense of making an impact. With regard to perceived injustice, Smilde shows how similar are the sources of indignation among evangelicals as compared with non-evangelicals: the causes, however, are traced back to an uncaring and Satanic greed rooted in alienation from God. When it comes to the sense of identity, evangelicals feel they are acting vicariously for "brothers who are still blind" and, as for impact, they are raising consciousness to stimulate reflection and a new spirit.

A key element in Smilde's analysis relates to the historic controversy over Latin America's path in contradistinction to the Anglo-American path which has a contemporary lease of life in the clash of nationalist and neo-conservative discourses. Neo-conservatives stress the impediments brought about by an Iberian heritage and the need for cultural and moral reform, in discipline, work-habits, individual responsibility – and in democratic procedures. Nationalists on the other hand blame foreign domination and so to the extent that evangelicals stress personal morality and individual motivation (more especially on the heels of perceived decline in Catholic collectivist radicalism) they are entered by casual onlookers in the neo-conservative column. However, Smilde's own conclusion rather stresses ambiguity:

> While criticism of the local sociocultural context is almost always an aspect of the Evangelical frame, it does not usually broaden into a general critique of Latin culture [and] emphasis on the supernatural only occasionally engages with conservative politics in any clear and consistent manner. More frequently it simply provides moral fervour to an individual's pre-existing political preferences (p. 139)

which in any case are rarely abstract and intellectually articulated.

Apart from work on Pentecostal politics, David Smilde has also looked at conjugal relations in Venezuelan Evangelicalism; and that makes a useful transition to the following section. He picks once again on the frequently debated "gender paradox" of Pentecostalism discussed, *inter alia*, by Salvatore Cucchiari, Judith Stacey, Elizabeth Brusco, and Bernice Martin.[21] This he relates to the economic crisis of the nineteen eighties and nineties which exacerbated the already difficult transitions in family structure, with increased employment of women and children, and a combination of male irresponsibility, violence, and loss of control in the domestic sphere. Evangelicalism is one way in which the resulting dilemmas and stress can be addressed.

The evidence Smilde presents confirms what has been argued elsewhere about patriarchalism in theory and consensuality in practice: a conservative tendency balanced by a revolutionary one based on spiritual equality. He cites instances of the inner independence and detachment of women when men act "outside the way of the Lord." There is in Smilde's view a transition from patriarchal submission to individual assertion "under God."

Family Ethic

Apart from his observation of Pentecostal political culture, Burdick also gives an account of the Pentecostal family ethic. He begins by utilizing the distinction between local cults based on residence and prior identity, and cults of affliction.[22] Catholic cults belong to the former, Pentecostalism and Umbanda to the latter. All recruit disproportionately from working-class women, and the stories of these women, as told by Burdick, underline the specific advantages of Pentecostalism. As families arrive in the city, internal tension rises. There is a threat to male prestige caused by unemployment, as well as a drain on resources needed for the children's education brought about by profligate male expenditure. And there is a general loss of parental control.

Now, it is taboo to raise domestic issues in the local Catholic Bible and prayer circles. The other participants are, after all, neighbors, and open discussion of problems would destroy privacy and encourage gossip. As for recourse to the priest, he is celibate and not likely to understand domestic or sexual problems. Traditionally, it is the Virgin who provides the primary source of relief and consolation, but she is approachable only in isolation and her only proffered comfort is resignation. Once upon a time the alternative source of relief for Catholics would have been the non-literate blessers and prayer specialists, who did indeed offer the advantage of secrecy. But they have been downgraded by the contemporary Church.

Within the Pentecostal community, however, the presbyter is a prayer healer who operates from his own home. He is himself a family man. This is where women can air their troubles in a supportive, understanding, and private atmosphere. Domestic troubles are defined as the work of the Enemy of Mankind and cure is by expulsion of the evil spirit. That means that each believer can start afresh.

Beyond that, Pentecostalism gives women authority "to speak out in the name of God and seek support in collective prayer." Faced with recalcitrant machismo, they can appeal to unequivocal religious norms of marital conduct, inside or outside the home. In this way they can influence the husband to better things, and may also reinforce their argument by inconvenient prophetic revelations. In the course of comparing Pentecostalism and Umbanda, Burdick suggests that the spirit world of Umbanda is morally ambiguous, while in Pentecostalism it is polarized into good and evil. The source of trouble for Umbanda is in another person. The medium can, therefore, advise on counter-measures, including justice or revenge. But there is no long-term solution.

The milieux discussed by Burdick are working-class. But in places like Chile, Brazil, and elsewhere an evangelical middle class is emerging for which a major dynamic is a therapeutic context for marital turbulence. It is not just a matter of reconstituting the families of the poor.

In an account of family therapies in a (largely) middle-class evangelical context, Jorge Maldonaldo describes the family as a locus of pain, crisis, despair, and disorganization.[23] So far as middle-class people were concerned, they encountered this crisis within their families at a moment when Catholicism seemed only to provide an impersonal supermarket in the sacraments. They sought real experience with a loving God and a meaning which could be fully appropriated. As comparable middle-class people in Santiago have commented, evangelicalism "got to me." And it reached them not through the mass media but through the testimony of others in the family, or relatives, or friends. They, therefore, enter the super-family of "brothers and sisters" in Christ, who will stand by them in need, whether financial or emotional.

Maldonaldo describes two communities where Pentecostalism has reached out to middle- and even upper-class people. The first is the Communidade Evangélica, which has grown from a tiny informal group to a membership of four thousand in fifteen years. Small prayer groups, many from broken homes, formed themselves into mutual-help communities. They found models for family life in their pastors and in evangelical literature (much of it North American). As elsewhere, such North American influence as exists is mostly located among the middle-class evangelicals. Husband-and-wife teams minister as a family to families, thereby breaking the norm of an all-male professional ministry. Many leaders run their own small businesses, or operate as couples with complementary professions. Above all else, they offer counseling, inner healing groups, and marriage growth groups. Also offered is counseling on sexual problems and help for the divorced. Since this evangelical community is not Pentecostal it is uninhibited about the value of training.

The other example is the Iglesia Pentecostal Las Acacias in a lower-middle-class neighborhood of Caracas, Venezuela. The church is a remodeled cinema, seating 2000 and taking up a whole block. It holds three services, each overflowing, every Sunday. Among other things it offers a "marriage involvement" program, with open discussion of all matters, sexual or otherwise, which might be relevant. A biblical literalism and a moral rigor are combined with a stress on female autonomy, not dependence. Many Pentecostal churches experiencing upward mobility have evolved in a similar manner. Parallels will be found in Nigerian material. In this particular group, nine out of ten began life as Roman Catholics and expressed their dissatisfaction in terms of lack of participation or of guidance in translating traditional Catholic symbols into a non-hierarchical, non-sacramental mode. In the evangelical community men learn to be husbands, to feel, to cry, to show affection, to be trustworthy, and to exercise family responsibility. Most members believe that men and women should work together for the economic maintenance of the family, in taking decisions, and in offering spiritual leadership.

One particular study by Cecilia Mariz and Clara Mafra addresses the neglected topic of family size and reproduction among evangelicals.[24] Historically there has been a difference between the more open historic Protestant churches and the conservative mores and dress code of the Pentecostals. However, matters are in flux, particularly maybe with the arrival of neo-Pentecostals.

The study was conducted in Rio de Janeiro, Brazil, where nearly one in six of the population is evangelical, divided among the Assemblies of God (31 percent), the Baptists (19 percent) and the relatively recent and expansive Brazilian church, The Universal Church of the Kingdom of God (16 percent). Of the rest 18 percent of evangelicals were in small Pentecostal churches, 7 percent in historic Protestant churches "in renewal" and 9 percent in historic Protestant churches. 70 percent of the evangelicals were women, and that figure was even higher – 81 percent – in the Universal Church. Of the women 61.4 percent are married or cohabiting, 38.6 percent "single" and (within that figure) 21.9 percent widowed, separated, or divorced. Overwhelmingly, Pentecostals came from the least educated and poorest sectors, whereas Baptists were relatively well-off.

With regard to family size and reproduction, the evangelical churches entertained diverse views, but overall were somewhat more inclined to birth control methods than practising Catholics. No literature prohibiting contraception was located. If one examines the average family size for evangelicals, it turns out not so different from the (falling) national average at 2.7, and the variation by denomination is related to education, except in the case of the Universal Church which appeals to a poorly-educated constituency. The Universal Church is at one and the same time in favor of male decision-making and vigorously anti-natalist. The ideal number of children preferred by evangelicals is two, so one presumes that their rate of reproduction will continue to fall. With regard to gender relations, the vast majority of evangelicals supported a common sexual standard. Most evangelicals see the man as the final source of decisions and at the same time consider that men equally with women should subordinate interests and inclinations to the needs of the family.

Diane Austin-Broos's remarkable study, *Jamaica Genesis,* relates to Anglo-America, not Latin America, but the cultural elements contain potent parallels with respect to the Jamaican poor, and exhibit the same ambiguity found in Latin American examples.[25] Part of the object of the analysis is to show how Pentecostalism has become indigenous and how revivalist Evangelicalism has mingled with African religion, through what Austin-Broos calls "the politics of moral order," more especially with respect to sexuality and marriage.

As with many other studies, the site of the research was a poorish sector of the principal city, Kingston, which Austin-Broos found was honeycombed with Pentecostal churches, large and small. She points out as a preliminary that whereas Rastafarianism is male-dominated and consists largely of males, Pentecostalism consists largely of females under the guidance of lower-class males. Women make up half the Jamaican work-force and one in three of all heads of households, and when not at work they are mostly engaged in church-related activity. Indeed, the Pentecostal Church *is* their organization.

In the earlier history of Jamaica under British colonial rule there was a superimposition of orders, in which color, power, and morality were highly correlated, with the subordinate groups consigned to immorality, more particularly sexual behavior outside marriage, for example, concubinage. However, the subordinate groups, in partial alliance with evangelical (largely Baptist) preachers, struggled for their own "possession of the sign," in particular understanding all too well the Hebrew narrative of an enslaved and exiled people and the Christian narrative of a lacerated and impaled Christ. On the one hand was a revivalist tradition of fall, including sexual indiscipline, offering individual redemption through ethical aspiration and pursuit of perfection, and on the other an African tradition of collective joyful celebration in which good and evil were ambivalent companions.

What Pentecostalism made possible on its arrival from the United States was the fusion of these two, empowering the lower class to conduct their own marriages, and elevating the "fallen" women of the old order as the perfected "saints" of the new. Guilt and sin were wiped away in mass baptism and in a joyous healing rite exorcising bio-moral malaise. People, especially women, were healed body and soul, and though the element of patriarchy was present with regard to male supervision that was largely a set piece overtaken by female practice. Thus

Pentecostalism became a site of genuine cultural creativity not simple hegemony, even though this was localized and unable to overturn the wider order. With respect to overt politics, this ambiguity was reproduced in that pastors saw the potential both to criticize and to reinforce the established order and from time to time took the one course or the other.

It is useful here to refer to two cognate studies, by Cucchiari and Toulis, bearing in particular on the status and role of women.[26] Toulis's study offers a natural complement to Austin-Broos, since it deals with an essentially black denomination made up of Jamaicans, the New Testament Church of God, in Birmingham, England. Those who belong to this church reject ethnic definitions in favor of a common "citizenship in heaven" and contrast their clean, warm, sharing, and sober enclave with the cold, grasping, and injurious world outside. Cleanliness, godliness, and honest work elicit God's material blessings, and male authority in home and church depends on faithfulness and responsibility. But though a man is formally "the head" the woman is defined as the neck, and she may preach, pray, and testify as well as exercising leadership on informal occasions. What Toulis stresses is the way Jamaican, and especially female Jamaican, identity is conveyed in the place accorded to food and through the dress code. Women preside over eating and sharing together in an atmosphere which recreates the Caribbean world. As for dress, the code is more precise for women than men: women dress attractively but modestly, and without resort to make-up or jewelry. It is precisely the control manifest in the criteria of the dress code which facilitates the spiritual and bodily abandonment when the Spirit declares its presence.

Cucchiari's study applies as much to Latin America as to its original locale in the extreme south of Italy, and also complements the argument of Austin-Broos concerning the way psycho-moral reorganization affects the place of women. Since his analysis shows how the loss of the Madonna is made up for by a transformation into Sophia we will give it at some length.

In a complex and subtle argument, Cucchiari suggests that Pentecostal conversion takes the convert *out* of the traditional moral and social order, with its duality of male honor and female shame, and reconstitutes the social and moral order in the eschatological church community and in the relationship with a transcendent God. The aim of that community is sanctification, which provides the sole criterion both for worth of self and for social worth, thereby bringing men and women together under a single judgement. From the non-Pentecostal viewpoint the woman is "shameless"; from the Pentecostal viewpoint she is a sanctified woman whose sense of shame has been reconstituted. This allows Pentecostal women to compete honorably even with men in the public arena in a way otherwise impossible for women outside the elite. But, of course, the Pentecostal community remains enveloped and partially infiltrated by traditional understandings. So while equality in the search for sancti-fication is acknowledged by the idiom of "brother" and "sister," the male pastor has to enact the traditional patriarchal role and protect "the honor" of the church family in "the eyes of the world." He is helped in this role by segregated seating arrangements in the church.

In Sicily, the hierarchy of gender has adapted itself to the impact of "modernization" so that the honor of men is still closely tied to their ability to control the behavior of their women, though that does not prevent a firm matriarchal control of the domestic economy. Class-based movements have not spoken to this cultural configuration, whereas, in Cucchiari's view, Pentecostalism is a gender system in the making. It is here that we encounter an ambiguity which is overlooked by designa-tions of Pentecostalism as merely morally conservative. As in all other spheres Pentecostalism is and must be ambiguous, as are all concrete social movements with a real potential for change. They must straddle to move, and they are, therefore, misunderstood and misestimated by those who tick off movements according to a check-list of progressive traits.

Let the ambiguity be set out clearly. At one level Pentecostalism can be seen as a conservative or even nativistic attempt to re-establish a stable patriarchal order within the boundaries of the church community. Yet Pentecostal women play major roles in the community, and even dominate some religious ministries. Moreover, Pentecostal religious dis-course contains non-patriarchal models and symbols of gender.

Here follow some highly relevant facts about the community studied by Cucchiari which could be paralleled almost anywhere in Latin America. Women not only out-number men by two to one, which is a standard proportion in all kinds of Christian community, but they are more active in recruitment and in participating in worship. Two-thirds of the house-holds represented in the community are represented by women, most of whom have become converted independently of their husbands. This leads to hostilities within the family and the labeling of the Pentecostal church as a den of "witches and whores."

The Pentecostal God is, of course, "the God and Father of the Lord Jesus Christ." But the imagery of worship is of the long-suffering, broken-hearted pursuer of human hearts – lover and mother in one. He is not afraid to be weak and to deal in the murky emotions of the heart; He courts the human heart, vanquishing it only by love. Whereas the mighty Word "leaps," names, and orders, as in standard Christian iconography, the all pervasive Pentecostal Spirit consoles and opens up the rivers of blessings, as well as bringing about the fluidity of prayer and song. This "fluidity" (or "anti-structural liminality" in Turner's phraseology) is paralleled very closely by favorite images of Latin American believers. Over and over again houses and churches are decorated with pictures of the waters of life and of comfort. Cucchiari suggests, and in my view rightly, that the activity of the Word is carried out mainly by males, and the activity of the Spirit (prophecy, healing) mainly by women. In order to surmount formal prohibitions against women prophesying, their activities are labeled "gifts" rather than "ministries." Women preach but do not call it preaching, and they do the bulk of proselytizing through their networks. Furthermore, the predominant background noise of worship is the undulating moaning and rhythmic sobbing of public prayer. The full range of emotions expressed takes in a maternal father and paternal mother.

Now, in Sicily, as elsewhere in the Christian Mediterranean, the Virgin is a member of the Celestial Family and so of the Domestic Trinity. It is this Domestic Trinity which provides the model for earthly relationships: the aloof and authoritative father, the pure, indulgent, and subservient mother, and the filial, devoted Son. In traditional iconography the Holy Spirit skirts the edges of this Domestic Trinity, thoroughly displaced from His original role in the New Testament. Clearly, Pentecostalism restores that role and one may recollect that Sophia, the Divine Wisdom, is linguistically feminine.

Pentecostals approach the "Father of all" through the feminine and fluid intimacy of the Spirit or through a feminized Jesus appealing from the heart to the heart. In subsuming the Celestial Mother into itself, the gender-amalgamated God of Pentecostalism suggests a communication and interpenetration of gender characteristics. Nor are there clearly separable internal and external aspects of the Pentecostal God – symbols of the domestic and public spheres in the Celestial Family. On the contrary, the Pentecostal community of brothers and sisters is the family fused into the church community. Clearly, these mutations provide spaces in which to negotiate new roles. It can do this, it would seem, precisely because the "Father" is not toppled; as ever, a revolutionary attack would generate the resistances which guarantee its own future rigidity, whereas a radical conservation allows space for changes which are masked for safety. As a result over time they become merely accepted. What Sicilian Pentecostalism in particular has to balance is a longing on the part of females as well as males for a morally conservative and secure traditional family system, including rigorous restrictions on abortion and divorce, and the provision of a space in which new relationships are negotiated and achieved. One might describe this as "revolutionary nativism." Or one might say that believing women see in the religious community a renewed, sacred super-family of which, according to older understandings, they are properly the active and moral center. It is also the place where they are reborn and liberated after the pain of failed romantic attachments. Men, for their part, see the religious community as the place where they receive traditional respect and, moreover, can absorb without discomfort the feminized subtextual images of Pentecostal discourse. The female is packaged in male forms for public consumption.

Such an analysis could be applied word for word to all the congregations observed in Latin America. It answers the question as to how they can bear the loss of the Blessed Virgin. The answer is that Mary becomes Sophia.

The Family and Healing

One of the main precipitating aspects of conversion is clearly healing, and the recent research of Andrew Chesnut in Belém, Brazil, gives healing a central place.[27] To raise the question of its importance in the immediate wake of discussion of the family is appropriate because the other main aspects (as cited, for example, in Kurt Bowen's study in Mexico) are trouble with spouses experienced by women and trouble with alcohol experienced by men.[28] For Bowen healing is one major element in a substantial minority of cases, whereas for Chesnut it is a central emphasis of his whole analysis.

This is not the place to discuss the etiology of faith healing or "miracle" in relation to standard techniques of modern medicine. Enough to say that there is a complex mind–body relation and there is no reason to cast comprehensive doubt on the ubiquitous accounts of healing. That there are charlatans and exaggerated claims no more supports comprehensive skepticism than the multitudinous misuses of psychotherapy invalidate therapy as such. What Chesnut properly draws attention to as crucial are what he calls the maladies of poverty, especially as exacerbated among the myriad migrants from the interior and workers in the informal economy by the debt crisis of the eighties. For Chesnut evangelical faith offers a transition from economic disfranchisement to divine empowerment, most dramatically initiated or manifested by healing. Nearly half the female converts Chesnut interviewed, and about a quarter of the male converts, came to conversion through illness. He underscores the lack of medical facilities and the frequency of misdiagnosis in a situation where people are dealing with all the maladies of poverty from worms and parasites to dehydration and undernourishment, from snakebite to ovarian cancer.

In a culture of machismo, drink, sexual conquest, and carnival, the faiths embedded in the lives of the majority have no defense to offer. The woman bears the brunt of caring for the whole family. The husband is often violent or sexually abusive prior to desertion, whereupon the wife or partner has to place children with the extended family while she takes multiple jobs just to survive. In that event children themselves graduate to gangs, delinquency, alcohol, and drugs. It is a contest between the home and the street, and what restores the home is the discontinuity and inner transformation offered by a demanding, disciplined faith with firm boundaries. And that is provided by the initiative of women. They are the movers and the shakers.

In such a situation Pentecostals seek out those in need where they are, and the need is often signaled by illness. Chesnut describes the Visitadoras as by far the largest and most dynamic form of missionary organization, and family networks as the typical channels of contact. All doors are closed until the evangelical woman comes through the door. The background as described by Chesnut is one where many churches even look like hospitals, where street fliers speak of the maladies of mind and body – fights, nerviness, vice, depression – and where there is a collective welcome of visitors to the church with the pastor and lay healers acting as "conduits of power." He argues that against such a background conversion is literally the capacity to turn things round and that is something the base communities find difficult to do. The convert is someone who has restored the home, holds the Bible fiercely in hand, and finds in the Holy Spirit the ecstatic lover of the soul and healer of body. For those whose words are discounted in the wider world He gives the Word as well as the tongue to express it.

Non-Evangelical Groups

There are, of course, other religious reformations capable of creating networks and of inculcating moral discipline and familial stability apart from the evangelical. Jehovah's Witnesses and Mormons are both active in Latin America. They are the potent rivals to the Pentecostals and other evangelicals, yet they offer life-worlds which are in some ways strikingly similar in their grain and texture. Both Witnesses and Mormons are much more directly connected with the United States than are most Pentecostals. In the material collected in Mexico by Patricia Fortuny, which follows, the comment on the family, moral, and work discipline of Witnesses is consonant with research on Mormons reported in an earlier study by Lawson.[29] At a rough guess Mormons and Witnesses have created constituencies which added together are perhaps one tenth of the evangelical total.

According to Patricia Fortuny, Mexico is the country where Witnesses have been relatively most successful. It is also a country where they are stigmatized as subversives, due to their attitude to the state and in particular to the flag. Witnesses do not vote or join political parties or participate in strikes. Fortuny sketches the familiar change from a peasant society to a complex urban environment, and indicates how the Witnesses provide a supportive network and a frame of meaning when poor people come to the city. As is the case in Pentecostal groups, the women are the ones initially interested, but when men are attracted they abandon the machismo way of life, devoting time and resources to the family – and the church. Moreover, the married couple come together to acquire various skills, notably literacy, and they also co-operate in teaching their children the virtues of orderliness, cleanliness, punctuality, and loving-kindness. Fortuny also refers to the way a liberal Catholicism can, by invalidating the worship of saints, or even the efficacy of confessional absolution, precipitate a crisis of faith which is resolved by conversion to a non-Catholic group. Typically the Witnesses find no spiritual assistance through the Catholic priesthood, and are very conscious of a lack of easy access to religious professionals, whereas in the Kingdom Hall they feel valued and can play a central role and make themselves heard.

As for material specifically on Mormonism, the most useful contribution has been made by David Clark Knowlton in his study of Chile.[30] Taking the published figures at face value, whereas in Mexico Mormons account for only 0.8 percent of the population and in Brazil only 0.3 percent, in Chile they account for 2.6 percent, which is about a third of a million. So while Mexico has been the most productive ground in Latin America for Witnesses, Chile has been the most productive for Mormons. The total number of Mormons in Latin America as a whole is perhaps three million – about 0.6 percent of the total population.

Missionary work began in Chile in 1956 through North American Mormons resident in Santiago. Further penetration was promoted by groups of foreign missionaries directed by the church bureaucracy and with an eye to converting relatively well-off and educated people who might act as leaders. Thus although nearly half of current members come from among laborers, or the unemployed, about one in six is a professional and one in four from the petite bourgeoisie. Again, though Mormons in Santiago are concentrated in the poor districts, nevertheless they are skewed towards the better-off among the poor. In the leadership there is a high proportion of educated and business people. This means that Mormonism crosses class lines in Chile in a way Pentecostalism has so far failed to do and, moreover, quite explicitly embraces formal business values. Knowlton suggests that the boom in Mormon expansion was linked to the period of maximum repression under Pinochet between 1976 and 1980.

The overall impression from this (and other evidence) is that the Mormons are the most distinctively North American in ethos of all the non-Catholic groups, and have the most overt links with North America. Not only do they facilitate social mobility but they have a greater degree of cross-class appeal in their pattern of conversion and a large proportion of middle-class persons in their leadership. (This is consonant with the evidence of Gooren cited earlier.)

A third important group alongside Witnesses and Mormons and almost equally marginal to Evangelicalism or Pentecostalism, is La Luz del Mundo or The Light of the World. What strikes one about La Luz del Mundo is the Zionist theme. As in the case of the Witnesses and Mormons there is a Judaizing tendency associated with the idea of being God's people and a distinctive nation. In part this arises from intense scrutiny of the Old Testament but it can fuse with a contemporary nationalism, as La Luz has done in modern Mexico, or it can generate a Third Testament validating a fresh People of God, as in the Book of Mormon. Further variants of the theme are present in the Brazilian group Renascer, in the New Israelites of Peru and, of course, in aspects of Seventh Day Adventism widely active in several Andean Republics. The parallels in African Zionism have complicated genealogies, including some in North America, and perhaps the closest African parallel to La Luz del Mundo is the Church of Simon Kimbangu in what is now the Congo Republic. Both bodies reproduce elements of the geography of the Holy Land and the Jerusalem Temple.

La Luz del Mundo has been extensively studied by Patricia Fortuny, as well as by Renée de la Torre and Bobby Alexander.[31] What follows leans extensively on their work, more especially that of Fortuny, together with some personal observation.

La Luz del Mundo is a startling projection of the religious imagination of a sergeant in the Mexican Civil War. His massive funerary slab proclaims that he was called by Christ in a vision to adopt the name of Aaron and to further "the great commission." This is religious entrepreneurship on a grand scale, *sui generis*, and it shows how vision can strike anyone and generate a community of many thousands centered around a major architectural creation. The guiding conception of La Luz del Mundo challenges comparison with Mormonism in its inventive, syncretistic grandiosity.

Though there is no established third scripture, like the Book of Mormon, there is an almost Ethiopian recollection of the signs and symbols of the Old Testament. Opponents see Aaron's son as embedded in a patriarchal genealogy, with the power to define, rule, and require, and irradiating a prophetic aura far beyond that of the normal pastorate. Courteous and articulate public relations men play down this aspect, but certainly the leader exhibits a distinct aura of sacred power. No doubt this sacred power helps maintain the notable discipline and cohesion of the group.

The area around the temple is a disciplined enclave, conceived and built as a new Zion in Mexico, with biblical street names like Gaza or Bethesda. Large-scale and colorful murals depict previous temples on the same site, or biblical scenes like the meeting of Jesus with the woman of Samaria. There is a school, an orphanage, and a hospital built by La Luz del Mundo, and special shops such as you might find at centers of pilgrimage, selling postcards, cassettes, and devotional literature. Perhaps one should add that this whole sector of town received privileged treatment from local government and tends to vote for the PRI – the Permanent Revolutionary Party. The Party and the church share a common genesis in the nationalism of the thirties, though the church is quite pragmatic and has been open recently to overtures from the PAN, the Catholic Party, to the considerable annoyance of the Catholic hierarchy.

The main enclave of La Luz del Mundo contains some 35,000 people, nearly 1 percent of Guadalajara, and clusters round a vast temple supposedly holding 15,000 or more. Each believer is expected to attend the temple once in the course of a day. The building itself twists sideways and up wards in smaller and smaller spirals which fade into a tower, from which flashes a laser light to "enlighten" the world. Once a year vast crowds gather for the Sacred Supper and once a year the "Prophet" stands immediately under a ray of sunlight which falls on a sacred spot at that and no other time. A sacred carpet is regularly laid down from the entrance to the raised sacred area, and on Sundays the leader, and he alone, walks along the carpet while outriders run on either side before him, and the congregation claps, cries, and exults. It is a sort of entry into Jerusalem. The leader then ascends the steps to a seat of authority behind the holy table, and speaks *ex cathedra* for anything up to two hours. The congregation shouts back answers to his sporadic questions. In images strikingly reminiscent of Revelation, he stands in front of a winged golden book with trumpets issuing from it on either side. Immediately following his entry the women begin to keen, and the more "lowly" they are, the more dolorous their keening has to be. Each is covered in a mantilla to signify their womanly subjection to their husbands. At some stage in the service they line up to offer their gifts. This is an obedient people, standing peaceably in almost Judaic order. The iconography, though it is said to be of little significance and not to be iconography at all, is also Jewish, with the Star of David and the seven-branched candelabra particularly striking.

Along the vast curved space behind the raised area are the flags of two dozen or more nations "conquered" for the faith, including Spain and the USA. Spain, they explain, has been visited by the peaceful "conquistadores" of the Light of the World. La Luz del Mundo is special. Believers quote the text of the Song of Songs: "There are many queens and concubines, but only one perfect one who is my dove."

Behind the tilted marmoreal headstone of the founder, half encircled by white pillars, is a strange manifestation of power: a zoo with any number of exotic animals, many of them gifts to the leader. A cramped lion prowls about in Ethiopian splendor. Guides abound carrying their Scofield Reference Bibles. They engage you in textual exposition, and sound a little as if they are deploying scriptural formulae gathered together to establish key doctrines. An "Indian" of the Nahua tribe approaches, Bible in hand, his eye on you and on the book. This book is his truth newly opened, newly owned, and never to be wrested away. He has the pride of the reader and will face down your suspected skepticism. Such newly acquired independence brought him into conflict with the Catholic priest of his village. He had a dream of the priest's altar as sprouting the horns of a bull and immediately fled the sacrilegious vision. The priest had him put in prison for contumacy before he escaped to the safety of his Mexican Zion. Clearly his visions are continuous with the visions of an older indigenous shamanism. The theology propagated may perhaps be Pauline, though with an emphasis on works rather than faith, and the enthusiastic ambience is Pentecostal. As so often with localized inventions, the use of the whole Bible results in a Judaic emphasis and tone. There is a sense of Solomonic power redolent of Ethiopian cults, while from the deeper psychic layers come architectural shapes reminiscent of the vast creations of Mayan and Aztec civilization, with their sun worship and their ancient priesthoods.

With regard to La Luz del Mundo, Bobby Alexander presents a variation on the theme of migration. The spread of the church in the USA is largely among Central American and Mexican migrants, to whom it offers stepping stones and helping hands both forward and back, especially through the annual pilgrimage to Guadalajara.[32]

In the context of Judaizing movements one has to refer briefly to the Israelitas of Peru, who have many analogues in contemporary Africa. Work by Michael Leatham and Damian Thompson underlines the way buried ethnic identities may be resurrected through identification with Israel in the Old Testament. The Israelitas have grown rapidly since the 1960s, to the number perhaps of 100,000, and they exhibit the usual gains of asceticism and work, such as delivery from the effects of alcoholism and crime. They are to be found in collective farms in the Peruvian jungle, which they identify as the Promised Land, and in the shanty towns on the outskirts of Lima. The Messiah of the Israelitas was for a while a Seventh Day Adventist until he received a vision of himself as a Second Christ, inaugurating a millennial kingdom and restoring the ancient Inca empire.[33]

Development Agencies

Something needs to be said about the various agencies operative in Latin America. These engage in development work, and also channel assistance in time of disaster. They deploy massive resources and have even been described as the vehicles of modern neo-colonialism.

The country most affected by such agencies is Guatemala, though they operate more or less anywhere in Latin America. So far as Guatemala is concerned, they are powerful in the media, in education, and in the social services.[34] A case in point is Pat Robertson's "Projecto Luz," which in its initial television programs reached over half of Guatemala's homes. By contrast, Roman Catholics control only 20 percent of religious television. There are also numerous evangelical radio stations, but their impact and ownership tends to be more local.

As for education, day schools in Guatemala are provided principally for the middle class, apart from some schools for the poor run by the Assemblies of God. There are also seminaries, Bible institutes, extension schools, and Sunday Schools. Another channel of influence is through a new breed of evangelical social-service professionals. The government happily tolerates evangelical schools and social services, such as orphanages, to remedy gaps in its own provision. It also tolerates curricula often based on cheap versions of North American models, and presumably values their emphasis on discipline, obedience, and self-control. Yet even in these spheres, North American influence is limited. Joseph E. Davis comments in the Jesuit journal *America* (19 January 1991) that "Although the mass crusades of prominent Protestant evangelists get the media attention, most Protestant growth moves along lines of personal and familial contact."

That is the crucial point with respect to an analysis of the growth of evangelical Protestantism. Any additional impetus provided by agencies, or by television, or by help in time of disaster, is extraneous to the main modes of recruitment. In any case, some of the results of work by development agencies are problematic from the viewpoint of local evangelists. They can feel themselves undermined, or bypassed, or find the disciplines of their people eroded by injections of money which dwarf the available local resources. David Stoll, for example, analyzes such a situation with regard to the respected agency World Vision in the context of the large-scale conversions among the Quechua.[35] Stoll sets the scene as one in which the Catholic Church, along the whole political spectrum, was trying to regain its central position as the core of Indian communal organization. That meant defining the evangelical segments as divisive, and also as individualistic, meaning likely to foster personal advancement. The alternative view was that the evangelicals were themselves part of the ethnic renewal, exactly as described by Swanson and other anthropologists such as Andrew Canessa and Blanca Muratorio.[36] The other actors in the struggle were the left and World Vision. The left found itself without an adequate vehicle for maintaining protest once the Quechua acquired modest parcels of land and some freedom. It also felt undercut by World Vision (and by the concept of "development"), rather like some of the local evangelicals. As for World Vision itself, it is difficult to offer a summary view, except to say that it felt scapegoated by people in all the other parties to the struggle, including rival agencies, and unable to act in a way which was unequivocally helpful.

To recapitulate, the crucial point is that the various elements inherent in such a situation exist whether an agency complicates matters or not. They are that the communal system is breaking up and its controls breaking down. Religious pluralism is part of this break-up, and the Catholic Church tries to reconstitute itself as the core of communal renewal, while evangelicals also act as vehicles of renewal. The Catholic Church retains some links, at least symbolically, with older, more comprehensive, forms of hegemony, and the evangelicals have some links with remoter forms of influence and power. As the localities are pulled into wider networks, whether these be national or international, evangelicals tend to have above average representation among groups which are more individualized, more detached from the older traditional system, more related to the commercial world of commodities and monetary exchange. As the local system differentiates, both Catholicism and evangelicalism fragment into distinctive sectors, which in Catholicism constitute rival versions of the one faith, and in Evangelicalism distinct independent bodies.

The Revolving Door – and Social Mobility

In the course of recent inquiries into evangelical expansion, frequent reference is made to the "revolving door" whereby people come out from, as well as go into evangelical groups, but there has been little precise evidence. Evidence collected on my behalf by the Centro de Estudios Publicos, Santiago, certainly shows a considerable exodus, at least for Chile. That is particularly interesting given that those particular churches are long-established and have experienced the advent of new generations, many of whom are nominal in their adherence. This does not mean they are unmarked by the experience of conversion: they depart through the revolving door as different due to their experience. Probably they do not return to Catholicism except, of course, by marriage.

Fortunately we now have firm data available from Mexico in Bowen's *Evangelism and Apostasy*.[37] Bowen shows by many examples how Evangelicalism spread initially by personal contact and cross-border migration, rather than by missions. He shows also that the Pentecostal majority of evangelicals has *never* been significantly reliant on foreign missionary support or direction. Everywhere evangelical successes and failures are primarily determined by indigenous situations. Bowen adds that the Catholic charismatic presence does not as yet compete seriously with the Pentecostals, being active principally among the urban better-off and subject to clerical control. It also seems from Bowen's account that the presence of a liberationist influence does not inhibit evangelical growth.

As to apostasy, Bowen provides initial comments on the Mormons, with an official baptismal membership in 1990 of 617,000. Bowen concludes that the active membership is about a quarter of that figure. With regard to evangelicals, Bowen agrees with those who state that the greatest growth is in the semi-detached south which contains many indigenes and is culturally linked to Guatemala. The growth is not in the megacity. It seems – and this is important – that there is no reason to suspect different birth, death, or migration rates as between Catholics and evangelicals. Evangelical growth rates were four and a half times greater than those of Catholics in both the 1970s and 1980s, though in the latter decade birth rates dropped for both communities.

With specific regard to apostasy, the figures cited reduce the otherwise very high rates of growth. There is, in fact, much fluidity and fragility, not to mention the fact that members of churches in the north often migrate across the border. A crucial statistic consonant with what emerges in the Chilean data is that 43 percent ceased to be evangelicals in the second generation, of whom the great majority described themselves as "nothing." Another nine percent attended between once and three times a month, while the rest attended at least weekly. Presbyterians and Baptists had lower drop-out rates compared with Pentecostals, which was only to be expected in view of their lower growth rates. When they switched they tended to shift to the Pentecostals, which hardly makes for Christian amity. Another striking feature also parallel to impressions in Chile is that nearly two in three of evangelical women stay committed in the second generation, compared with only one in three of men. The fiesta and football no doubt beckon, and inevitably marriage to a Catholic woman makes a big difference. Bowen's overall estimate is that about half of evangelicals are first-generation converts and he goes on to argue that the problem is precisely "the revolving door" rather than the problem of lessening zeal in the group as a whole with the arrival of a second generation. The apathetic leave, the newly zealous arrive. Nevertheless Bowen concludes, both with respect to census data and his own chosen congregations, that 1970–90 represented two decades of remarkable growth and vitality.

One telling point made by Bowen concerns the "opportunity cost" of the priesthood of all believers and of substantial local autonomy. It is the availability of the Spirit which drives forward and vitalizes the evangelical movement but inevitably it leads to a clash of rival charismata. The result is schism and contention and in the subsequent abrasions quite a number retire hurt and disillusioned. Competition is not all gain.

The theme of the revolving door is closely bound up with social mobility, and in that respect the work of Kurt Bowen in Mexico serves to firm up the rather fragmentary evidence cited in *Tongues of Fire*. Moreover, it had the advantage of picking up shifts between generations during that chaotic period in the eighties when merely to stand still and survive might be counted an achievement.

The Mexican evangelical converts studied by Kurt Bowen were mainly from the poorer classes, and somewhat more so than the average for the Mexican populations as a whole. At the same time, perhaps one in ten were in the less prestigious reaches of the professional groupings, and about one in six were small shopkeepers, office workers, or people in minor supervisory occupations. Among the evangelicals the Pentecostals were relatively depressed socially, apart from a (so far) smallish group of neo-Pentecostals, while there was a rough upward gradient running from Adventists to Baptists to Presbyterians.

With regard to economic improvement, Bowen identified as crucial the evangelical refusal of drink and the withdrawal from the costly sprees of the *cofradías* (fraternities). This was particularly important among the indigenous groups, and it freed some 25 percent of total income for other uses. In Bowen's sample more men than women reported improvements in living standards, a difference due to women being out of the labor force or dependent on someone not a convert. It follows that much of the improvement was brought about by better use of resources, although over five years one man in five also experienced straightforward upward mobility.

When, however, it came to shifts in mobility over generations, the proportion of unskilled workers fell from 39 percent to 22 percent. Bowen concludes that overall, evangelicals experienced a widespread though modest measure of mobility over generations. As might be expected, economic advancement was more marked in the historic denominations. Nevertheless, one in three Pentecostal converts agreed that their standard of living had risen since conversion. Their population of professionals trebled in the second generation, while the number in unskilled occupations fell by about half. Bowen concludes that "Asceticism may, therefore, be a cost or price that erodes the commitment of some, but it reaps benefits for others over the long haul, which may embrace commitment."[38] And this came about in the difficult conditions of the eighties. Setting aside certain conversions directly in the middle class, more especially in Guatemala by free-range charismatics, this is the observed pattern of empowerment.

Mobility, Pragmatism, Character: an Ambiguous Conclusion

Whence comes the energy propelling social mobility? Evidently such energy has its genesis in the kind of character promoted by Pentecostalism, and for that we turn to evidence of its persistence since the earliest days of the century and the initial revivals in Los Angeles, Kansas, Wales, and elsewhere. Grant Wacker in an insightful study has shown just how ecstasy and technical rationality go together, along with a potent union of participation and authority, joy and discipline.[39] After all it requires a literally ecstatic group to make the leap on to the raft which sails to the Isles of the Blessed, and to batten down all baggage against inevitable turbulence. Once on board, technical skills are highly advantageous, as well as efficient systems of communication, since it is well known that the Lord helps those who help themselves. If you are praying for a miracle you are expected to ease its passage. Hence the title of Wacker's piece, "Searching for Eden with a satellite dish."

Pentecostalism comes out of that movement for stripping away of the extraneous, known as primitivism, whereby the believer transcends tradition to re-enter the New Testament. In the New Testament world the Holy Ghost ruled, with "signs" following, and truth was untainted by relativity. The contemporary believer retrieves the primitive condition to construct a garden in the wilderness of modernity. And yet in so doing there is no surrender to other-worldliness, in spite of all the hours spent in earnest prayer and ecstatic praise. The romance of the divine love is pursued within a confident calculus of reward and pragmatic ambition. The same goes for lesser loves and for finding a serviceable spouse. People are in everything ambitious "in the Lord." As Wacker phrases it, "A scenario of mundane sagacity and this-worldly hard-headedness dominates the picture."[40] Pentecostals are cunning and shrewd and apt for whatever is useful and to hand. So it is no wonder one of them was the first to launch a privately-owned communications satellite.

Grant Wacker comments that when combing the biographical data one is struck by a maverick defiant temper, a bravura style, and an unwillingness to be frustrated by past convention. Pentecostals accepted no other criteria or discipline but their own and never suffered self-consciousness or embarrassment. Indeed, they do not know what embarrassment is. They are full of holy boldness, taking up their own beds to walk with alacrity. They accept responsibility without ever considering themselves victims of circumstance, and they will alter such circumstances as are in their control without waiting for the illusory promise of politics. Their objectives lead them to found periodicals rather than to attend schools.

Finally, the saints persevered. "Wilfulness," says Wacker,

> fired stamina. . . . There is good reason to believe that significantly fewer of them endured debilitating illness than the national norm. Moreover, virtually all enjoyed stunning divine healings in their own bodies. . . . Thus wilfulness – defined in this case as a determination to believe that one had been healed, regardless of symptoms, or the certainty that one had been divinely commissioned to do the Lord's work, come what may – ignited and sustained extraordinary levels of physical exertion.[41]

Clearly from the Pentecostal perspective, "All things work together for good, to them that love God." Or at least, with faith, enough "things work together" to sustain hope, and in these circumstances there is no more vital virtue.

Family Likenesses? An Ambiguous Conclusion

A concluding theme present in some recent understandings of Pentecostalism is that of family likeness – and difference – compared to the base communities. One analyst stressing notable likenesses is Daniel Levine. Levine's main argument in his "Protestants and Catholics in Latin America: a family portrait" is that change does not occur only or even mainly by direct attack on the supposed central redoubts of power.[42] Change can flood in quietly, surrounding these redoubts and undermining them through mutations of culture. So far as these mutations are concerned, the base communities and Pentecostal groups have much in common. In the first place, in the majority both are composed of women, who have their own interpretation of the world and their own priorities. This, incidentally, means that *most* base communities are *not* directly political but religious, and if political they usually focus on local concerns like sewage or transport or lighting. Both Pentecostals and members of base communities seek intense religious experience in small groups, through a focus on what they regard as the liberating power of the Word.

There are continuities with this approach in the recent work of David Lehmann, notably his *Struggle for the Spirit*.[43] Lehmann speaks of the way people are distancing themselves from the hostile approach to Pentecostalism which used to be sociological orthodoxy. His own approach remains ambivalent, however, and his generalizations based more on the Universal Church of the Kingdom of God rather than the Assemblies of God. The consumerism to which he refers characterizes the former much more than the latter.

Lehmann reiterates the shared commitment to the Word and the shared identification among Pentecostals and base communities with the Children of Israel. However, in the case of the base communities, this identification is at the level of God's elect who have the real key to the text, whereas in Pentecostalism it is straightforward continuity. Among members of base communities there is a self-conscious hermeneutic as to political applications, whereas among Pentecostals literalism implies direct individual access, even though the denominational apparatus does in fact reproduce a shared, authoritative interpretation.

Both movements are international, but in the case of liberation theology it is located in a wider idea of *"basismo"* promoted among loose networks of experts and academics. Both movements were initially generated outside Latin America, Pentecostalism in Anglo-American and Scandinavian culture, *basismo* in France and the Low Countries. This, however, introduces the principal difference because *basismo* was developed among Latin American intellectuals, and it involved a veneration on their part for an "authentic" popular culture which was in part merely a mirror of their own aspirations. Pentecostals make a clean break with this dialectic of popular and erudite. They conduct "an onslaught" on popular culture, nevertheless using its own language and (at least in the case of the Universal Church) appropriating many "popular" elements. Pentecostalism rejects good taste and the tutelage of the intelligentsia, and for Lehmann that is their radical achievement.

Pentecostals and members of base communities all share sharp images of the Enemy, in the one case the Devil, in the other case capitalism and the USA. Pentecostals locate evil in demons to be exorcised, while members of base communities locate it in structures to be struggled against. Good for Pentecostals is identified with a "very present" transcendent help, whereas for members of base communities it is located in an abstract figure of Christ and communal integration. However, the members of the base communities only appropriate the ideology of struggle tangentially. Most surprising of all perhaps, especially in view of old stereotypes, the ideas of *basismo* are financed to a large extent elsewhere, whereas the Pentecostals, more particularly those in the Assemblies of God, are urged to sacrificial giving. Pentecostals are for the most part independent in every way of external financial assistance, even from that icon of plenty, the USA.

Finally, John Burdick sees most supposed likenesses as superficial.[44] Only a minority in the base communities respond as progressive clergy expect. The power of Pentecostalism resides in relieving the sufferer by throwing the burden of wrong on to the Evil One. The weakness of members of base communities resides in making demands for struggle on those already deep in the struggle for daily survival. Because base communities are continuous with "the world"around them they reproduce that world, including its inequalities. Because Pentecostals are separate, they produce an unself-conscious counter-discourse. Continuity and separation both exact their respective opportunity costs.

The most successful response to the Pentecostal challenge is clearly charismatic Catholicism. Beginning in the North American middle class in 1967, and spreading to the South American middle class, it now outnumbers the base communities by at least three to one. As Pentecostalism moves up the social scale so charismatic Catholicism has moved down, using the same methods as its rival but sharply differentiating itself also by increasing devotion to the Virgin and indeed overt hostility to Pentecostal "wolves." The most intriguing fact about them is that in the most recent presidential election in Brazil, charismatics were more inclined to vote for Cardoso rather than Lula, the Left-wing candidate, than Pentecostals. But then even among members of the base community Cardoso received 40 percent of the vote and Lula only 31 percent: yet another myth undermined.[45]

CHAPTER FIVE

indigenous peoples

This chapter explores the theme of radical religious change among indigenous peoples marginal to the major cultures and civilizations in which they are situated. It does so solely in the context of "Latin" America in order to provide a model of the way indigenous peoples seek distinctive religious definition and the reversal of negative stereotypes as they enter global modernity. It also shows how rival sectors within an indigenous people may define themselves against each other, one adopting evangelical Christianity and the other not. Clearly the processes outlined here parallel those observable in other continents, in particular Asia. As other chapters indicate, the model here is transferable, with appropriate adjustment, to different contexts such as Nepal and the Philippines.

The appeal exercised among the indigenous peoples of Latin America by evangelical and Pentecostal faiths has given rise to a great deal of controversy, much of which has focused on two slightly eccentric missions, the New Tribes Mission and the Wycliffe Bible Translators. But missionaries in the old-fashioned sense are marginal to most of what is now going forward. Indeed, the contexts in which conversion occurs are extraordinarily varied, ranging from the myriad smaller groups to the major indigenous peoples in Guatemala, Mexico, Peru, Ecuador, and elsewhere. What follows in no way attempts to summarize the large number of studies now available, some of which were, in any case, discussed in *Tongues of Fire*, but aims rather to select material from some recent contributions which add something fresh to our understanding.

Two assumptions have to be challenged: first, that indigenous cultures can be sealed off so as to preserve intact the relation of a local faith to a local social fabric, and second, that Evangelicalism is necessarily more remote from indigenous faiths than Catholicism.

The notion that Evangelicalism and indigenous faiths are at opposed poles gives special interest to a study by Tod Swanson of the Puruhá, a Quechua-speaking people in Ecuador who up to the 1960s were virtually impervious to evangelical expansion.[1] Swanson bases his analysis on a polarity of drinking/not drinking which dominates Puruhá language and culture. While for evangelicals refusal of alcohol is central, for the

Puruhá rum is an omnipresent sacred fluid. How, then, did the Puruhá reverse their symbols? And was it a sharp break or a development?

The traditional religious institutions of the Puruhá were centered around the ritual exchange of alcohol in order to gain *suerte* or good fortune, in which was included economic power. Drinking contests served to maintain a circulation of juice and wind and power between the people and the spirits. Strong brew was drunk only at sacred times and under priestly aegis, and it involved a contest with the spirits of the mountains. Sometimes the shamans won, sometimes the mountains.

But then the good fortune or power of the Puruhá began literally to run out. Traditionally, the main check on drunkenness, and therefore on indebtedness and alcoholism, had been supply. Once, however, alcohol was offered on credit, things began to deteriorate, and the Catholic priests were viewed as implicated in that deterioration. They had, so it seemed, set up the Puruhá leaders as sponsors of drinking contests and fiestas which could not be won. Furthermore, they had kept to themselves the book containing the secret of the true power of Christ. Once the Puruhá saw how power had been wrested from them by the white priests in league with the white vendors of alcohol, they saw how they might win it back. They must gain control over the power of Christ in the holy book, and manifest that power through control of their own religious music and preaching. Leadership among the Puruhá now shifted from elders to deacons, and the old contests were replaced by conferences at which adjacent kin groups competed in displays of vocal power, in eating and in drinking non-alcoholic beverages. Instead of powerful liquid pouring down their gullets powerful sounds emerged on their lips. The music itself differed very little from the old music of the fiestas, but the lyrics were different. The rivals in the new version of the old contests were the Catholics and the unbelieving white world in general. Indeed, the *conferencias* amounted to a display of the absence of whites. Once the symbols had been reversed, the other collateral benefits of modernity, such as education, electricity, and toilets, could be attributed to turning to Christ and turning away from alcohol.

Swanson goes on to analyze a further and wider layer of contestation between a political federation of Indians led by a liberationist priest and a federation led by evangelicals, in which the stakes are the right to negotiate with outside agencies for monies, and the right to be considered the legitimate representatives of the Indians. As seen by the evangelicals, the Catholic claim to provide the sole legitimate representation is precisely the old hegemony in new guise. As seen by the Catholics, the prosperity of the Puruhá is a North American pay-off for abandoning their true culture and so delaying the return of true good fortune. Swanson insists, however, that this Catholic claim is very doubtful

and criticizes attempts to portray evangelicals as dupes of foreign interests. They are now part of a mass movement of hundreds of churches
and constitute "modern representatives of the Indian tradition that will
not go away."

In his study of the Otomi Indians of Mexico, James Dow controverts
the notion that conversion is in any serious way due to missionary
activity. On the contrary, it arises out of economic and demographic
circumstances, and especially from the effects of migration.[2] Dow begins
by describing how in the public religion of the Otomi, men and their
families were appointed for a year or two to carry out religious obligations (cargo) which were burdensome and expensive. Only if you had
discharged these obligations and supported a fiesta could you be heard
at a public meeting.

Then, as the economic prosperity of Mexico City and surrounding
areas increased, Indians with only a few years schooling were welcomed
on the farms which provided for the burgeoning urban population. Those
engaged in this work, along with others who had migrated for periods
to Mexico City itself, objected to the cargo system. They preferred to
improve their own standard of living rather than shore up the authority
of the elders. In any case, the demographic balance was turning in favor
of the young, who were more likely to be skeptical about the value
and legitimacy of the cargo system. They, therefore, became part of a
shift from a system where prestige came from redistribution of wealth
to one where prestige came from accumulation. It was not so much
that Protestantism favored capitalist accumulation as that it was bound
up in the rejection of traditional redistribution.

Evangelical Protestantism made its initial impact when two men
founded a Bible study group, which appealed to the discontented younger
men. They felt happier with a faith based on a wisdom to be gained
through literacy. They were freed to think about their social obligations
in new ways and the cargo system simply collapsed, though the progress
of Pentecostalism was slowed down by a new Catholic movement which
likewise rejected the cargo system. This example indicates how a faith
based on a choice exercised through becoming literate is compatible
with changes in a local economy, and in no way necessarily requires
stimulus from external sources. Migration is a quite sufficient explanation on its own, though it by no means follows that all evangelicals are
on the move. There still remains a great deal of localized stability.

The next example bears directly not only on the question of missionary visitation from outside but also on a notion quite widely canvassed
in the Guatemalan situation which relates conversion to militarization
and violence, and to fear of identification with a rebellious Catholic left.
In a study of a Mayan village in Guatemala, Duncan Earle argues that

the impact of missionaries was slight and indirect, the impact of violence and militarization nil, and the Weberian process of economic shifts too late, and in part dependent upon Protestantism rather than the reverse.[3] The point about the independent economic impact of Protestantism must certainly be noted, but the points about missionaries and violence are specially interesting as coming from an anthropologist who judges the advent of Protestantism negatively because it is associated with a fragmentation which undermines any united cultural resistance to outside influences.

Earle points to a general increase in social fission and conflict, and underlines the role of Catholic Action in initiating breaks with traditional religious organizations and its shamans. The impact of Catholic Action clearly deserves considerably more attention than it has yet received in creating channels later widened by Pentecostalism. At any rate, there is now a breakdown of legitimate authority and its capacity to adjudicate disparities, and Earle sees evangelical Protestantism as part of that breakdown. At the same time, it picks up attractive aspects of traditional religion while "promoting an ideology more immediately successful in making coherent – and conforming to – change."[4] Protestantism is running *pari passu* with a splintering of local society and a weakening of solidarity and cultural resistance that facilitates capitalist penetration, the commodification of the land base and a ceding of land which may in the end be tantamount to ceding control of the municipality itself. In short, the local system is fragmenting internally and being absorbed into wider systems.

The Maya villages of highland Guatemala had the fiesta or *cofradia* system earlier described among the Otomi, but the revolt of the young and under-franchised was, in this case, not initially associated with Protestantism. It was associated rather with the introduction of political parties and the promotion of Catholic Action by activist priests. Catholic Action sought improvements in local economic conditions and education and it extended economic activity beyond the cornfield and the village, but it also increased internal divisions (or was sucked into them) and exacerbated external conflicts with the Ladinos who controlled many of the towns. Catholic Action effectively brought down the sacred ceiling, especially the links between the authority of the elders, the shamans, the saints, and the ancestors. By attacking the cult of the saints it laid bare and open part of the sacred world. The process of fission and collapse accelerated alongside increasing divisions in Catholic Action itself, the division of the Catholics into charismatics and traditionalists – and the arrival of a second evangelical temple.

Earle refers to evangelical involvement in the conversion of communal land along the shoreline into property saleable to outsiders. Profits from sales went to help build the second temple and to acquire the amplifiers and band equipment so attractive to the young, especially the young who had left their patches of communal cultivation to work as year-round day laborers and "guardians." Conversion, therefore, assisted the conspicuous consumption of the males. It also allowed expiation of the feelings of ill-will and tension engendered in these changes.

Earle concludes that evangelical Protestantism helps to rally kin around a sub-group, where locals can be in control. Each person in the group is a brother or sister, and the Maya can once more feel good about themselves. But, of course, they are now exposed to a wider economic system over which they exercise little control. The community could well end up providing services for the owners of holiday homes.

Timothy Evans is a Catholic monk and sociologist, also studying religious changes in Guatemala, particularly among the Indian populations, and his conclusions reinforce those of Earle to a remarkable degree, but with significant extensions.[5] Evans takes off from a point made by Sheldon Annis concerning the higher proportion of Protestants among cash croppers than subsistence cultivators and among women who made textiles for sale than those who made it for home use.[6] This reinforces Earle's comments about the greater distance of Protestants from the communal system and proximity to a wider more capitalistic system.

Evans agrees with Earle that there has been little connection between oppressive military violence and Protestant conversion, and adds there has been no connection with the mere fact that for something over a year the regime was headed by the evangelical general Rios Montt. In line with Earle's analysis, Evans singles out the role of Catholic Action. Where Catholic Action left the fraternities and traditional customs intact, Catholicism survived better. (Indeed, there must be another story here in that fraternities have resented the full imposition of clerical control over a long period.) The work of Catholic Action was seen as foreign and alienating in spite of the support it offered to Indian activism and basic education. The parallel here with events in the Ecuadorian highlands is striking because in Ecuador it was precisely the disorientation brought about by Catholic agrarian reform in a situation where the pastoral coverage provided by the Church was weak that opened up a space for evangelical conversion. Clearly, in Guatemala reform broke down the boundaries of the sacred, giving the profane an opportunity to pour in. Churches were cleared of pious bric-à-brac, the images declared dead, and intercessions to the saints curtailed. Pentecostalism, however, restored the palpable presence of the sacred, particularly through tongues, and in that respect acted to conserve the sacred. Evans emphasizes (in a somewhat different context) just how thoroughly indigenous is this re-assembly of the sacred. Many Protestant homes retain the family altars, though without the image of the Virgin. Evangelical spirituality is thus a form of moral conservation running alongside the break-up of the primal solidarities. Indeed, evangelicalism makes way in part because of the contrast with local Catholic ambiguity about morals.

Evans identifies two groups as more North American in style: the Mormons and some Neo-Pentecostal churches like Agua Viva. The Mormons were widely regarded as spending the highest number of dollars per convert, and certainly offered spectacular churches with unique amenities. The Agua Viva church had a particular appeal to business people and apparently set forth a living triumphant Christ in a manner remote from any understanding of crucifixion and suffering.

Pentecostalism and Evangelicalism have a greater appeal to the "Indians" than to Ladinos, and those Ladinos who are converted are often Ladinoized Indians. Evans distinguishes two appeals: one to the moral conservatism of the poor, especially the Indians, the other to the political conservatism of Ladinos. Among Ladinos many middle-sized landowners, small business people, and factory workers felt they had some sort of stake in the system and reacted to liberation theology with alarm.

Evans points out that with the arrival of a second generation of evangelicals, a Protestant nominalism emerges parallel to Catholic nominalism. Yet he stresses the dynamism of Pentecostal worship and its capacity to fulfil the worshippers. It generates power and allows all to relate their own personal autobiography. Spiritual power is of the essence. "One female dancer stands out in my mind. She was the lead; her face projected such inner rapture and bliss that the impact was startling."[7]

This is not to say that the Catholic Church is bereft of power. Evans, together with Edward Cleary, emphasizes the emergence of kinds of Catholicism parallel to Pentecostalism, such as *New Evangelization 2000*.[8] Indeed, Cleary holds that there is a general religious revival in Guatemala, generating a similar language and parallel conversion experiences, and that both Pentecostalism and revitalized Catholicism can offer vehicles of ethnic renewal, bridges between tradition and modernity, and a new sense of self and responsibility.

The work of Carlos Garma Navarro is interesting partly because it suggests differences between rural and urban Protestantism, and partly because it indicates how it can galvanize the identity of indigenous people over against the economic power of *mestizos*.[9] Carlos Garma Navarro compares a rural region in the mountains of northern Puebla, and Iztapalapa, a municipality in Mexico City containing the highest number of Protestant temples.

With regard to the Protestant people of the mountains, they are a socially mobile group who reject alcohol and the traditional fiestas, and adopt an economic and personal discipline. There is no observable difference in mobility as between the various kinds of Protestant, though Pentecostals are often small businesspeople, functionaries, providers of services, and proprietors of small engineering workshops. In this urban area Pentecostals are largely lower middle class and only Jehovah's Witnesses seem to have penetrated the working class.

Carlos Garma Navarro notes that miraculous healings under the aegis of the Holy Spirit characterize Pentecostalism wherever socially located. The main difference between town and country is organizational: in the former there is a larger scale and more bureaucratic organization involving ministerial training, and in the latter the organization is more autonomous and charismatic. Nevertheless, the overall unity of Pentecostalism enables migrants to move easily into the atmosphere of urban churches and is a major factor in Pentecostal success.

Garma Navarro also describes how the Pentecostals of the rural area found themselves faced by a group of *mestizo* middle-men, operating between them and the market and between them and the dominant political party. In response, the Pentecostals joined a union and affiliated to the Partido Socialista Unificado de Mexico. A parallel point is made by Susanna Rostas with respect to Protestant conversions in a traditional community in Chiapas.[10] Having noted that all services take place in Tzeltal and that the evangelicals are predominantly not *mestizo*, she comments that to become an evangelical is both a move towards *mestizo* culture and a redefinition of indigenous identity. She characterizes the evangelicals as more interested than others in cleanliness, hygiene, tidiness, and health, in the domestic appropriation of resources and individual responsibility.

A slightly different angle emerges from a study conducted by Lesley Gill in La Paz, Bolivia.[11] Gill focused on the role of Aymara women in a smallish Pentecostal church on the margin of the city. Agrarian reform fragmented land holdings in the countryside, and many Aymara women migrated to La Paz where they eked out an isolated and vulnerable existence as domestics and vendors. They could not rely on their men and were often the principal wage earners, or if single or abandoned, the sole wage earner. These women find in the Pentecostal church a haven in which to pursue various activities, which can even, on occasion, include preaching. As for the converted men, they become sufficiently rehabilitated to channel their resources to their families, but they also encounter enough traditional teaching about the female role not to feel threatened. The homes of the believers are now islands of peace. The women rediscover themselves by reworking their biography and by taking part with other women in networks of support and information. Inevitably, such a community is too impoverished to harbor entrepreneurial aspirations, but it does validate the life of the respectable Aymara poor and it inculcates a practical economic discipline. Moreover, in the context of their little churches, Aymara people, scattered all over the fringes of La Paz, find their life, identity, and language accorded a new dignity.

Research by Andrew Canessa amplifies the work of Gill with respect to evangelical expansion among the indigenous peoples of the Northern Highlands of Bolivia.[12] It appears that in these areas evangelicals make up some 15–20 percent of the population and are often the majority of active believers. The largest group of evangelicals is still Adventist, representing a late harvest of a century of dedicated work, including extensive medical and educational provision. In common with Gill, Canessa links the success of the last forty years to the social changes following the Agrarian Reform of 1952. These not only destroyed the social controls and domination exercised by Hispanic and *mestizo* elites but also stimulated major migrations to urban areas as agriculture ceased to be capable of providing a viable existence and as new communications offered a way out.

In this way the growth of evangelical Protestantism complemented the break-up of a local agricultural community and of the burdens and obligations of fiesta and fictive kinship. Fictive kinship in the locality was transmuted into evangelical brothers and sisters in the process of migration. Much depended on whether evangelicals represented a critical mass, which they more often achieved in areas close to the new roads. Otherwise they were likely to be extruded by community pressure because of their non-compliance with obligations central to local survival.

Evangelical Protestantism was also part of an affirmation of Aymara identity over against the thrust of Hispanic nationhood, as this was exercised through the school. Though the indigenous population had acquired formal equality, in practice this meant the right to be at the bottom of the same heap as everyone else, made worse by an explicit denial of ethnic status. By adopting an evangelical identity, Aymara leapt over the local national identity to a wider "western" identity, symbolized in dress and by a reversal of the contemptuous stereotype harbored by the wider society. The Aymara were now conspicuous for their refusal of coca and stimulants, their honesty, cleanliness, and tidiness, and their rejection of male violence within a newly integrated family.

Other sidelights on Pentecostalism and Evangelicalism among indigenous peoples are provided in studies by Rita Laura Segato, Fred Spier, Frans Kamsteeg, and Roger Kellner.

Segato's study of evangelicals in indigenous communities in Argentina high up on the Bolivian-Chilean border sets them in the context of long-standing polarizations between those people established in leading positions over some time, and more recent, more migratory, more marginal individuals.[13] There is an alliance between the Roman Catholic Church, symbolizing the long shadow of the colonial state, and the school, symbolizing the outreach of the contemporary national state and its attendant chauvinism. This powerful alliance is further linked to a cult of the Virgin that has pre-Hispanic roots but now conveys a nationalistic input. Evangelicals, many of them young, many of them small salespeople, repudiate that alliance and vigorously reject the Argentinean national state and its patronizing inclusion of their ethnic identity in the folkloric activities of the school. The evangelicals' own assertion of identity is established precisely through a rejection of the ethnicity promoted by the tourist brochure, and through a rejection of incorporation in the nation. At one and the same time they repudiate the old local gods and the newer national ones, to embrace an international identity beyond Argentina or Bolivia or Chile. They lie on an untenable cultural fault line high above the world and have to leap a long way to discover themselves. At the same time they declare the local humble equal to their proud neighbors. Periphery challenges center.

This double rejection of patronizing nationalism and the organic ties that bind them to local subordination is expressed in various ways, for example, dissociation from the ritual communication of wine. But even more important, the timid acquire the powerful and authoritative speech of the Bible, together with its distinctive vocabulary, and link themselves to the biblical version of a universal history, which includes remote time as well as linear, forward-looking time. Evangelicals become actors by walking up on to the biblical stage, and by studying a script (or a scripture) which they independently read, act, and know as the truth. In this way myth is the basis for becoming historical, allowing evangelicals to separate themselves from cyclical nature, Mother Earth, and sacrosanct limits and taboos.

Such a shift, achieved through abandonment of local identity, runs in parallel with new non-Catholic, non-local strategies of regional articulation. These take the form of political alliances, a flow of resources (including information and assistance to employment) and a leadership which helps redistribute these resources and assist with health provision and cheaper goods. Evangelicals manipulate a world of goods which is quantifiable and exchangeable, and so enter super-regional markets.

In making this move these Quechua Indians resemble the Mapuche of Chile. And in that respect they go in quite the opposite direction to those Afro-Brazilians who adopt spiritism. Afro-Brazilian spiritism is an unstructured pluralism within a restricted ethnicity. Evangelicalism is a move in the direction of a singular claim linked to an identity without frontiers. Thus the *cambio religioso* is to be understood *como idioma de rebelion.* As the evangelical respondent told the researcher, "Do you think we wear plumes, Miss?" Once again the logic of "my enemy's enemy is my friend" is vindicated.

Spier's work in Zurite and Katañiray, in the southern Andes of Peru, is interesting in its documentation of evangelical failure where the converts did not manage to attain a critical mass.[14] He describes how prior to the land reform of 1970, Indians were semi-slaves working the harder soil, and effectively prevented from the exercise of religious options by social enclosure and the joint supervision of clergy and landed establishment. After 1970, however, the division of land and the ideas gained through school or radio or visits to Cusco, the regional capital, increased personal independence, loosened the local social structure, and widened horizons dramatically. All this activated a desire among young people, including the intelligent and independent, for a better life. For some of these young people evangelical Christianity might help satisfy their aspirations. But that meant opting out of drinking relationships and the obligations of the cargo system and godparenthood, which in turn meant dissociation from their biological and classificatory family. So massive a shift could not be carried out by half a dozen youths on their own, especially as the older villagers became very anxious about loss of the social security built into godparenthood. The initiative, therefore, collapsed.

Things were different in the hamlet of Katañiray. The evangelical church was founded on the initiative of a comparatively well-off Indian family after the mother of the family had been succored in her illness by missionaries of the Iglesia Evangélica Maranata in Cusco, and it offered a book shop and medical post. The interior of the church was sober and tidy, with flowers and a representation of the difference between the broad and the narrow way. The congregation was well dressed and spruced up, and provided with Bibles proudly indicating their ability to interpret God's Word for themselves. This advent of individuality is important, and it is reinforced by the idea of the personal remission of sins, hitherto unappealing among Indians.

Spier makes some crucial comments congruent with massive analytic testimony elsewhere. In his view evangelicals are looking for new ways to interpret changing conditions, and to have any success you need self-discipline. They are typically those who already have or actively seek wider horizons and rely on themselves rather than have recourse to the saints. Interestingly enough, the local priest took the same approach about the same time, refusing drink and distancing himself from the festivals of the saints. Protestantism does not necessarily work simply by people becoming converts. Nor is it the only way to modernization. It is rather one route available as peoples strive to rise morally and socially, maybe to become farmers and release themselves from the controls of the in-turned peasant existence into wider networks. But a critical mass is essential.

Kamsteeg's study of an evangelistic campaign led by a Puerto Rican preacher in the southern Peruvian town of Arequipa offers one particularly interesting point.[15] Though this campaign was well attended and a putative 15,000 "won to the Lord," these people were in fact indicating their (highly traditional) interest in being healed rather than in being converted. Even with regard to the few converted in the sense intended by the campaign organizers, their distribution among competing churches in varied parts of the city proved a thorny problem. The main positive effect of the campaign had been to draw evangelicals together, though the issue of the distribution of converts presumably made some inroads into unity. The message itself had problematic elements. The links suggested between sin and illness ran into many difficulties, and threats of earthquakes have varied implications in a region where they are all too likely to happen. But more of a misjudgement from a social point of view was the way the oratory fell into a pattern of rhetoric from outsiders ignoring the marginality of the many Indians present and their dissociation from an Arequipan identity. (The relative ineffectiveness of the campaign in this instance fits with much other evidence of the ineffectiveness of campaigns in general.)

Roger Kellner's study is of Pentecostalism among the Mapuche of Chile, who for long maintained the largest intact indigenous society in South America.[16] Kellner emphasizes that Pentecostalism spreads most readily by local people converting other local people, often along kinship lines. This means that the structures of the faith (and of its social boundaries) are smudged by local practices, notably by belief in embodiments of evil such as Mapuche witches. Indeed, because Pentecostals interact with each other more than outsiders interact with each other, they tend to generate precisely those tensions which give rise to witchcraft accusations. What Pentecostalism brings in particular to its Mapuche congregations, apart from a sense of imminent judgement of the Dies Irae, is a shift away from honor and shame to inward moral scrutiny and personal responsibility for wrong-doing. In short, they strive for consistency between an outer face and an inner essential self maintained over time.

Summary

These studies taken together present a clear picture. Evangelical Protestantism is one potent element in a whole series of changes – acting upon them and acted upon by them. These changes are inevitable, short of cutting off contact with the outside world. They include changes in Catholicism itself which undermine the old pattern of the sacred in a way which facilitates evangelical entry, and which may also generate a reformation running parallel to Evangelicalism and even rivaling it.

The old local solidarities are breaking up and people are taken into a wider sphere of commerce and communication. This process involves migration and where there is migration the people do the moving themselves and do not need missionaries to come to them. Evangelical Protestantism is a faith chosen rather than received, by people on the move, conceptually and physically, and in terms of rewriting their own autobiography. The converts are not necessarily better off, because they may on occasion have been marginalized and squeezed out of the local system by sheer hardship. But they are, one way or another, on tip-toe at an edge, picking up new vibrancies which may help them to survive immiseration or to grasp new opportunities. They are helped to survive and/or to initiate change by new priorities and disciplines, by a sense of responsibility, by concern with cleanliness and health. They are also assisted by the restoration of peace in the home and the return of males to their family responsibilities. They acquire networks of mutual support, and these are especially advantageous when they move to the larger urban centers. Once they arrive in these centers, they quite often encounter an ever wider network through large-scale churches with international connections. This should be seen as connectedness, not as external missionary domination.

As people possessed by a new sense of identity they revive their own culture and assert their independence at the same time as they initiate processes which may in the end lead them to become more *mestizo*. They are often able to speak for their people through their ability to speak for themselves. Part of this recovery of ethnic identity occurs through vigorous moral and linguistic conservation and through a relocation of the sacred. A bridge is created between tradition and modernity, though traffic across that bridge also involves a certain degree of secularization in the second generation of converts. Such bridges involve some secularization at the modern end, and notable continuities at the traditional end. All kinds of continuities are possible, including continuities with indigenous dreams or flickers of millennial hope, or with spirit worlds capable of being harnessed to a faith in one Holy Spirit. Almost anything is possible. In Chile, for example, Cristián Parker (in a personal communication) has discerned continuities with nativistic cults of resistance under the aegis of the Virgin.

It is also important to keep in mind the ubiquitous logic of "my enemy's enemy is my friend." There is a series of superimposed and rival groups, ethnic or economic, or simultaneously ethnic and economic, running from the smallish indigenous groups to much larger ones, extending further to *mestizos* and Hispanics and ultimately to North Americans and

Europeans. North Americans play negative or positive roles as saviors or oppressors according to how they are placed, and how they place themselves, in these multiple hierarchies of exploiter and exploited. In local contexts the exploiter or cultural intruder can as easily be defined as Catholic, *mestizo* or Hispanic as North American. Cases can be cited of economic resistance to *mestizo* exploitation or Hispanic domination which work through a repudiation of local bonds in favor of international connections. By a symmetrical logic, liberationist attempts to utilize old solidarities can be viewed as re-assertions of comprehensive hegemony. Each context needs to be understood historically in terms of a field of alliances. After all, *Latin* America is itself a recently coined concept from the nineteenth century which still expresses a hegemonic social and religious idea.

CHAPTER SIX

africa

Africa is, of course, very different from Latin America, and what follows has to include contrasts as much as comparisons. The most obvious contrast is between an extension of Latin Christendom under the aegis of a single church, however heterogeneous the reality on the ground, and a multitude of peoples and cultures previously under colonial rule for varying periods of time, and living in political units not necessarily related to patterns of ethnic settlement. The nearest approximations to Latin American conditions are in areas of Hispanic or Portuguese colonization, though the associated Christianization there has always been very patchy. French colonization was in a way an "enlightened" version of the comprehensive imperial concept because it inducted Africans into the French linguistic community and the African elites into a metropolitan civilization. But the cultural war over religion in France meant that both Catholicism and anti-clericalism were exported to Africa, at least in areas not predominantly Muslim. In much of the rest of the continent the British method of indirect rule, which could sometimes mean restrictions on missionary activity, prevailed. From the imperial perspective missions might mean advancement in culture and welfare but equally could lead to unpredictable changes, especially through the disruption of the traditional authorities or the creation of elites imbued with revolutionary ideas. Pentecostalism in particular was viewed in the inter-war period as subverting traditional chiefly power. Christianity might be appropriated by Africans for their own needs and purposes, leading to separatist movements and disruptive prophetic outbreaks. The intermittent millenialism of Latin America might equally emerge in Africa.

There was, therefore, both complementarity and disjunction between the colonial project and the missionary idea, and in the event the Christianity of the post-colonial era took off on its own in "critical solidarity" with the new states, many of them led by Christians. By the end of the millennium Christians numbered over three hundred million and represented a major shift in the global constituency of Christianity.

Two major currents in African Christianity are relevant to the current discussion: the emergence of the independent churches and the arrival of Pentecostalism. The former mingled African elements with the Christian repertoire. Since Africans had the biblical text in their own hands they read it in the light of their own situation, which might mean the appropriation of prophetic themes, as in the cases of Simon Kimbangu or the Prophet Harris, or adoption of ancient Jewish practices close to their own, or identification with the idea of a Chosen People. African religion had always been fluid, and African independent churches added to the flux.

Pentecostalism arrived early in the twentieth century but its massive expansion came in the seventies, a decade or so later than in Latin America. When it did so it tended to undercut the independent churches as well as the historic denominations. As in Latin America, Pentecostalism benefited from the cultural radiation of the USA and that included some appropriation of prosperity gospel. At the same time African religion was concerned with "goods" and needed little prompting in that respect. The prime appeal of Pentecostalism (and of associated movements) was to groups who were anxious to share in what modernity has to offer but through the lens of a spiritual and inspired understanding. Whereas the independent churches pursued Africanization to this or that degree and the historic churches, at least at leadership level, combined a critical political perspective with inculturation and cultural retrieval, the Pentecostals cared for none of these things in their intense desire to repudiate whatever they saw as holding them back and embedding them in local practices that inhibited their mobility, freedom, and advancement. In their view the old powers were both real and regressive, too real for comfort, and too close for nostalgia. As for the political world, it was far above them and initially a realm dominated by "the principalities and powers," though with increased mobility and confidence they might aspire to enter it and – as in Latin America – add their voice to the Babel of competing interest groups. Characteristically, there were two stages, one of humble withdrawal behind the protective fence of the "household of faith," and one of assertion in which leaders spoke for a new presence and sometimes a new generation, contesting the older establishments and even offering alternative props to political leaders.

The broad background is the weakness of the African state, vast indebtedness, and a corrupt clientism, which means that churches become the main mediating institutions and Christian appeals count as major arbiters of political legitimacy. Churches become alternative communities wielding power through non-governmental organizations, and Pentecostals may sometimes act as alternative oppositions, picking up the sentiments of the excluded. Inevitably this leads to tensions, and these tensions are exacerbated where one form of Christianity becomes associated with particular tribal or regional interests and another form with its rivals. Perhaps one should add that even the leaderships of the mainstream

churches may sometimes need the stimulus of an attack on their interests to engage in criticism, and that they do have the advantage of
transnational personnel, whereas Pentecostals are often locals finding a
voice for the first time and so striving for recognition. Something parallel to this happens among those indigenous peoples of Hispanic America
whose habitats are likewise athwart political frontiers.

In Africa, Islam is a massive presence, especially in the north and
along the east coast. Thus Pentecostalism encounters two zones, both
mainly Francophone, but one comprising a north-central belt of Catholicism and the other a belt of Islamic minorities shading into the huge
area of essentially Muslim states. Where the Muslims are a minority
there may be straight competition in which Pentecostals (and other
Christians) do well, but penetration beyond that can lead to serious
cultural conflict, as happened in Kano, Nigeria. Milder versions of this
cultural conflict might also be encountered in the Coptic sectors of Egypt,
Ethiopia, and Eritrea, though a version of the charismatic movement has
been influential in Egyptian Coptic Christianity.

Recently Pentecostals have made progress, along with other evangelicals, in the ruinous emplacements of the Portuguese ex-colonies, which
are sparsely Christianized and have been wracked by civil war. Here the
cultural and political frontiers are porous and there has been a notable
increase of Pentecostalism in the Mozambique–Zimbabwe border areas,
as well as considerable activity in the country by foreign evangelical
non-governmental organizations.

These introductory comments are intended to suggest spectra of
appropriation of Christianity by Africans, and so to locate just where
Pentecostalism finds its optimal niche between the "historic" mainstream
and the independent churches. Two suggestions now follow as to where
Pentecostalism is located, one which is general, but focused on East
Africa, and one which selects a local situation in South Africa.

Creative Appropriations

Recent work on East Africa presented under the editorship of Thomas
Spear and Isariah Kimambo gives an idea of the range of appropriations,
more particularly with respect to charismatic motifs as they affect historic churches.[1] In Tanzania, with its distinctive Lutheran traditions, for
example, there is now a fresh awakening which looks back to revivals in
the period immediately after the second world war. People in the older
denominations give a cautious welcome to the awakening but feel considerable unease about the growth of semi-independent cell structures
and interdenominational mass rallies. These are just the changes and
anxieties now experienced in Argentina. The overall tone is charismatic,

with choruses, testimonies, exorcisms, and healings, and the movement probably picks up energies otherwise likely to flow into Pentecostalism proper or perhaps into the independent churches.

Similar undercurrents have affected the Roman Catholic Church, and they represent a "bottom-up" inculturation. Traditional Catholicism combines with African tradition under the solvents of charismatic practices, creating on the one side a discourse of spiritual warfare, fastings, exorcisms, and healing, and on the other side a discourse of family integration, mutual support, discipline, and hard work. The conclusion one draws is that what is currently outside the Catholic Church in Argentina can, *mutatis mutandis*, just as easily exist inside. Devotions center on the rosary and the Blessed Virgin, and include the role of the Virgin as protectress of the chosen nation of Tanzania, freed from colonial bondage under Nyerere. Similar developments, testifying to the failure of top-down inculturation, have come about in the Catholic Church in Uganda. In that country there has emerged a spirit-empowered people active in the extra-sacramental sector of Catholicism. They cater for local needs with respect to healing and witchcraft, imputing their own meanings to Catholic resources, as well as attracting press criticism for their mass appeal and alleged greed.

Movements which have picked up evangelical and Pentecostal motifs more tangentially are located in the Holy Spirit cults of Kenya, for example the Arathi people. The Arathi approached the Bible rejecting traditional culture and western understandings alike. They saw themselves as a separate nation on the Jewish model, defined by appropriate rituals and taboos. They combined that with a New Testament eschatology which demonized the colonial power and gave to them a spiritual empowerment in visions and healings, prophecies, signs, and wonders.

To give some idea of the wider range of appropriations, the Congo has seen a Comtean version of Judaism, taking off from the Church of Simon Kimbangu but based on its own prophet and scripture, and a holy city situated in northern Angola. As in Guadalajara, Mexico, with respect to La Luz del Mundo, so also in northern Angola. The movement pursued linguistic revival and worships a trinity of love, intelligence, and power (or religion, science, and politics).

In all these varied responses we have the creative approach of African lay people to the resources at hand and a profound indigenization of biblical themes, Judaic and Christian, which owes nothing to theory and everything to need. These resources are deployed to build up new kinds of voluntary community with or without an ethnic base or reference to the national solidarities promoted in the post-colonial period. What is in train is the accelerating extension of options, the crossing of denominational boundaries, and frequent creation of extra-ecclesiastical structures

and fellowships. African practice and Christian charismata offer empowerments in all the problems and griefs of everyday. These are especially
potent for women no longer embedded in systems of bride wealth,
polygamy, or assigned marriage partners. In this area of family and
reproduction the key is knowledge, and Christianity is a major source of
it, as well as of new norms and individual choice.

The Pentecostal Location in Mobile Society

An idea of the spectrum of appropriation on offer in a particular area is
provided by Rob Garner's study of an urban sector in South Africa,
presented here with some supplementary material taken from Karla
Poewe. The main focus of Garner's work is on the motivation to social
and economic mobility, and so there is a parallel between his findings
and those of Gooren in Guatemala City.[2]

Garner cites research by Anderson in another peri-urban sector near
Pretoria, which shows that Black South Africa is 90 percent Christian,
and African Independent Churches as now larger than the mainline
churches combined.[3] The fastest growing churches are Independent Pentecostal Churches and Zionist-Apostolic African Independent Churches
stressing charismatic worship. This parallels national trends suggesting
that Pentecostals increased from half a million in 1966 to two and a half
million in 1990. Spirit-focused religion, both in predominantly western
(Pentecostal) and predominantly African expressions (Zionist-Apostolic)
is the dynamic force in contemporary South African religion, seemingly
at the expense of mainline churches. Moreover, the levels of commitment and practice were much higher than in mainline churches. Garner
adds that in his area and Anderson's, as well as nationally, the mainline
churches had more of the better-off, and the African Independent
churches least, with the Pentecostals in between. Non-affiliation is associated with *low* income; and both Jewish whites and Muslim Indians
tend to have high income.

Garner discusses the relation between mainline missions and on the
one hand legitimation of a modern capitalist economic ethos in terms of
mobility, education, discipline, all kinds of betterment, and respectability, and on the other hand the generation of protest. It is these mainline
churches which created leaders and intellectuals, including liberationists,
challenging the previous political system of apartheid as well as its economic assumptions, unlike the ANC intellectuals who mostly dropped
their economic critique once their political aims were achieved. Mainline
churches also lost interest in conversion understood as personal transformation. However, as one might expect, the mainly middle-class laity
accepted the legitimation while ignoring the critique, although they did

share to some extent in the validation of, and nostalgia for, African forms. Crucially Garner points to the way the expanding Pentecostals have picked up the older Methodist stress on respectability and socio-economic advance. They are, as it were, the next cohort in line, picking up where Methodism left off.

What then, of them? The answer thus far, is too little, partly because they will account for not more than 10 percent and partly because sociologists are drawn more to the African Independent Churches (and sometimes see Zionist-Apostolic Independents as to some extent a variety of Pentecostalism). Pentecostalism can be portrayed as an American import inclined to facilitate American foreign policy objectives, especially in the form of prosperity teaching and in those white churches which can be identified as a New Religious Right. However, Garner points to a much more ambiguous relationship, and what he has to say fits with André Corten's discussion of the intellectual "unacceptability" of these churches.[4] They are simultaneously rafts for the survival of the poor, taking them to destinations somewhat better than survival and they tend to be positive about capitalism. Garner also quotes Anderson's own "pneumatological" approach, stressing the essentially religious aspects of a transforming potential, which is further associated with a rejection of ancestor reverence and sacrifice. Presumably this association is part of a modernization, breaking with the elders and the past.

Beyond the Pentecostals are the African Independent Churches of the ultra-poor, who like the Pentecostals have been politically passive. As in Latin America there is a characteristic gap between the intellectual option for the poor and the options of the poor themselves, though it is always possible to see Independent Churches as coded resistance through healing practices and an alternative holistic spirituality. More prosaically, Zionist Independency is part of a quest for belonging and cultural conservation in which the church provides an organization for material help and some control over adverse circumstances. Prosperity is hardly in their sights. The focus is rather solidarity, discipline, and networks under a strong and centralized leadership.

At this point one arrives at Garner's own local study, which exemplifies this broad picture and, indeed, provides a guide to the Pentecostal phenomenon more generally. In the sector he studied there were nearly a hundred churches, half of them Zionist-Apostolic African Independent. At one end are mainline churches, like the Anglican, where there is an educated lay leadership, little personal contact or participation or talk of conversion, and (among African intellectuals) some advocacy of traditional African culture. At the other end are various kinds of independency, usually poor, often neat, orderly, and sometimes uniformed, with a division between those stressing formality and those swaying and clapping with healings, testimonies, frenzied prayer, acute awareness of the demonic – and ancestor worship. Leadership is male and women are restricted to singing and prophecy. Music is central. There is, of course, a wide range of practices here, but the emphasis is on authority and cultural conservation.

The Pentecostals are also very varied. Though there is a conservative view of women in fact women participate vigorously. Leadership tasks are widely distributed and include women. Often the music is contemporary and there is a strong dualistic sense of the Satanic element in "the world." The prophecies and prayers are humble and mundane, usually to do with health and safety, and there is some modest reference to giving and to prosperity, and to faith healing. Pentecostals include educated members and stress tithing, Bible use, learning English, mutual trust among the brethren, and rejection of idolatrous practice, i.e. they promote commitment and advancement. Garner notes in a general way the division between holiness and prosperity types and concludes that it is the Pentecostals (with the Apostolics) who have advanced furthest from the status of their parents, who stress education and discipline and insist on a break with Zulu culture.

Here it is worth mentioning the broader penumbra of charismatic Christianity, as discussed by Hexham and Poewe, among others.[5] In the eighties many whites left mainline denominations to find the close relationships offered among charismatics, and some have accused them of being insecure and neurotic religious "consumers" while in the view of Hexham and Poewe they showed themselves creative, optimistic, as well as firmly against racism and more open in their attitudes than their peers. What Hexham and Poewe describe is the emergence since the mid-sixties of large super-churches in dormitory areas, parallel to those found in many other parts of the world from Atlanta to Seoul. In these, new personae are negotiated with prophecy, healing and weeping, hope and celebration, in a way which parallels the traumas of the country at large. Biographies have to be reconstructed as well as social systems. Furthermore, women find an affirmative atmosphere in such churches, helping them through difficult experiences, including single parenthood. At the same time there is an overtone of prosperity gospel, and whereas the Protestant Ethic was held to help entrepreneurship, such bodies are themselves interesting cases of business administration and marketing.

Indigeneity, Africanization, Autonomous Space

We turn now to some studies of appropriations in various parts of Africa with some particular interest in the question of indigeneity. The issue of indigeneity and local context as contrasted with foreignness is a major focus of the Nigerian material recently analyzed by Ruth Marshall-Fratani.[6] Of course, that is not the only axis around which her evidence is arranged, but she does refer specifically to those scholars and religious leaders who are "tempted to view the rise of these churches solely from the point of view of their foreign origins and connections."[7] Ruth Marshall sees Pentecostalism very differently.

> With its central theme of personal and social rebirth [it works] both as a powerful metaphor for new types of practice, as well as a symbolic and material resource for the elaboration of a conceptual challenge to the power monopolies, for the creation of "autonomous spaces" of practices which defy the oppressive logic of current power monopolies (in which state violence and economic exploitation figure prominently) and for the articulation of strategies to create, exercise and legitimate new power relations and new opportunities for survival.[8]

What follows in her analysis echoes Latin American evidence. She distinguishes two layers, closely parallel to layers in Latin America: one consists of denominational mission churches like the Assemblies of God, and their indigenous counterparts, drawn principally from the literate and semi-literate poor; the other consists of a transdenominational charismatic movement, appealing particularly to the young and the mobile, and having a strong base in the universities. The former are well-organized, and at least up until recently, have been ethically rigorous and withdrawn from the world, while the latter have often been inclined to the "prosperity gospel." All have a very strong sense of community and see themselves both as an international movement and as able to act as a pressure group with the government. They all react against "nominal" orthodox churches and against connections with tribalism or with "heathen" practices such as might be found in the Aladura churches. They are participatory in style as well as strongly hierarchical; and they wear western dress and listen to western gospel music as part of a self-conscious modernity.

The background for the growth of the poorer churches is not merely economic decline and the increasingly abrasive struggle for survival, but the use of power and influence at every level for personal pillage, so that subordinate groups are burdened with a sense of forces out of control. Hence, narratives of conversion contrast helplessness with empowerment, and this empowerment is not some unreal world of atavistic escapism, but rather "an expressive and pragmatic" act of individual and collective restructuring.[9] People find in these churches an equality and sense of worth outside the categories of material success or the hierarchies of age and wealth, and also a rudimentary social security, a pooling of resources, and access to counseling on financial and marital matters.

In the better-off churches, material successes are not shunned but seen as marks of divine favor, and pastors like to show that they have received these marks. Ethical discipline ensures that appetite for mammon is under control and "goods" kept circulating in not too hurtful a manner. Those living triumphantly "in the power of Jesus" have to abide by the rules or face ruin. Clearly, in the born-again community as a whole, there is a network of patrons and clients whereby the born-again prefer domestics or secretaries or business contacts who are likewise born again; and there is a parallel network of private hospitals, maternity wards, and kindergartens, as well as a born-again record company called Selah. Born-again people and institutions are considered more reliable and trustworthy. One slogan is "Jesus is our Lord, Catering is our business."

In the poorer churches, women are expected to be domesticated and to obey edicts about dress and comportment; in the middle-class groups, however, there is little endorsement of the withdrawal of women from the work-place. In the spheres of marriage, family, and sexuality one finds born-again doctrine and practice not only transforming them quite dramatically, but also in ways that are highly attractive to young urban women. Once again, one encounters the potent ambiguity of Pentecostalism. For example, women may gain by merit what they otherwise are obliged to seek by trading sexual favors; again, birth control is allowed, even advocated, even though abortion is sinful; and the infidelity of men and women is judged according to a common standard. Moreover, the maintenance of such rules in the community is matched by a respect accorded by outsiders to the "spiritual power" of being born again. (Ruth Marshall-Fratani herself found she could deflect unwanted attention by claiming to be born again.)

Furthermore, the churches offer a place in which to find a relatively reliable spouse and, in particular, peaceable husbands who will treat wives with consideration and not use them as baby machines. Marital disputes are regularly brought to the pastor or to his assistants for adjudication. Wedding ceremonies are reasonably modest; choice of partner is up to the individual; and this choice more easily crosses ethnic lines than elsewhere. Among the better-off, women discover chances for mobility and achievement, in the public as well as the private sphere. But even among the poorest born-again people, women are increasingly encouraged to take pride in their own achievements. To be born again is to have the power to "construct a space" for freedom and dignity, and to exercise authority, by prayer, by exorcism and by averting misfortune.

The reorganization of a chaotic moral field enables Pentecostals to participate in popular discontent with government. Most born-again Christians do not bribe officials or even tolerate such behavior, and they also articulate an indirect critique of state-sponsored violence and the operations of the fraternities. They wrestle against principalities and powers, and that means spiritual and satanic wickedness in high places, i.e. big and evil men. They are armed with countervailing power and their struggle on the spiritual level is all of a piece with their refusal to "play the game." There are signs that this spiritual contest with corruption and with the violence and lack of accountability of the powerful may grow into a more institutional participation in politics – though the Brazilian experience indicates how this may narrow and blunt the edge of witness. Clearly, this cannot be a homogeneous movement precisely because evangelicals express different sets of interests in their opposition to corrupt elements in the social order. Nevertheless, they are part of self-conscious regulation of practice "in an ongoing process of social transformation".

Some of the points just made can be illustrated by material from another African context analyzed by Birgit Meyer.[10] She studied religious change among the Peki Ewe of south-eastern Ghana over the past century or more and the processes run parallel to those in Latin America, apart from the absence of an established church. The original Christian missionaries arrived in the mid-nineteenth century just as the Protestant "historicals" also arrived in Latin America, and they brought with them a long tradition of German Pietist awakenings. For these missionaries, themselves of very modest background, health and wealth were mere outward things compared with healing of the heart and inwardness of conviction. However, the Africans they encountered appreciated goods of whatever kind and in the early stages tended to be men dissatisfied with their position in the old order who were attracted by a worship without expense. Converts saw missionaries as agents of modernity and of the future, as well as visitors from a more powerful global reality. They embraced Christianity pragmatically in terms of their needs, which included goods here and hereafter, as well as educational opportunity and scope for enhanced individuality. There is a contrast here not only with the inner transformation required by their Pietist mentors but also with that achieved by classical Latin American Pentecostalism. But it is at least clear that African traditions, in Africa itself or in Brazil and the Caribbean, do not require external and foreign stimulus to appreciate a message of prosperity.

In Birgit Meyer's view, the ascetic ethos of the missionaries complemented the emergent capitalist economy, but that complementarity was qualified by their reservations concerning worldly and external things, including the fragmentations of mass consumption and of political liberalism. They were also unwilling to impart the prophylactic resources of their own Christianity in case the unleashing of the Spirit might undermine godly order. For the missionaries Satan had traditionally been

important as representing the sin of idolatry, and in Africa they re-
phrased that to mean the attraction of the old ways. Yet by attributing
diabolical attraction to the old gods they also confirmed their reality.
The traditional gods became integrated into a Christian discourse and in
this way an Africanization was achieved quite different from that later
proposed by African theologians.

When Pentecostalism emerged it took over this conceptual Africanization, but whereas the leaders of the mission churches envisaged a once-
for-all transition from heathendom to Christianity, Pentecostals maintained
a continuous fight along the border between the new power of the Spirit
and the genuine powers of the old satanic order. In staging this dramatic
contest and projecting it in stories and media presentations, Pentecostals
revived the healing practices of Christianity, as well as offering vibrant
and colorful services without a written order. The original fears of the
missionaries were, therefore, realized. Their godly order was indeed
subverted by the freedom of the Spirit and their theological training
undercut by demotic availability.

It turns out, then, that there are two channels of Africanization. One
is produced from above by African theological intellectuals and the other
builds up from below by incorporating the old gods in satanic guise. The
former ignored the actual operation of the mission churches at the grass-
roots level and dismissed Satan as a superstition which was, however,
part of a traditional culture nourishing benign elements. The latter accepted the reality and power of the old gods in the course of demonizing them and exorcising them. It is precisely this frank acceptance of
the power of the old and the embrace of a Christian prophylaxis which
moved many to secede to the Pentecostals. In this way much of the
older practice was incorporated in the new, including bodily movements
and gestures. Thus by breaking dramatically free from the past, believers
can revisit it, experiencing forbidden desires without being responsible
for them.

If one accepts this analysis, the notion that Pentecostalism is simultaneously ancient folk religion and new gospel gains fresh plausibility. The
same paradox is most obviously present in Brazil in the practice of the
Universal Church of the Kingdom of God which combines a rhetoric of
Christian prophylaxis with a dramatic war against the real powers of the
old spirits. At the same time as it conducts this war it pursues all the "goals"
of modernity with abrasive sophistication. It seems that Pentecostalism
articulates the transition from traditional to modern by symbolizing and
expressing all its tension-ridden ambivalences, and does so without the
kind of disenchantment which expels the world of the spirit as such.

In viewing Pentecostalism as a version of Africanization from below,
Meyer clearly rejects the idea that it is an alien import. Rather it provides

a discursive space and initial practice enabling believers to negotiate modernity. This negotiation is particularly potent for women needing to achieve multiple adjustments within the family. Troubled relationships with fathers and husbands manifest themselves in headaches, confusion, and weight loss. They dread the way their everyday life pushes them towards dependence, but they also fear what independence may bring. So what Pentecostalism offers are the spiritual resources and the communal backing of the circle of believers to help them stand on their own two feet.

At the fundamental level, according to Meyer, Pentecostalism assists believers to become individuals by loosening their ties to the family and the wider group and offering the infilling of the Holy Spirit. At the same time, it deals with the tensions of new conditions by mediating between individual success and family loyalty, and moderating the raw experience of a random economy with notions of a proper and limited pursuit of godly betterment. A collective fantasy of devilish riches both releases a desire for what is realistically unobtainable and criticizes the rigors of the capitalist system. People strive for the good and the goods which may be attendant on it, while rejecting the purely worldly pursuit of riches and success. Meyer concludes, in line with the argument above, that Pentecostalism not only crosses boundaries but enters deeply into a particular locality because it is able to confirm individual existence without linking that to any particular community outside itself.

What, then, does such an example show? It demonstrates the flexibility of Pentecostalism as it relates to a particular time and place. In this case time and place run parallel to the Afro-Brazilian situation and the specific variety of Pentecostalism has an affinity with the *cura divina* of the Universal Church of the Kingdom of God. As argued above, Pentecostalism confirms the local even in the course of crossing boundaries, and subsumes the older tradition while setting it in a new frame. It also deals with the ambiguity of modernity and with the mingled promise and threat of capitalism by allowing hope to burgeon without selling out to worldly seductions. In the course of achieving this it confirms men and women in their personal identities and reintegrates the family.

As a footnote to the analysis by Meyer it is worthwhile citing material from Embu District, Kenya, by Miriam O'Neill,[11] who emphasizes a marked discontinuity between Pentecostalism and the past, and the strong boundaries erected between Pentecostal believers and the outside world. Pentecostalism in the Embu District began in the 1930s as a series of breakaway movements from mission Christianity which were identified as anti-colonial and as seeking cultural autonomy. This identification of Pentecostalism as anti-colonial was, in fact, widespread at this time, especially as it subverted the tribal authorities who were the props of indirect rule.

During the post-world war "emergency" many Pentecostal churches were banned but that phase concluded and with the arrival of independence Pentecostal growth took off. Nowadays Pentecostal churches may well form the dominant grouping. O'Neill suggests that with regard to contemporary politics Pentecostal churches are largely uninvolved and, in any case, Pentecostals tend to feel they are too lowly to be critical in a situation of attenuated democracy. The general focus of Kenyans is local and has to do with the working community not the political tribalism of an invented nationality. A complicating factor is that a vigorous Christian profile was adopted by President Moi which had some success in attracting Pentecostal support.

Miriam O'Neill deals with one or two other controverted issues. She argues that Pentecostals are deeply rooted in Embu identity, but that their methods of healing were strongly opposed to involvement with the ancestors, and their espousal of the ethics of hard work involved a "refocusing" of Embu values. With regard to ideas about prosperity, O'Neill emphasizes their origin in African sources, especially in rural areas, and the existence of a critical approach to them. In general, salvation was understood as a source of social betterment, so that socially believers "go up a class" and are cleaner. Pentecostals adopt a helpful discipline which bolsters the integrity and economy of the family, they encourage self-help groups, and promote independent initiative and equality within the social space provided by the church.

Media and Imagined Communities

Rosalind Hackett takes up a rather different theme showing how the Pentecostal fascination with the media, so evident in Latin America, and especially Brazil, is also evident in Africa, especially Nigeria.[12] What began two and a half centuries ago with George Whitefield "peddling divinity" to crowds of twenty thousand in Philadelphia is now vastly amplified by television and electronic synthesizer. As in other spheres, the American connections are palpable, but the users and usages are local. In the early seventies it might have been Pat Robertson or Oral Roberts but now it includes a host of Nigerian – and Ghanaian – voices. As in Brazil this is an attempt to re-present popular culture in Christian terms acceptable to the "born again." It suggests that West African Pentecostals increasingly reject their traditional withdrawal into enclaves of faith and are inclined rather to contest public space. There they are in direct and successful competition with secular media, for whom they are natural targets whenever there is the slightest suspicion of graft or vulgar aggrandizement or sexual misconduct. A pastor is often also a presenter or a writer of manuals of conduct. Pentecostals are also in direct competition with the elites of the state and education because they wholeheartedly embrace western modernity and dress rather than promoting the retrieval of "pagan" customs and festivals as is now required in the schools. Once again, as in Brazil, they are refused sponsorship, yet they grow nevertheless. Here one identifies a triangular field of contestation: the state, the religious community, the mass media.

What Pentecostals (and charismatics more generally) create through the mediation of television, stickers, videos, and tapes, is a loose community of like-minded people moving across local and denominational frontiers, who immediately recognize each other's style, aspirations, and language. They appeal to the young, and especially to young women, disillusioned with the moral claims of the older generation of leaders in churches and politics. In one sense this is a community of equals because spiritual gifts trump wealth and connections; in another sense it is focused on charismatic icons deploying a lurid imagery of spiritual warfare not unlike the imagery of popular western comics about cosmic conflict. Such a combination of charismata and equality realized in communities without clear organizational borders is very reminiscent of contemporary Argentina. The charismatic spirit is globally recognizable but made manifest in all kinds of small and local groups, including families gathered around the magic lantern of television.

The basic units of this kind of religion are the family, the church and the conference (or camp-meeting), and the world. The extended family is sometimes rejected (with its cult of the ancestors) where it is seen as embedded in gerontocracy, though it can also be cultivated as a link between the rural and the urban existence. The world is embraced because that is where the transnational trails lie, in London perhaps as students or lawyers, in the Netherlands maybe with fellow Ghanaians in diaspora. Charismatic Christianity is the portable identity of people in diaspora. Matthews Ojo, himself someone who is from time to time in London and in Nigeria, has given illuminating accounts of the style of fellowships among young well-educated Africans and the kind of marital disciplines and professional ethics they promote.[13] As the poor rope themselves together on slippery slopes so, too, do the middle classes and emergent counter-elites seeking insertion into the public realm. And maybe their "imagined communities" have a salience and importance as great as the public realm of the state.

Economic Ethic among Mobile Disembedded Young

In his work on Zimbabwe, David Maxwell develops the issue of a Pentecostal economic ethic which I raised in *Tongues of Fire*.[14] Selecting from Maxwell's varied concerns, he gives an account of the prosperity teachings propagated by the Zimbabwe Assemblies of God Africa (ZAOGA), a body claiming to have a constituency of about ten percent of the population of the country. He contrasts his view with the arguments of Paul Gifford who stresses the indebtedness of African Pentecostals to American sources and possible vulnerability to the American New Christian Right. Maxwell is clear that concern for betterment has deep African roots and that prosperity teaching is focused on local concerns. He says that for some they have engendered social mobility, for others provided a code helpful in avoiding destitution, and for yet others a pattern for dealing with modernity and benefiting from it.

The origins of ZAOGA lie in the aspirations of urban artisans struggling for recognition in Highfields Township, Salisbury (Harare), which was also the birthplace of Zimbabwean nationalism. As usual there is a tale of confused genealogies and breakaways. ZAOGA grew from a breakaway from the Apostolic Faith Mission, joined up with the South African Assemblies of God, and then broke away once more. Paralleling so much Latin American experience, the church expanded along the networks of labor migration into the urban cities and along international migrant networks in Mozambique, Malawi, and Zambia. Its leader, Ezekiel Guti, formed a relationship with the Christ for the Nations Institute in Dallas, Texas in 1971, which has been of some importance even though American influence is regularly castigated. After Zimbabwean independence in 1980 the church mushroomed again, rather like the expansion of the Mossi tribe of Pentecostals in Burkina Faso, setting up networks in Botswana, Zaire, South Africa, Rwanda, Tanzania, and Ghana.

The development of ZAOGA can be compared with the trajectory followed by the Assemblies of God in Brazil. It is a familiar story of a transition from egalitarian revolt to bureaucratic structures under the authoritarian control of a small group gathered around a charismatic personality. Participation remains a core activity but the church also pursues political influence in promoting a moral agenda, and seeks recognition and respectability. These aims are helped along in this case by the fact that the present wife of President Mugabe is a member, and that Mugabe himself is happy to raise his hands in prayer before so numerous a constituency. What I termed a "revision of consciousness" in *Tongues of Fire* begins as an individual conversion, realized in domestic and business relations, especially as young males give up violence in the peer group and reject traditional practices to pursue literacy and education. Debt and waste are shunned as sin, and money spent on alcohol, tobacco, and women is channeled into useful goods and savings.

Men and women reject possession rituals and witchcraft as demonic, rather as Methodists once rejected rural pastimes, and they show their new self-respect and solid achievement by their dress and demeanor in the assembly of the godly. If a break is to be made with the past, and with the pull of local ties and obligations, then the extended family has to be transformed into the Christian fraternity. Local ties drain resources and restrain individual initiative, whereas the church encourages accumulation and the virtues of responsibility, such as thrift, mutual assistance in employment and in welfare, hard work, and trustworthiness.

The economic ethic of ZAOGA is summed up in a doctrine of talents, which includes explicit encouragement for business women, teaching them self-reliance should they face desertion. Start-up grants are made available and earnings are recorded by computer. Money is not just accumulated but accorded moral meaning through the ritual cleansing of notes and coins. Members testify to God's blessings on their endeavors, and these are often impressive.

Dreams and visions of betterment achieve practical realization through self-actualization and black pride – notions which also draw on American sources but are tuned to context. Release from the spirit of poverty is release from the pollutions of the backward countryside, and it entails the reversal of older negative stereotypes. You must learn how to be courteous to women and manage your bank account. *Do ut des.* You are delivered by the blood of Jesus, and deliverance is marketed in homely familiar idioms. Conspicuous consumption of blessings in the leadership should be matched by conspicuous giving, though that kind of giving may be easier to orchestrate among the members than to practice consistently. The orchestrated displays of conspicuous giving among members resemble those of the Brazilian Universal Church, and give rise to similar criticisms.

David Maxwell concludes that while Pentecostalism rejects modernity in the form of moral relativism (which plainly they could not afford) it embraces it as a repudiation of traditional hierarchies and legitimations. The price paid for participation and advancement is tight control at the top of the organization. That now attracts criticism from mobile young Turks in the mould of the original urban artisans, recalling the movement to an older and humbler populist Pentecost. But their success is not guaranteed: those presiding so successfully over the phase of betterment will not concede so easily.

Just as there is this cycle shifting from revolt and equality to a kind of bureaucratic platform for charisma and personal authority, so there is another cycle in which the young men and women break from the gerontocracy of the elders to occupy their own free space, and then in turn the men become gerontocratic. Maxwell traces this process in his *Christians and Chiefs in Zimbabwe*, showing how women in particular have much to gain from a once-for-all release from witchcraft accusations, given that a free exorcism is always available. He also comments on the way Pentecostals – in this respect like the Jehovah's Witnesses – delegitimated chiefs by demonizing ancestor religion. This was the context which, on the one hand, gave young labor migrants anxious to retain their wages legitimate reasons to break free from traditional commensality, and on the other hand enabled young women to challenge patriarchal authority. Clearly an "inculturation" which included the ancestor cults would have made such major shifts towards generational mobility and an increased range of options impossible. Exactly the same considerations apply in Latin America with respect to the communal obligations of the fiesta and godparenthood.

Pentecostal expansion in Burkina-Faso is especially interesting since it occurs in a country tucked under the lee of Islamia. Burkina-Faso is a country of ten million people, half of whom are Muslim and about one in six Catholic.[15] Pentecostalism arrived in 1921 through Sierra Leone, and half a century later the Pentecostal community, largely belonging to the Assemblies of God, numbered only 125,000. Yet since the mid-eighties it has soared towards half a million, some three to four percent of the population. The context here is the usual one of a failure on the part of the state and of rapid urbanization, especially round the capital. Clearly people are experiencing a rapid extension of horizons in time and in space through migration and communications which gives resonance to a universal and powerful monotheism. Running in parallel is a tearing of the local fabric which undermines the structure of ancestral power, witchcraft, and familial coercion in favor of choice. Clearly this is popular among females since they may choose marriage partners, but young males are also attracted. Such changes alter conceptions of responsibility and culpability, and the new consciousness of voluntary agency comes into being, exercised, fostered, and canalized within the disciplines of a voluntary religious group. However, since all revolutions must at the same time reproduce familiar elements from the past, the hierarchical sectors of previous social structures are mirrored in Pentecostal organization, notably in the elite groups comprising the pastorate. Indeed, young men coming to church "with a view" will apply to the pastor to know whether the young lady in the choir is free or engaged. Pastors may shoulder the task of calming down relatives resentful that their daughters have moved away out of their control and repudiated the alliances entered into without their consent.

The Pentecostal community provides a mobile and dynamic mirror of elements previously localized, and in turn sustains its own rigorous discipline. The new spiritual powers in the new family of brothers and sisters incorporates and engages in a duel with the powers of the previous order – itself *not* static – treating them as real but demonic. This simultaneous incorporation of and duel with the powers of the old order runs exactly parallel to the observations of Birgit Meyer.

Mobility takes many different forms. For example, because Pentecostals have been concentrated among the Mossi people, the expansion of Pentecostalism in neighboring countries like Benin, Ghana, Togo, Senegal, Niger, and Mali runs in parallel with Mossi patterns of migration and itinerancy. As usual black carriers are at the heart of this expansion. As for social mobility, it is connected to a complex and varying dialectic of individual equality with corporate discipline and pastoral power and authority. The equality is expressed in access to gifts such as healing and exorcism, exercised especially in prayer groups. But it is always important to recognize the power of the pastorate and the shadow images of traditional hierarchy which in time may migrate back to gerontocracy. In the countryside in particular, pastors create a new space identified as an installment of modernity. In the expanding urban centers there are miraculous manifestations of the Spirit, and there are Bible Schools and colleges which train catechists in basic literacy. Literacy includes French in one direction and translation into the vernacular in another. As mobility gathers momentum, the sphere of politics ceases to be seen as demonic and becomes an arena of agency and action. Naturally this appropriation of spiritual and educational resources and attendant opportunities for leadership generates rivalries over who is in control and therefore leads to schisms. Dynamism means schism. Self-proclaimed pastors owning the biblical vernacular create rival communities, often in their own homes, and attract vigorous anathemas. In short this is a paradigm case of the geography of the divine undergoing reconfiguration but without loss of solidarities or global secular standardization.

Political Interventions

A different approach is offered by Paul Gifford. He focuses on national political cultures in Ghana, Uganda, Zambia, Cameroon, and Liberia, and sees a mainly Anglophone Africa deluged by a "faith" teaching about prosperity, more especially in megachurches appealing to the emerging middle classes.[16] This is not so much the dualistic withdrawal from political life previously criticized, as a newly confident entry looking for social validation. Whether from elsewhere or indigenous, the new-style charismatics tend to refer to models in the Hebrew Scriptures, sometimes with a theocratic element, and they entertain a tincture of Christian Zionism such as also exists in Latin America.

As noted elsewhere, the charismatic churches appeal to young men and women, representing their ethos and interests over against older generations and older elites. When mainstream churches are co-opted as non-governmental organizations, Pentecostals and charismatics can constitute a religious opposition, and when mainstream churches offer a critique they, by contrast, may offer a legitimation, not only to Chiluba in Zambia but to Moi in Kenya and Rawlings in Ghana. They simultaneously draw from the mainstream and the independent churches, and also influence the mainstream bodies, especially the Baptists. What they provide is a modern image, vibrant expressive worship, and a family discipline. Like Renascer in São Paulo they operate as large-scale religious businesses: not so much what religion does for business as what business can do for religion. Though the organizational models may be North American the approach to the demonic is African. Again, like Renascer, they engage in relief work and mutual benefit activities, teaching know-how and promoting technology; their leaders form an international, much traveled elite, sometimes competing, sometimes cooperating. Given this international perspective, they assist the spread of English. (The point about English is even true in Spanish Guinea where enrolment in a Pentecostal Bible School provides a step in communication, fusing religious motives and linguistic competence. Naturally this is not so much the case in Francophone Africa, especially given anticlerical attitudes found there.)

The political interventions of evangelicals and Pentecostals in Africa are too complex for summary here, but the Zambian case discussed by Paul Gifford is instructive and worth further elaboration.[17] Zambia became independent in 1964 under the leadership of Kaunda, a former Methodist lay preacher who promoted a United Church to complement the united nation. This church in fact became a quasi-establishment, though Kaunda's own rather varied religious explorations gave rise to some tension. Kaunda's opponent and critic, Chiluba, came through the Zambian labor movement, and his movement towards multi-party democracy gained momentum with economic decline and a regime of statist regulation and corruption. Newspapers were mostly state-owned, giving Christian organs a role in expressing desire for change. It seems that when it came to the 1991 election some United Church pastors openly campaigned for Chiluba, and some born-again leaders also did so, since Chiluba confessed himself as such. However, Chiluba's victory was (as one might expect) marked by various problems such as economic instability and business cronyism as well as a curious relationship of evangelicals to politics and to Chiluba's designation of Zambia as a "Christian Nation." Just what is happening here is unclear, but one has the sense of Chiluba leaning towards "born agains" in a way they find both seductive and embarrassing, and of a jockeying for position among Protestants in which "born agains" have acquired parity with the older mainline constituency. Some have offered Chiluba overt support, including support against criticism from the mainline. There are also elements of Old Testament theocratic notions present in the evangelical constituency and of dispensationalist Christian Zionism, which may have links with friendly overtures to Israel.

The overall impression derived from the Zambian case, as indeed from roughly parallel situations in Kenya, Zimbabwe, and Ghana, is that the access of "mainline" churches to dispositions of political power is under pressure, as is their religious constituency, from new groupings with a born-again (or Pentecostal) commitment. The mainline mode of operation has been more mature, established, and invisible, as well as more critical of government, while the born-again mode has been more naive, obvious, and clearly open to political manipulation. The "born again" may represent new groups not sufficiently conscious of the dangers of an identification between Christian commitments and particular policies or identification with leaders like Chiluba claiming Christian validation. Indeed, Chiluba's own overt association with Christian ideals renders him vulnerable as well as attracting support for his rhetoric of unity and pulling together.

Summary

How, then, can we best bring together this selection of African material, and what are the main emergent themes? The rationale behind working through a select number of studies has been to expose a thematic index, beginning with the economic ethic.

If firms beyond a certain size are dependent on trust, and if micro-enterprises are dependent on thrift, probity, fair-dealing, and saving, then economic life is likely to be furthered and enriched by the expansion of Pentecostalism. Taking David Maxwell's study in Zimbabwe as typical, the consequences of Pentecostalism are indirect yet cumulative. They cluster around the sayings "My word is my bond" and "Honesty is the best policy." To live a disciplined life without waste or dissipation in a secure home and environment, to learn skills of administration and to exercise responsibility, to gain a good reputation, to belong to useful networks: all of these are economically advantageous. They make survival more likely in bad times, and motivate believers to take opportunities when times are better.

The paradigmatic changes concomitant with Pentecostalism are the trek to the urban center and megacity, the trail of migration, and the rending apart of the fabric of extended kin settled in a given place with associated obligations, above all to elders and to ancestors. In the course of that psychic experience of new birth in order to face the death of an old world and the arrival of a new, the individual gains the freedom to choose and to act responsibly. He or she is now controlled by inward shame as much as public honor, although the fraternity of believers acts as a new point of moral reference and repute.

The seeds of these changes may arrive from far away many decades before they burgeon under the impact of new circumstances. Traveling long distances in Africa by indigenous carriers, they divide and mutate, picking up new elements and responding to fresh needs, yet always recognizable. Maybe just one element will be incorporated into the tight capsule of an independent church otherwise devoted to cultural conservation. Maybe elements will emerge in an historic church like the Catholic Church and there combine with highly traditional elements, or they may lodge in an ethnic group to create a Judaic sense of peoplehood. The overall tendency at middle-class levels is to form free-ranging networks, cells, or fellowships, sitting loose to denominational affiliations, and capable of crossing ethnic boundaries. The means of evangelization are found in modern technology and media, and "imagined" quasi-communities come into being around the tighter nuclei of explicit church membership.

There are some characteristic developments, in particular the shift from a humble egalitarian fellowship to a bureaucratic church under an authoritarian personality. There is also a shift from a space opened up for young men and women to a narrowing down of that space as gerontocracy again sets in. Nevertheless, there is rarely any serious loss of room for participation, for the acquisition of social skills, and for religious ecstasy.

Pentecostals lie in between the independent churches, carrying the old world with intimations of the new, and historic churches effectively in the new world, including its available political critiques, but looking back to an old world in the spirit of retrieval. Pentecostals are those close enough to the old order to fear its gravitational pull and *sotto voce* to believe in its powers. They therefore incorporate certain aspects of that old order, so that, for example, traditional hierarchy reappears as pastoral authority. They also demonize the old "powers," sometimes incorporating practices relating to them, but pointing in the reverse direction. Beyond that, Satan may provide a comprehensive explanation of all that is untoward. Pentecostalism in Africa is a collective raft pointed with determination towards modernity. As for its politics they are those of a voluntary organization with a moral agenda and institutional interests. These interests it defends like any other pressure group.[18]

CHAPTER SEVEN

asia

Asia is distinguished by the pervasive presence of major historic civilizations defined by or linked to religion, in particular Buddhism in all its
variants and popular forms, as well as Hinduism and Islam, though
Christianity also has its ancient presenses. With the emergence of nationalism the religion of the majority has linked popular culture to ethnic
and state definition, which has meant that the enclaves of Christianity
are found either among those excluded from social honor as, for example, the Dalits (Untouchables) or among peoples on the margin as,
for example, the Nagas and others in north-east India. That has also to
be true of Pentecostalism and its penumbra of associated movements,
even though Pentecostalism has a relatively greater capacity to break the
bounds of the enclave.

Moreover, the stimulus given to the historic faiths by Christian
competition has had various consequences: an emphasis on elements
analogous to the unique selling-points of Christianity or movements of
counter-definition, especially the firming up of ethno-religious borders.
That has in turn pushed Christian minorities towards a defense of their
own communal stake and in some cases towards their own version of
ethno-religiosity. That is, for example, true in India, Pakistan, Malaysia,
and Indonesia, so that in the last two instances there is a considerable overlap between Christianity and Chinese ethnic identity. The most
obvious exception to all that is, of course, the Philippines, which is
sociologically more part of Latin America than Asia. The islands of the
Pacific are also quite distinctive and could as easily be discussed in the
context of the Atlantic islands.

Pentecostalism and charismatic Christianity are inevitably affected by
these pressures, to the point where they can find themselves in sufficiently sensitive situations to prefer their progress to pass without
academic note. At the same time it is one of the characteristics of charismatic Christianity to push against the lines of ethno-religious definition,
particularly when associated with emergent middle classes. There are
several places in Asia, from Seoul to Manila and Singapore, where
freewheeling charismatic churches have burgeoned in company with
social mobile groups, and these churches are close cousins to similar

ones found in Lagos or Buenos Aires. Furthermore, the historic churches have felt themselves drawn to emulate the charismatic style or simply encountered it as a tendency embraced by many of their own members. The Roman Catholic Church, for example, in India and Malaysia, has simultaneously sought to foster and control an inner Pentecostalization in a manner parallel to the Catholic movement known in Latin America as "New Evangelization." All this implies that in these new middle classes, denominational borders have become porous to transnational movements of "spirituality," some of them not linked to ecclesiastical forms and sometimes created by freewheeling religious entrepreneurship.

Turning first to India, this vulnerability of Catholicism to Pentecostalism is very clear. However, it is also the case that Pentecostalism in a narrower sense can boast roots in India which go back some way into the nineteenth century, and would even support the claim that the movement was as much generated there as among North American poor whites and poor blacks. There were also revivals in India in the years 1905–7 apparently quite independent of American contacts, and since that time, recurrent revival has given rise to a community of some three million.

Indeed, one distinguished commentator, R. Frykenberg, has suggested that the single most sweeping movement of conversion in India is Pentecostal. He describes long processions of people clad in snow-white garments, often long tunics and saris, and (deploying research such as that of Lionel Caplan) he identifies these as the urban poor and powerless who are more responsive to healing of body and exorcism of demons than to liberal programmes.[1]

Susan Bayly points in a similar direction. She says that a large proportion of professing Christians in South India is now associated with activist churches which have charismatic leaders and emphasize the Bible and the gifts of the Spirit, including constant prayer, exorcism, healing, and prophecy.[2] Such churches promote corporate and individual discipline and seek out the presence of the supernatural in everyday life. They are built up around individual lay people's assemblies and lay leadership, and are hostile to established hierarchies. Women find these churches highly attractive, partly because many of them have husbands away working in the Persian Gulf, but also because they appreciate the opportunities offered to lay female adepts.

As in Latin America, there are parallel changes taking place inside the older ecclesiastical bodies, and these also affect commercial and professional middle-class people, for example, among the St. Thomas Christians present in India from the earliest Christian centuries. As for the Roman Catholic authorities, they have responded by encouraging parallel manifestations of an emotional lay piety, including healing, more particularly under the aegis of the Velankanni Virgin. A major problem for all the conventional religious authorities is that they tend to look relativistic, liberal, compromising, and weak, especially when faced with militant Hindu communalism and with the very specific and concrete powers of non-Christian deities. These new movements represent a defense of a fragile but genuine Christian stake in the social order, a marking out of identities, and a very Indian reclamation of living presences and concrete powers, even if some of the organizational models were clearly made in the USA.

The situation in Nepal provides an interesting addendum to India, particularly with respect to minorities. Nepal is a country where religion may only be spread by personal contact. Nevertheless, there are many dozens of churches run by Nepalese in Katmandu and at the same time rapid shifts in the remote Tibeto-Burmese valleys.[3] Lines of Christian conversion in the valleys conform to differences of lineage, and sometimes whole villages may convert under local leadership. Where habitation is dispersed, conversion is of individuals or families. Pastors tend to be hostile to lamas as the legitimacy of traditional sacred powers is put in question. The groups operating in this area are the Nepalese Christian Fellowship, Gospel for Asia, and Baptists of the New Life Mission, equipped with educational and health facilities.

China poses the largest question mark for Pentecostalism (as for Christianity at large), since it contains one in six of the world's population and is currently in flux as a rampant capitalist development ruptures a social fabric still under autocratic control by Marxist political elites. Marxism itself is now no more than the prayer wheels of administration, and the vacuum is palpable.

Christianity in China is divided into those bodies granted some marginal acceptance even in the most repressive period of communist rule, and an extensive underground church which is conservative and evangelical. The latter are by now the larger, and the mid-century ratio of Catholics to Protestants has been reversed in favor of the Protestants.

Much of this underground Christianity goes on in house churches, and those involved in it are frequently subject to sanctions such as denial of access to educational or health facilities. The main areas of expansion have been in the south-eastern coastal provinces where they overlapped areas of earlier Christian activity, but in the eighties there was also rapid growth in inland rural provinces, which included some subsumption of folk practices. There is a plethora of kinds of conservative Evangelicalism, such as the "spirit-filled" Little Flock which tends to pacifism and is prone to schism, the Jesus Family which is small and communitarian, and the True Jesus Church which is anti-western and has its headquarters in Taiwan.[4]

The house-church movements have a lay character with many female workers, and characteristically offer healing, exorcism, and spiritual gifts in the Pentecostal style. Spiritual gifts were evident in recent revivals along the Korean border in the north-east. Quite how many evangelical Christians there are is impossible to estimate securely, though some have suggested thirty to forty million or more. The expansion is at any rate large enough to arouse government concern, particularly after the political crisis in June 1989. It has been suggested that Christianity substitutes for village folk religion and follows the huge influx of Chinese into the cities. Once again it accompanies the great trek of modern times, and again females are very much in the majority.

Alan Hunter and Kim-Kwong Chan suggest that governmental unease and suspicion is much moderated by the ability of evangelical Christianity to ameliorate family conflict and to control alcoholism and "peasant selfishness." It creates trustworthy workers at a time when the decline of traditional culture and supportive structures gives troublesome vent to materialism and consumerism. Evangelical faith is practical and a source of psychic and physical relief, in particular through holistic healing. Christian rites are widely regarded as efficacious against evil, and the virtues of honesty and restraint are enforced by church discipline and the nurture of inner conscience and conscientiousness. Alan Hunter and Kim-Kwong Chan also point out how a non-Han ethnic minority can enter modernity through Christianity without Sinization.[5] The minority finds an alternative identity in the biblical narrative, and also acquires a script and a history.

The query that hangs over China also hangs over the vast diaspora of the overseas Chinese, some no longer separate from China, as in the case of Hong Kong, or, as in Taiwan, culturally Chinese while (mostly) preferring political autonomy. Taiwan is best held over to be included in a comparison with South Korea and Japan. It is meanwhile worth noting the rapid changes which have occurred in Singapore.

The work of Michael Hill and his associates in Singapore indicates that Christianity there makes headway mainly among the Chinese, though it includes a significant Indian minority.[6] After independence from Britain the primary aim of Singaporean policy was economic advance, but then there was a turn to the moral dimensions of nation-building and some interest in Confucian ethics as conducive to order, nationalism, and commerce. The government held Muslim Malays suspect because of possible attachments to neighboring Malaysia, and suspected Christians of social activism, so Confucianism held political attractions.

In the late eighties a dramatic change began among young, high-status Chinese, educated in English, and many of them gravitated to charismatic Christianity (or alternatively to Buddhism or secular irreligion).

They set aside the amorphous Daoism of their parents and today perhaps one in four of those in tertiary or university education is Christian. They saw their new spiritual home as orderly, rational, English-speaking, and international, yet offering much opportunity for personal expression and for musical catharsis in a democratic atmosphere. At the same time there was continuity with the older spiritism in anticipation of mundane benefits.

Malaysia and Indonesia are both states with Muslim majorities, though the overt role of Islam is much greater in Malaysia than it is in Indonesia, which has aimed at a multicultural approach. The Malays in Malaysia are somewhat over half the population, and as Muslims they are automatically off-limits to conversion. At times the Chinese have been under pressure from the Malay majority on account of their economic success, and those Chinese who are Christian have certainly been conscious of the pressure of communal politics. In both countries communalism ensures that religious belonging can constitute a political act. This is particularly dangerous where, as in Sarawak, Christians have increased relative to Muslims in populations belonging to neither faith. Malaysia is a country of some twenty million, where Christians represent some seven percent, about half of whom are Roman Catholic. Amongst Christians at large there is a strong representation of Chinese, with some Indians as well.

The largest group experiencing charismatic renewal is Catholic. Sometimes renewal occurs in extra-denominational organizations where it meets official disapproval, but more often it occurs in parish groups meeting in homes to carry on ministries of healing and deliverance. All the mainline denominations find themselves hoist between attempting to maintain their traditions and stemming a loss of members by emulating charismatic styles. In any case they are being rapidly overtaken either by independent charismatic and Pentecostal churches or by offshoots of (often) recent Anglo-American denominations – a situation also not unknown in Singapore. This proliferation, taking place in shophouses or office blocks, bothers the Muslim government because it resists regulation and restriction.

In Michael Northcott's account, Pentecostalism has a particular appeal among the recently urbanized poor, but economic growth has also created an urban middle class, and for both the Pentecostal experience offers a voice and access to spontaneous experience. The middle-class people are attracted by a Neo-Pentecostal (and sometimes American) emphasis on prosperity, and you pick up its flavour in the style of the Full Gospel Business Men's Fellowship: *do ut des*. In particular Neo-Pentecostalism expresses and justifies the prosperity of the Chinese Malaysians as they face governmental threat to their economic position.[7]

The relation of charismatic and Pentecostal groups to ethnicity is complex, because conversion of Malays or Hindus is interpreted as undermining ethnic solidarity. At the same time Christian mobilization may itself be partly a response to Muslim revivalism and Malay ethnic assertion. It may also be that the sense of call and even the apocalyptic strain among Indian and Chinese Christian charismatics is related to this economic and ethnic pressure. Observers comment that charismatic groups cross inter-ethnic lines more easily than the traditional denominations, and even have some appeal to young Malaysians educated in the common national language – a situation paralleled in Singapore among young people speaking English. Another contested area concerns attitudes to the layer of shamanistic spiritism. Pentecostals both draw on this and define it as a sphere of demonic power from which believers require deliverance.

Indonesia is currently a country fearful of fragmentation. It is the most numerous of predominantly Muslim nations and has so far managed to avoid the explicit adoption of an Islamic identity, though communal clashes have increased in areas where there are substantial Christian populations, often in peripheral areas and the islands such as Ambon. There is also some insurgency among Christians in Irian Jaya, close to the border with Papua New Guinea. Pentecostals have been active since the sixties in West Timor, and this activity has spread to Java. Perhaps the main impact of Pentecostalism has been in the Chinese minority, currently under some social pressure, and the community may now number some six million in a total Indonesian population of nearly two hundred million.[8]

Rather than attempt a superficial survey of several countries in South-East Asia with mainly Buddhist traditions, I select Thailand, as studied by Edwin Zehner. He touches on older shifts among non-Thai (and Northern Thai) peoples, but concentrates on recent developments in the capital Bangkok.[9] One of the missing elements in Asian material has been detailed ethnography of religious change, and Zehner's work offers a useful ethnographic dimension. It also focuses on widely noted characteristics of conversion, one being the way Pentecostalism keys in to local cultural forms, in this case the Thai hierarchy of merit, and the other the concomitant and parallel changes occurring in the majority faith of Buddhism.

Christianity in Thailand had its initial successes among marginal peoples and among the Northern Thai, who were distinct from the central Thai, and who for a while held on to their administrative autonomy, even though paradoxically it was Bangkok that pushed for freedom of mission activity. Interestingly, the thrust of mission included the association of Christianity with medicine and science, which worked better in the "superstitious" north than in Bangkok, where local elites regarded

Buddhism as more open to science than Christianity. In any case conversion was slow, especially when confronted by a union of Buddhism and nationalism and indeed by reconversion to Buddhism due to anti-Allied feeling in the period 1941–4.

At the end of the second world war, most of the less than 10,000 Christians belonged to the largely Presbyterian Church of Christ. At that point new missions began to arrive, including missionary personnel expelled from China, and then from the 1960s on, Pentecostals of various kinds arrived. Conversion was relatively successful among non-Buddhist highlanders such as the Akha, and the rates speeded up in the late 1970s and early 1980s, until by 1990 the Church of Christ accounted for less than half the Christian population of (perhaps) 150,000, while Pentecostals and charismatics accounted for some 25 percent. Other shifts were from over-representation of Chinese and Sino-Thai to Thai among Christians in Bangkok, including some from the educated middle class. These shifts ran parallel to increasing mobility, delegitimation of sacred authority, democratization, individualism, and increasing awareness of choice. Just as Catholicism in Latin America underwent differentiation, including an emphasis on individual heart-work, so too did Buddhism in Thailand, though among some in the elites what Buddhism offered was ethical rationality. The appeal of Christianity was similar to its appeal in Singapore: ethical discipline rather than corruption (and exploitation of women), personal and affective relationships rather than social atomization, and – for some – a divine empowerment to overcome stress and achieve. Both outside and inside the Church of Christ, charismatic and revivalist styles gained ground, often of North American provenance. Some charismatic leaders ran sizeable churches, one with a membership in thousands, and in this sector particularly the demonic was acknowledged as needing to be subdued and exorcised. Though to be a Christian in principle gives some immunity from the demonic, devotional protection and exorcism might also be required through fasting and prayer in tongues. Some Protestant leaders are considered especially gifted in these matters, which underlines the contrast with the nineteenth-century approach whereby the spirits were banished as superstitious delusions.

Zehner contrasts the modes of relation between evangelical Christianity and modern and traditional Buddhism. With regard to traditional Buddhism most evangelicals morally reclassify local spirits, though a minority of them join with modern Buddhists in denying this kind of supernatural power. In the main a Christian discourse about spirits recasts traditional spiritism very much in the manner analyzed by Birgit Meyer in Ghana, which appears more effective than the older "Victorian" dismissal of "superstition."

Zehner also analyzes the appearance of large Pentecostal churches in Bangkok in the late 1970s.[10] He stresses both their independence of mission sponsorship and certain parallels between the church's organization and personnel ranking system and the modes of ranking promoted historically by the centralizing Thai monarchy. Such rankings are still potent today. Whereas foreign missionaries are disinclined to deploy Thai-style charisma to construct a Thai-type of organization, the autonomous Pentecostal leaders have done precisely that. Their administration exemplifies a mode of ranking based on childlike subordination and trusting obedience. However, since "merit" is theologically unacceptable, the internal structure of dependence is recast as the "covering" offered by divine anointing, spiritual maturity, and the outpouring of the Holy Spirit. This combination of replication with displacement parallels other findings showing how Christians have retained many Buddhist traits through the whole radical process of conversion. Pentecostalism clearly represents a radical break with Thai culture yet as regards charisma as well as the discourse of spirits it is closer to Thai culture than many of its earlier Christian rivals.

Tripartite Comparison

It is useful to discuss South Korea in relation to Taiwan and Japan, since all three have mixed Confucian and Buddhist traditions, but only one, South Korea, has proved vulnerable to Christianity, including Pentecostalism, though Presbyterianism is still the largest single Christian church. What is interesting turns on the "new religions" of Japan and Taiwan, which are neo-Buddhist, yet exhibit some of the same characteristics as the "new religion" of Christianity in South Korea. As new religions in Japan have been extensively studied, I prefer to take a Taiwanese "new religion" as my functional equivalent of Christianity in South Korea.[11]

In *Tongues of Fire* (1990) I argued that Korea offers a case of a whole nation of considerable importance made marginal by existing at a crossroads between Chinese and Japanese, and from time to time culturally or politically subject to one or other influence. The crucial difference with Japan in respect of openness to Christianity turns on the fact that the USA has been in different ways positively associated with Korean aspirations to be free of Japanese imperialism, while for Japan it figured as the threat and the conqueror, and its religion as irredeemably alien. Attempts at indigenization did little to reverse that alien character. This is not to say that Japan has not been influenced by Christianity, but Christians have tended to be concentrated in educated enclaves, and it has been left precisely to the Pentecostals and holiness churches, some of which were indigenous, to make some impact on the poorer urban areas. Post-war urbanization in Korea offered fertile ground for a Christian expansion to about 25–30 percent; in Japan it facilitated an expansion of neo-Buddhist "new religions" to about 20 percent, and these expansions resemble each other in their emphasis on experience, exorcism, charismatic leadership, and zeal to convert. Both the evangelical expansion in Korea and the neo-Buddhist expansion in Japan offered a spiritual and social mobility, empowering and educating their members within vigorous protective frameworks with much opportunity for participation, exercise of spiritual gifts, and a sense of collective presence.

In Korea, Presbyterian and Methodist missions of mainly American provenance were major players in creating the modern educational structures of the country and in nurturing nationalism, even though that put the missionaries in a difficult dilemma in relation to the Japanese authorities. Today there is a large and educated Christian middle class with many members critical of undemocratic practice, in particular through the rather cerebral form of liberationism known as "Minjung theology." The problem here has been a chronic fear of communism, particularly among those, many of them Christians, forced to flee communist North Korea. Many people accepted corruption and dictatorship in the time of the Methodist president, Syngman Rhee, as the price of physical defense and economic advance. The result was intense emotional division when a pro-democracy movement propagated anti-American attitudes which opponents argued could expose an unshielded country to aggression. One important element in the pro-democracy movement was the Catholic Church which, particularly through the foreign-based orders (such as the French), helped shore up the highly emotional commitment of radical Korean students. Though Catholics have been a minority among Korean Christians they have expanded of recent years, while Protestants have stagnated. Indeed, Buddhism has also revived and now emulates the Christian use of the media.

Like South African Pentecostals, those in Korea have not made much of a contribution to this current of socio-political criticism, being more of a vehicle for the survival and advancement of the poor. In common with Korean Christianity as a whole, the Pentecostal scene has been marked by schism and the canalization of spiritual power through rival charismatic leaders. Contemporary Seoul has seen some of the largest ever evangelical rallies and its charismatic megachurches, built on a cell structure, are among the largest in the world. The Full Gospel Church in particular shows the effects of expansive "positive thinking" in the mode of church growth experts and Robert Schuller. It aims to "find needs and meet needs" and is not shamed to fuse revivalism and prosperity theology with shamanistic practice.

It is with regard to shamanism that the ambiguities of indigenization are most obvious. The issue can be argued in several ways, so that shamanism can be positively valued as a female practice or as an expression of "the oppressed," and from such perspectives one would expect the Pentecostal adoption of (for example) pilgrimages to the prayer mountain to be applauded. Another aspect of indigenization is the distinctly Confucian interest in examination success, in mutual care and wellbeing, and the evident reverence for pastors. Of course, Pentecostalism is noted for its ability to "inculturate" but in the Korean case the applause of other Korean Christians has been rather muted, even though they have themselves extensively adopted many features of the Pentecostal style.

Taiwan is an interesting case, especially when compared with Korea and Japan. Like them it has been exposed to intense cultural radiation from the USA, but the Taiwanese seem to have responded like the Japanese by emphasizing their own cultural roots. Perhaps they were repelled by the association between Christianity and the nationalist forces which took over Taiwan after their expulsion from the mainland. One of the most interesting developments has been the meteoric expansion of a Taiwanese neo-Buddhist "new religion" quite distinct from the popular utilitarian religiosity of the temples.

The movement in Taiwan most clearly analogous to Pentecostalism, but drawing on the resources of Pure Land Buddhism, is known as the Compassion Relief Foundation.[12] It is led by a charismatic woman (as the Japanese New Religions mostly were not) and it is essentially lay, although it has a core of nuns. Compassion Relief took off noticeably after the end of the military regime and now comprises about a million people, most of them women. After dramatic increases in the late 1980s and 1990s, it acquired a bureaucracy and also developed provision for males, notably by offering training in martial arts. The group meetings are marked by much ecstatic shedding of tears by the women, though recently that has been balanced by uniforms and what is known as "silent melody": rhythmic, feminine, and orderly body movements to cues provided by electronically amplified lyrics. The crying is brought about by many stimuli, for example, the sight of the leader, but it also erupts at all evocation of home-coming. That homes could have this powerful effect is especially interesting because so many females are the only members of the group in households where their attachment arouses male hostility.

The boundaries of the movement are not as clearly marked as in Pentecostalism, and there is much coming and going, but the movement is unique in Taiwanese Buddhism in its public presence, comprehensive benefits (medical and educational), and extensive charitable work, all related to its capacity to create wealth through sacrificial giving. Although it employs traditional Buddhist sutras, memorization is not necessary, because this is yet another religion of the heart. In that, as in its appeal to women, its accent on mutual assistance, its expressive and lay character, the Compassionate Relief Foundation is a Buddhist equivalent to Pentecostalism with the additional advantage of relating directly to national tradition. According to Robert Weller and Chen-Yu Julia Huang, its power lies in the universalization of women's family concerns and evocation of their immediate experience. It also deals with loss of communal values in a manner closely parallel to Pentecostalism. The final similarity is the way its wealth arouses newspaper criticism.

A mere 1.3 percent of the population in Taiwan is Protestant, and of those one in three (some 100,0000) are involved in inter-denominational charismatic activity. Some groups are indigenous, others, like the Assemblies of God, are of American provenance. The Prayer Mountain Revival movement echoes Korean Christian spirituality and it may be that charismatic Christianity provides the kind of bridge between East and West that it offers in Singapore.

The Philippines and Other Pacific Islands

Sociologically the Philippines is half-way to Latin America, due to its centuries of Spanish colonization and consequent Catholic hegemony. However, the Spanish–American war at the beginning of the twentieth century began a process which made English the lingua franca and introduced many new Protestant groupings, so that perhaps 8–9 percent of the population today is Protestant. The Philippines illustrates the global circulation of evangelical messengers and messages, in that there are currently a thousand Korean evangelical missionaries active in the country. The Assemblies of God is a large body, but there are many independent religious enterprises, such as the Cathedral of Praise in Manila with some 14,000 members. As in Korea, believers are often organized in cell groups. Apart from the urban churches, there are numerous missions active in the ethnic sub-groups, especially in the north, some of them quite remote, but anthropological studies are lacking as to how appropriation of evangelical themes has proceeded. In default of an ethnography, however, it may be helpful to summarize material from Jungja Ma derived from her study of the Kankana-ey tribe in the northern Philippines.[13] She argues that Pentecostalism is particularly potent in an animistic context lacking basic medical services. It seems that early preachers worked in the open air proclaiming healing power (based on Mark, chapter 16) and found their message carried through local testimony. Particularly effective was a team led by a widow missionary, and whole households were converted through what Jungja Ma calls a "power encounter" with her. She concludes that this kind of Pentecostalism finds its natural provenance in rural areas, presumably by contrast with the style of the urban megachurches.

Material by Jae-Yong Jeong on Filipino Pentecostal spirituality in rather similar contexts suggests that though the original imports of Pentecostalism were of American origin, the principal carriers were Filipino migrants to the USA, returning home in the inter-war period. The expansion in the last quarter of the twentieth century was relatively centralized in the urban contexts but quite fragmented in the rural areas with their considerable linguistic and cultural variety. The competitive entrepreneurialism of work in rural areas involved greater adjustment to local practices and led to the emergence of powerful charismatic leaders, often lay and often ruling with the rod. As is so frequently the case, Pentecostalism both resonates with an indigenous "spirited" world-view and breaks with it, validating its message with "signs and wonders" and healings.

Again, as elsewhere, Pentecostal practices have been adopted by other churches, and the international charismatic group El Shaddai (active in Guatemala) has a particular appeal among Roman Catholics. Pentecostal groups provide some social relief, more especially to Filipino migrants abroad. There are numerous house churches. Interesting aspects of Jae-Yong Jeong's material are the pursuit of wider scholarly validation by some Pentecostal leaders without succumbing to rationalistic frameworks, and the embrace of a Filipino nationalism over against colonialism, linked to the resonances with indigenous spirituality.[14]

Other aspects of the religious situation in the Philippines are extensive activity by liberation priests in trying to raise social and political consciousness among people exploited by landlords, as well as a considerable to-and-fro traffic of North American evangelists. It has been suggested that this has a political aspect, though in the nature of the case *sub rosa* activities are difficult to document.[15] There are, of course, particular parts of the world, such as Liberia, Puerto Rico, and the Philippines, with a long history of American political involvement which presumably continues. The precise role of evangelicals in all the geopolitics of the Pacific is unclear. What arouses anxiety in this and other contexts is the simple equation in the minds of some international evangelists between American interests and the Kingdom of God.

The Pacific Islands are also culturally distinct from Asia, but largely on account of Anglo-American influences rather than Hispanic ones. Alan Davidson says that the style of missionary work created what was almost a "Christendom" model of collective identity associated with a given denomination admixed with expectations of pay-back and betterment in return for devotion.[16] What happens now is precisely the break-up of this collective identity, for example in the Solomon Islands where twelve new groups emerged after the second world war and another nine in the seventies and eighties. The dominance of Methodism in places like Tonga and amongst indigenous Fijians is threatened. The Kiribati Protestant Church, to take another example, finds itself competing with Adventists, Bahais, Mormons, and Pentecostals, some of whom have considerable financial resources. The reasons for all this are quite standard: educational and social mobility, the weakening of local sanctions, modern communications, and individualization. What the Pentecostal churches offer to uprooted young people is warmth and personal experience, authoritative guidance, participation, lively music, spiritual power, and (perhaps) prospects of prosperity. The young are incorporated in a mobile "new tribe" where those who carry the new messages may be returning migrants or even people who have never left their native island. As always globalization overlaps Americanization. The traditional churches (who after all were also accused in earlier generations of eroding local culture) are left looking as though incapable of stimulating personal transformations though perfectly able both to legitimate and to criticize local political arrangements.

If one were to seek for relevant comparisons then one might find them in other island communities rather than the major civilizations of Asia. In the Atlantic world one would find parallels in the corrosion of what has been the dominance of two or three denominations in Jamaica by Pentecostalism, or the corrosion of Catholicism in the Cape Verde Islands.[17] As in Jamaica, so in Cape Verde there was a sexual economy of surplus white males and slave females who could not marry. In the twentieth century that has meant the migration of impoverished people from Cape Verde in search of betterment, and the arrival of new religious groups, first Adventists, then Mormons and Witnesses, and most recently *cura divina* versions of Brazilian Pentecostalism offering the poor healing and hope of worldly benefit. What groups like Mormons and Witnesses may offer women facing the consequences of male irresponsibility is indicated by the woman who said, "I wish my man would join the Witnesses because then he would stop visiting his other woman and marry me." In each local situation there are specific circumstances, but global pluralism is similarly active in the islands of the Atlantic and Pacific, breaking up local communal identities and offering mobile communities of choice and personal transformation.

Returning to the overall picture, Pentecostalism in Asia clearly finds niches in marginal and borderland peoples, and displaces folk practices (for example in China) with the great trek to the city. It seems that the repudiation of folk practice is not so vigorous as in Africa, perhaps because shamanism can be subsumed in a Christian practice of healings and exorcisms, though veneration of ancestors poses rather more difficult problems turning on what is meant by "worship." Nor is Pentecostalism so clearly demarcated from other Christian bodies as in Africa. Instead one sees a Pentecostalization of historic churches, including the Catholic Church. That also occurs through Asian variants of freewheeling charismatic movements active in the emergent middle classes, mostly Chinese, in places like Singapore. These movements are part of a transnational outreach, related to the acquisition of English, visible from Lagos to Seoul and Guatemala City to Durban.

CHAPTER EIGHT

trying conclusions: a global option?

Even though the argument of this book is embedded in a large number of studies, reinforcing, qualifying, and amplifying one another, its drift is sweeping and dramatic. We have in Pentecostalism and all its associated movements the religious mobilization of the culturally despised, above all in the non-western world, outside any sponsorship whatever, whether of their own local intelligentsias, or of the clerical and secular intelligentsias of the West. John Wesley and his associates started it, out of materials provided by Pietism. The Evangelical Revival then set off further mobilizations which in the course of experimentation cross-bred the religion of poor whites with the religion of poor blacks to create a potent and ambiguous mix capable of combustion on a global scale. Wesley had, after all, declared that his message was to *all*, not just the Elect. Meanwhile the Methodist movement he founded, having carried out the initial mobilizations, most dramatically on the American frontier, moved back under clerical sponsorship until today it is embarrassed to acknowledge what it fathered. Most of the features of Pentecostalism tell tales of Methodist paternity, but fatherhood is only rarely acknowledged.

Pentecostalism is the Christian equivalent of Islamic revivalism, and as such part of the awakening self-consciousness of the "rest" of our global society. But it operates in a completely different mode, following the logic of a fissiparous pluralism, not of a "fortress Islam" militantly entrenched in a unity of people and faith. That is another way of saying that it is not inherently political, even though it trails the political and economic implications which follow from a competitive pluralism. Pentecostalism is very specifically a cultural revolution, and one undertaken from below, with no political theory to guide it and no political ideology to promote. What motivates the rival religious entrepreneurs who guide the revolution is pursuit of a particular kind of personal transformation, and their language is couched in personal stories and imagery rather than in abstract propositions. Because Pentecostalism is personal and cultural it does not need to deal in the violence intrinsic to political action, which is why it is virtually unnoticed by the western media, and comes as a surprise to the western academy.

The story which Pentecostalism promotes unites theology and social aspiration, by anticipating, in hope and trembling, an end to the current world order. When spiritual gifts descend on the ignorant and the unlearned that in itself foreshadows the new order of things: it is understood as an earnest of the "last days." When the spiritual gifts include "tongues" transcending the Babel of conflicting languages, then one has a "third sacrament" of global aspiration embracing all humankind, and the emergence of a "new voice" which is both individual and communal. Pentecostalism, like Methodism, is about finding your voice, which is why it is sung as much as it is spoken.

To be baptized in the spirit in this way is quite different from orthodox baptism, because priestly mediation gives you a "name" embedded in a community of continuing time and settled place, whereas a new name in the spirit is the choice of those whose times and seasonal rotations have been ruptured and who have been disembedded from the ties of place, for example the fiesta or ancestor veneration. Their brothers and sisters are now a supportive community of those born by the spirit not the biological flesh. Their notion of a people in exodus and *en route* runs parallel to and fuses with the great trek to the modern city. The result is a realization of the ancient idea of theosis – the human infused with the divine – but the idea has been made dynamic and energized. If putting it this way seems a diversion into theology it is important to realize that what moves people on the move and turns their atomized being into a corporate movement is a repertoire of religious images corresponding to their circumstance. If you do not read their images you do not understand their story.

So, what is that story? It is that tens of millions on the move know themselves to be released from ascribed categories and indelible markers into a dangerous and bewildering open-endedness which has been made meaningful and purposeful by a discipline that offers a destination. You cannot make this trek through the wilderness without a set of disciplines and a sense of a good "end" in view. For safety's sake the disciplines will err on the side of rigor, and believers will accept new markers of identity in exchange for the old ones, to show to what company of wayfarers they belong. They will also exchange the authority of the elders or patrons for the charismatic leadership of the pastor, who marks out the route and the rules but is in all things else like themselves, speaking their language. In one sense you follow the injunction to the original wayfarers in the Gospels to call no-one father or master, so symbolically abolishing all hierarchies and mediations, but in another sense the unity of the people is vested in the authority of the pastorate. On a crowded raft in a turbulent sea the law of survival depends on the exercise of authority. By a parallel paradox the inclusive has to be nurtured in the exclusive and the bounded: the seed of a new fraternity requires the protection of borders distinguishing Church from World.

In such examples one sees how doctrine and the exigencies of social reality are fused together in symbol and image. So to elucidate the social reality in a theological register, or to hint as to the resonances of that register, is only to do sociology in an unfamiliar key. Read the signs simultaneously at the social and the theological level and you see why Pentecostal iconography takes the form it does: the faithful have been cleansed from the dirt of the old in the limpid waters of the new. As in so many radical movements, the master image is of almost involuntary pregnancy forcing its way through to deliverance, and delivery is embodied in the physical movements and outcries of those who make the passage from death to life. The believers are moved in the depths of their being.

Earlier in the argument, stress was laid on the ambiguity of Pentecostalism. Ambiguity is more potent for change than confrontation of the status quo in the name of certified rectitude. By indirections we "find directions out." Of course, the existence of ambiguity means that one researcher is impressed by Pentecostalism as belonging to the ancient layer of global shamanism, whereas another sees it as the religious version of "The Expressive Revolution." On the one hand you can, if you will, insist that Pentecostalism belongs to a wave of fundamentalism sweeping world religions in a last-ditch defense against modernity. Or you can see it as an adaptable form of heart-work and spiritual self-exploration breaking free of the restrictive protocols of enlightened reason into a New Age of post-modernity. Or, again, Pentecostalism has been dismissed as old patriarchy revived, but that has to be set against the "gender paradox" analyzed by so many researchers, and the fact that this is a woman's movement. In the accelerating mobilization of those not heard from before, the women are the movers and the shakers.

Yet another instance of ambiguity is the coming together of the local and specific with the global and open-ended. Pentecostalism keys in to local cultures but it is sufficiently adaptable to forge links with very different social formations: the Chinese rural workers, the Singapore business elite, the West African transnational intelligentsia in Lagos or London or Amsterdam, the ex-drug addicts of Rio de Janeiro. Contemporary global dissemination means that whatever the initial effervescence in Los Angeles at the beginning of "the American century" the movement of Pentecostalism is multi-centered, and the spiritual contagion spreads in Burkina Faso or Korea or Guatemala. Seeds may have been dropped by Americans in the early twenties, but then they are taken hither and thither by indigenous carriers until they suddenly burgeon perhaps half a century later. Indigenization and autonomy are essential. And it is precisely that indigenization and "acculturation" that generates the observation that Pentecostalism can exhibit the qualities of Thai schemes of merit or Brazilian clientage or Korean shamanism. You cannot go everywhere and not be changed.

Notoriously the Catholic Church has assimilated many cultural traits in just this way, but it has done so as an absorbent system, whereas Pentecostalism is a prolific set of burgeoning affinities constituted by recognition of kind. It follows there is scant chance of some hierarchy of religious (or temporal) power canalizing the flow of energy and controlling it for its own ends. Of course, bureaucratization occurs, affecting this or that branch of the movement, and small leadership groups arrogate power to themselves, including the power to trace correct spiritual genealogies and define who or what is in or out. But the movement itself simply runs riot in any number of alternative channels.

Once the Bible is your text there are as many interpretations as there are readers, and the Spirit is unbound. Traditionally that has been accounted one of the disadvantages of Evangelical Protestantism, since it replaces one Pope by a multitude, and dissipates energies in passionate dispute. In today's world, however, where the niches and needs are so varied, Pentecostalism works by constant adjustment on the ground. The slogan of one of its most successful Korean entrepreneurs was to "find need and meet need," and one of the consequences of that is a dynamic of schism. Leaders with rival charismata try out their messages for resonance and live or die by the consequences.

Inevitably the historic denominations, overseeing what have been relatively stable constituencies, feel undermined by these shifting sands. Flows of spiritual energy simultaneously smudge and erode their own boundaries while creating any number of new forms on the market. In parts of West Africa, for example, the older churches face the reality of youthful generations sucked away into new forms of religious organization. But wherever the crisis occurs, in South India or the South Pacific, the options available to them are quite limited, and since context is crucial no one solution applies across the board. If the Roman Catholic Church finds particular compartments flooded and its structures strained by the exuberant pressure of lay networks at the margin of oversight and control, then the only alternatives are dangerous expulsion or dangerous emulation. If the changes initiated by the Second Vatican Council in the sixties did indeed evacuate the tangible power of older devotions, rendering Catholicism vulnerable in places like East Africa, then it is the market which dictates the local response. Perhaps, as was the case in Argentina, legal constraint is temporarily available and partially effective, but in a global situation markets can no longer be cornered. The forceful solutions of the Counter-Reformation are not available. Perhaps one way of looking at matters is to recognize churches as controlling spiritual energies at least much as they express them, and when vast and youthful populations suddenly come to self-consciousness the institutional frames simply cannot contain what must then transpire. As in the Reformation itself, wineskins break where the young are so much in the majority.

Pentecostalism, then, belongs by nature to open markets beyond all sponsorship, and even where it aspires to the exercise of social power it remains incurably pluralistic. However, that market analogy also implies that the spiritual goods on offer may as easily fall out as fall in to fashion. The statistics of the revolving door and of dormant customers might support that view, as does the history of previous revivals. Triumphalism can be very short-lived and regions may be "burnt over" until they are burnt out. The relative stagnation apparently observable in some of the most dramatic cases of advance in Korea and in Guatemala may indicate that ceilings have been reached, rather as British Nonconformity reached a ceiling in the mid-nineteenth century. At the same time one recollects historically that what appeared to be *the* Great Awakening or *the* Reformation was also a chain reaction of awakenings (i.e. re-formations).

In the developed world, roughly between Los Angeles and West Berlin, the sixties inaugurated a cultural revolution based on the power and self-consciousness accruing to the new post-war generation, and the long-term consequences turned out to be a combination of what Talcott Parsons called "the Expressive Revolution" with the disciplines of the free market variously conceived. Socialist parties in particular were nearly everywhere forced to a pragmatic accommodation by the threat of irrelevance; and neither the economy nor personal behavior could any longer be made subject to control in the interests of social engineering from above in the name of those below.

In an important way a populist Pentecostalism belongs to this developing scenario because it embodies the release of spirit in harness with the discipline that work and the market demand, above all where life is precarious. It is animated and animates, but at the same time it makes demands, not by way of direct response to economic requirements but by a discipline of spirit which finds a profound affinity with those requirements. There is, of course, mutual interaction, so that the randomness of market relations in (say) Rio de Janeiro finds a mirror in the random donation of goods and "gifts" proffered by the Universal Church of the Kingdom of God. Yet spirit levels are more than mere indices of external pressure. What is undeniable is that if you can both release the spirit by animated participation within the controlled and protective space of the assembly, and adopt a discipline of life and family, then you are better placed to survive the exigencies of your situation and to take advantage of such economic and social opportunities as may occur. This is so whether you are a hard-pressed executive in Brazilian banking or a migrant from the Andes to La Paz or from rural Zimbabwe to Harare. Trust, fair dealing, the rejection of dissipation and waste, and above all the struggle for the integrity of the family, are simultaneously virtues and "for your own good."

If this sounds like a sugared utilitarianism, and a questionable conjunction of the virtuous, the enjoyable, and the gainful, then in terms of philosophical and theological argument one is bound to agree. But in the situations where Pentecostalism takes off, the conjunction is workable and eminently plausible, and believers find ingenious ways of coping with the exceptions. The Psalmist so much quoted by Pentecostals may not be strictly correct in claiming the righteous never "want for bread" (given that there are plenty of instances where "the wicked flourish as the green bay tree"), but the conjunction of virtue and personal survival and betterment at the precarious margins of our global society is true enough to sustain confidence in the invisible hand of Providence. By a reinforcing spiral a kind of confidence is created which fulfills its own prophecies. To adopt Bernard Shaw's rather cynical comments put into the mouth of the Archbishop in the Preface to *Saint Joan*, that is part of the meaning and experience of miracle. Pentecostals are adept at usefully placing themselves in the path of the miraculous and are often duly rewarded. Liberals by reason of their disbelief receive no such reward and therefore remain confirmed in their faithlessness.

Included in the experience of providence and miracle is healing and expulsion of the demons that bedevil lives. Here the happy conjunction is (once again) ancient and modern. The linkages of mind and body, however exaggerated, especially with respect to "battling" against diseases like cancer, are genuine, and the healing of mind and body offered by Pentecost is simultaneously shamanistic and holistic. Such an approach is arguably feminine rather than masculine. Andrew Chesnut is surely right in claiming that the Visitadora, the lady who visits when you are ill, bringing with her physically or psychically the collective support of the sisters and brothers, is the most effective of all missionaries.[1] Spiritual autobiographies contain numerous accounts of bodily and spiritual upheaval and portray people literally fighting for breath against the weight of guilt and anxiety lying so heavily upon them.[2] People cannot deal on their own with their inner oppressions, and cannot or dare not even name them, so that a rite of authoritative naming and expulsion in the Almighty Name is their only efficacious resort. If such expulsions work among the shamans of the mountains of central Japan they also work in the favelas of urban Brazil.

The obvious question concerns the future of Pentecostalism (and its associated movements) and whether it will continue to be a global option. Perhaps the first point to be made about that concerns the main competitors and what their alternative advantages and disadvantages are. Taking the religious competitors first, they are Islam and Buddhism, Catholicism and Liberal Protestantism. Buddhism, for example, is clearly capable of various responses: providing the religious vesture of a nation-state and ethnic group, generating voluntary movements analogous to Pentecostalism, and sustaining a kind of austere humanism appealing to eastern elites and indeed western elites as well. As for Islam, it seems more capable of providing a frame for the nation-state than of generating voluntary movements, though Sufism does have some marginal appeal to intellectuals. The forte of Islam seems to lie in mobilization to influence or dominate civil society. As for Catholicism, the time when it provided frames for nation-states and ethnic groups seems to be passing. Today in its heartlands of Latin Europe and Latin America it suffers all the disadvantages of establishment in various stages of dissolution, whereas in Africa and Asia it can sometimes make rapid headway as a voluntary group exercising a critical voice. Its intellectual sector tends to be divided between strong conservatives and strong radicals, lacking the untutored pragmatism of the Pentecostals. As for Liberal Protestantism, it belongs to sectors of the developed world which lie at some social distance from Pentecostalism but have a leaky border with humanism or apathy.

What this implies for Pentecostalism is roughly as follows. So far as Buddhism and Islam are concerned they can firm up and activate their ethno-religious constituency (as can Hinduism also, though it has a weak underside in the numerical size of those it downgrades religiously and socially). Buddhism can compete directly with Pentecostalism when it comes to voluntary movements, as the examples of Taiwan and Japan indicate, though there is a huge area of traditional syncretistic religiosity infiltrated with Buddhist elements which is vulnerable to conversion once disembedded from traditional contexts. With respect to Catholicism, the major vulnerability lies in the disintegrating establishments of Latin America, where the spiritual premise is still automatically assumed and the old "tangible" Catholicism has to some extent been dismantled. Liberal Protestantism is not really a competitor at all, given its social provenance, though it does pick up quite a number of those intellectually dissatisfied with conservative Christianity. It might also make sense to place "New Age" phenomena adjacent to Liberal Protestantism, in particular a post-modern interest in "spirituality" which has a certain overlap with charismatic Christianity in its more unbounded, free-floating manifestations. There is a border here where evangelical experience shades into experimentation and the Spirit melts into spirits and spirituality.

That leaves secular alternatives which are different in kind from each other: international business culture, the liberal humanism of the academy, and Marxism. In the first two cases their social provenance puts distance between them and Pentecostalism, though business culture can effect junctions with charismatic and evangelical Christianity, so making God's business its own. Liberal humanism, with its ideological dominance in western elites, is perhaps a major reason why educated people are so little conscious of the size and impact of Pentecostalism in the non-western world. It provides the glasses through which we misread or edit out much of what is going forward there. As for Marxism, it used to be deeply implicated in the promotion of ethno-ideology, but that staple of the Soviet system is now openly mere nationalism, even in China. So Marxism has returned to being a scheme whose remaining appeal is to intellectuals, including Christian ones. Its performance as an economic system, which it made the test of its truth, has hugely reduced its popular appeal, and that means that Pentecostalism may experience less and less difficulty with an ideologically inflected hostility from left-wing parties. Mutual repulsion might well decrease. In Guadalajara, Mexico, for example, a conference of pastors concluded with a presentation of the seductions of consumerism, while in Brazil candidates of the Left make approaches to the Pentecostal constituency.

However, those are simply dispositions on a map of religious and ideological powers, and what finally remains to be explored is how one might frame the Pentecostal future, and what social evolutionary paths might be envisaged for it. One such path, long envisaged in social scientific theorizing, has been the transition from pre-political mobilization to secular politics, which can be linked to another transition from charismatic fervor to bureaucratic rationality and "unenthusiastic" faith. If one takes first the proposed transition to politics (and to secular theories of social change), there are various difficulties.

The first is that while religion is closely interwoven with politics and its fundamental images have political implications, it is nevertheless a distinctive mode of understanding. That means that the imagery of faith is not waiting for the politically correct translation, but is rather an independent resource for political thought. Moreover, that resource is cast in personal terms and visionary panoramas which resist redirection to abstract propositions or policy calculations. In short, picture thinking embedded in the intricate logic of symbols is a mode not a stage. Its time is now and eternity, not the medium term of the five-year plan.

The second difficulty relates to political thought itself, since it cannot be reduced to a science, but is rather a form of practical wisdom. There are, of course, all kinds of empirical relationships and guidelines, with their calculable costs and opportunities, but the ensemble cannot be subjected to a comprehensive and commanding viewpoint only awaiting full knowledge and proper application. Indeed, the political field is itself undergirded by a rhetoric rooted in picture thinking and fundamental imagery, which is, of course, precisely where the linkages lie with the imagery of religion, and some of these are as dangerous for the conduct of politics as they are inevitable.[3]

If these, then, are the difficulties, then religion is not an interim vent for energies whose eventual destination lies in the political realm. No doubt energies may be focused on the one rather than the other at particular times and under particular circumstances, and leaders who find their metier in the field of religion in one generation might in another generation find it in politics. There are complex interchanges here and their nature alters with processes such as social differentiation. But that still does not mean that Pentecostal leaders are blinded guides prior to proper enlightenment, or that the Pentecostal way of being in the world is a somnambulism waiting for the dream to vanish in sober reality. Such a notion of a true political epiphany to come, and a crucial transition to be made, has its roots precisely in the dangerous linkage of religious modalities with political ones. That means, at the theoretical level, that so far as the relation to the political realm is concerned, Pentecostalism is not predestined to undergo an emptying out into politics. Furthermore, the delusions fostered by that type of view have now been exposed by experience, given that the twentieth century was conspicuously bedeviled by violent politicized millenarianisms.

It is here that the Pentecostal lack of theoretical thinking actually has advantages as well as disadvantages. The advantages lie in a pragmatic attitude, which may be connected with the discrete empiricism and distinctly modest "enlightenment" of its North Atlantic cultural origins. However that may be, those nurtured in biblical perspectives, and above all those long practised in the everyday politics of survival and betterment, are not easily seduced by large-scale theoretical schemes and the political promise. Indeed, they share the well-schooled and grounded popular skepticism about politicians and the political realm. Rather their main temptation lies in pay-offs and trade-offs of negotiation for social space and recognition. This is where pragmatism is no protection against seduction. The disadvantages of the pragmatic Pentecostal mode emerge from a comparison with the Roman Catholic Church, in that Pentecostals have not built up over time a set of understandings about political action and influence and, moreover, cannot transfer these understandings from one situation to another through international linkages, especially through the religious orders. The insulation of celibate fraternities and sororities has its justification.

However, there are other difficulties with the transition to a bureaucratic rationality and to rational modalities in general which are not subsumed under the notion of the transition to politics. With respect to bureaucratic rationality, there are plenty of examples of the bureaucratization of Pentecost parallel to the earlier bureaucratization of Methodism, which means that Pentecostal churches acquire experts, departmental organizers, and specialists of various kinds. On the other hand, Pentecostalism is not *a* church or any kind of system, but a repertoire of recognizable spiritual affinities which constantly breaks out in new forms. This repertoire generates endless schism as well as self-help religiosity expressed in many thousands of micro-enterprises. For each instance where enthusiasm cools into settled forms and rationalization, there are others which break the moulds, above all in the huge population of the non-western world.

With respect to rationality in general (of which political rationality is only one aspect), the question of the future of Pentecostalism becomes assimilated to the question of the future of religion. That in turn has to do with the dominance in so-called post-modernity of the more restrictive protocols of rationality espoused by western elites, above all in the academy, and with the retrieval of alternative modes, analogous to the arts, in particular the logic of symbol, image, and icon. Clearly Pentecostalism, in common with Christianity generally, offers a narrative of transformations and transfigurations rather than a logic of linear implication or a theoretical rendering of tested empirical linkages. You can dismiss these modes as superstitions, illusions which mysteriously linger into what ought to be an austere and rigorous human adulthood (perhaps because compensations are still required), or you can suppose that there are other forms of encounter through testimony, gesture, song, and healing, which do not lie under the guillotine of progress but are intrinsic to the human condition.

notes

Preface

1   It was through the generous funding of the ISEC that I was enabled to undertake further research, subsequent to *Tongues of Fire*, likewise funded under the aegis of Peter Berger.

Chapter 1:   A cultural revolution: sources, character, niches

1   Schmuel N. Eisenstadt, *Fundamentalism, Sectarianism, and Revolution* (Cambridge: Cambridge University Press, 1999). Eisenstadt regards all varieties of fundamentalism as essentially modern, though often with roots in "the Axial Age" 500 BC–AD 500 , but it is clear that the violent "Jacobin" element he identifies in fundamentalism is absent from Pentcostalism, as indeed his comments on it indicate. Eisenstadt has important things to say about the locus of such movements in the monotheistic traditions, particularly where a transcendental and transforming utopia is projected. He makes a contrast with the "communal" fundamentalism of Asia consonant with the argument here. What Eisenstadt has to say about the role of "disembedding" provides a further context for that argument. Cf. also Melvyn Reader, "The rise of Protestant fundamentalism in world politics," Southampton University, Ph.D. thesis (1998). Steve Bruce in his forthcoming essay on *Fundamentalism* (Polity Press, 2000) omits Pentecostalism altogether.

2   James Davison Hunter, *Evangelicalism. The Coming Generation* (Chicago and London: University of Chicago Press, 1987). There is a huge literature here touched off by the work of Dean Hoge but including major contributions by Rodney Stark, Steve Bruce, Robert Wuthnow, Richard Quebedeaux, Wade Clark Roof, and others. Cf. Joel A. Carpenter, *Revive Us Again* (New York and Oxford: Oxford University Press, 1997) and John G. Stackhouse, *Canadian Evangelicalism in the Twentieth Century* (London and Toronto: University of Toronto Press, 1993); David Maxwell, "Delivered from the spirit of poverty," *Journal of Religion in Africa*, 28:3 (1998), pp. 350–73. Cf. David Maxwell, "Catch the cockerel before dawn," *Africa* 70:2 (May 2000), pp. 249–77.

3   This is widely stressed by Harvey Cox, Walter Hollenweger, and others but see in particular André Corten, *Le Pentecôtisme au Brésil* (Paris: Karthala, 1995). The fact that the fusion with popular spirituality in

Latin America is also stressed elsewhere indicates how complex and multiple these fusions are. Cf. Jean-Pierre Bastian, *Le Protestantisme en Amérique Latine* (Geneva: Labor et Fides, 1994).

4 David Martin, *Tongues of Fire* (Oxford: Blackwell, 1990), Part V.

5 David Lehmann, "Fundamentalism and globalism," *Third World Quarterly* 19:4 (1998), pp. 607–34.

6 David Martin, *Tongues of Fire*, and *Forbidden Revolutions* (London: SPCK, 1996).

7 Nathan Hatch, "The puzzle of American Methodism," *Church History* 63:2 (1994), pp. 175–89, esp. p. 185. I am very grateful to David Hempton for his advice and note the similarities discussed in his *The Religion of the People. Methodism and Popular Religion c. 1750–1900* (London: Routledge, 1996). The point about order and fecklessness is developed in Timothy Jenkins, *Religion in English Everyday Life* (Oxford: Berghahn, 1999).

8 Grant Wacker, *Present Tenses of the Everlasting Life: Pentecostals and the Future* (forthcoming 2001). Cf. William Kay, "Pre-millennial tensions: what Pentecostal ministers look forward to" in Martyn Percy, *Calling Time* (Sheffield: Sheffield Academic Press, 2000), pp. 93–113. This article shows that Pentecostal ministers expect the Millennium, but that is perhaps not the same as its immediate salience. It also provides confirmation of continuing belief in the Parousia.

9 Harold Bloom, *The American Religion* (New York: Simon and Schuster, 1992), p. 171.

10 André Corten, *Le Pentecôtisme au Brésil*, and "Le Pentecôtisme: Les Paradoxes d'une religion transnationale de l'émotion," *Archives de Sciences Sociales des Religions* 105, Jan.–Mar. 1999.

11 Diarmaid MacCulloch, *Tudor Church Militant* (London: Allen Lane, 1999). Cf. Kristin E.S. Zapalac, 1990: *In His Image and Likeness. Political Iconography and Religious Change in Regensburg 1500–1600* (Ithaca: Cornell University Press, 1990).

12 David Maxwell, *Christians and Chiefs in Zimbabwe* (Edinburgh: Edinburgh University Press, 1999) and "Catch the cockerel before dawn", pp. 249–77.

13 Bernice Martin, "From pre- to post-modernity in Latin America" in Paul Heelas (ed.), *Religion, Modernity and Post-Modernity* (Oxford: Blackwell, 1998), pp. 102–46; and Paul Heelas, *The New Age Movement* (Oxford: Blackwell, 1996).

14 Donald Miller, *Reinventing American Protestantism* (Berkeley, CA: University of California Press, 1997); Martin Stringer, *On the Perception of Worship* (Birmingham: Birmingham University Press, 1999).

15 Murray Dempster, Byron Klaus, and Douglas Petersen, *The Globalization of Pentecostalism* (Oxford: Regnum, 1999). Cf. Elaine Lawless, *Handmaidens of the Lord* (Philadelphia: University of Pennsylvania Press, 1998); Robert Beckford, *Jesus is Dread* (London: Darton, Longman, and Todd, 1998).

16 Simon Coleman, "Words as things, language, aesthetics and the objectification of Protestant Evangelicalism," *Journal of Material Culture* 1:1 (1996), pp. 107–28. Cf. Simon Coleman and Peter Collins, "The 'plain' and the 'positive': ritual, experience and aesthetics in Quakerism

and charismatic Christianity," *Journal of Contemporary Religion* 15:3 (2000), pp. 317–29, and Stephen Hunt, "'Winning ways': globalisation and the impact of the health and wealth gospel," *Journal of Contemporary Religion* 15:3 (2000), pp. 331–47. Stephen Hunt indicates how far the model of expansion based on American cultural radiation has to be qualified by "globalization" and "reverse globalization" whereby (for example) Nigerians bring prosperity teachings to Britain. He makes interesting points about Britain's resistance to over-emphasis on the theme of faith and wealth and the infiltration of spiritual enterprise culture into the charismatic movement more generally.

17 Ibid., and Bernice Martin, "From pre- to post-modernity in Latin America."
18 Loris Zanatta, *Dallo Stato Liberale alla Nazione Cattolica* (Milan: Francoangeli, 1996).
19 Michael Novak, *This Hemisphere of Liberty* (Washington: AEI Press, 1990).
20 Eamon Duffy, *Saints and Sinners. A History of the Popes* (New Haven, CT, and London: Yale University Press, 1997); José Casanova, *Public Religions in the Modern World* (Chicago and London: University of Chicago Press, 1994).
21 Anthony Gill, *Rendering Unto Caesar. The Catholic Church and the State in Latin America* (Chicago and London: University of Chicago Press, 1998).
22 John Burdick, *Looking for God in Brazil* (Berkeley, CA: University of California Press, 1993).
23 Michael Fleet and Brian Smith, *The Catholic Church and Democracy in Chile and Peru* (Notre Dame, IN: University of Notre Dame Press, 1997).
24 First draft of "Christianity without Frontiers" (2000). Introductory comments to work on Shona missionaries and transnational Pentecostalism. In this paper Maxwell shows how a body, ZAOGA, developed from loose networks of labor migrants with links to Christian Independency to a transnational bureaucracy around a charismatic leader and his connections. Black missionaries are sent out and subordinate pastors played off against each other; global charismatic Christianity is drawn upon *and* neo-colonialism repudiated.

Chapter 2:   North America and Europe: contrasts in receptivity

1 Lawrence James, *The Rise and Fall of the British Empire* (London: Abacus, 1994).
2 Mark Noll, *A History of Christianity in the United States and Canada* (London: SPCK 1992). On the growth of American religious institutions during the "modernization" of the country, I am conspicuously indebted to Jon Butler, *Awash in a Sea of Faith* (Cambridge, MA: Harvard University Press, 1990), and to numerous pioneering studies by Rodney Stark and his collaborators, whose gist is to be found in Rodney Stark and Roger Finke, *Acts of Faith* (Berkeley, CA: University of California, 2000).
3 Harry S. Stout, *The Divine Dramatist: George Whitefield and the Rise of Modern Evangelicalism* (Grand Rapids, MI: Eerdmans, 1991); Frank Lambert, *Pedlar in Divinity* (Princeton: Princeton University Press, 1994).

4   John Keane, *Tom Paine* (London: Bloomsbury, 1995). I am grateful here for discussions with, and material provided by, David Hempton and John Walsh.

5   Ronald Inglehart, *Culture Shift in Advanced Industrial Society* (Princeton: Princeton University Press, 1990).

6   Lyle Schaller, *The New Reformation: Tomorrow Arrived Yesterday* (Nashville, TN: Abingdon Press, 1995).

7   David Maxwell, *Christians and Chiefs in Zimbabwe* (Edinburgh: Edinburgh University Press, 1999).

8   James Piscatori and Susanne Hoeber Rudolph, *Transnational Religion, Fading States* (Oxford and Boulder, CO: Westview Press, 1994).

9   Marie Howes, "Priests, people and power: North Peruvian case study" in Susanna Rostas and André Droogers (eds), *The Popular Use of Popular Religion in Latin America* (Amsterdam: CEDLA, 1993), pp. 145–60.

10 Steve Brouwer, Paul Gifford, and Susan Rose, *Exporting the American Gospel* (New York and London: Routledge, 1996). For sharp qualifications to this approach, cf. Stephen Hunt, "'Winning ways' globalisation and the impact of the health and wealth gospel," *Journal of Contemporary Religion* 15:3 (2000), pp. 331–48.

11 Harold Bloom, *The American Religion* (New York and London: Simon and Schuster, 1992), chapter 10.

12 Donald Miller, *Reinventing American Protestantism in the New Millennium* (Berkeley, CA: University of California Press, 1997).

13 Paul Freston, *Evangelicals and Politics in Asia, Africa and Latin America* (Cambridge: Cambridge University Press, 2001).

14 Timothy Jenkins, *Religion in English Everyday Life – An Ethnographic Approach* (New York and Oxford: Berghahn Books, 1999).

15 Roger O'Toole, "Religion in Canada: its development and contemporary situation," *Social Compass*, 43:1 (1996), pp. 119–34.

16 George A. Rawlyk (ed.), *The Canadian Protestant Experience* (Burlington, OH: Welch, 1991).

17 Diane Austin-Broos, *Jamaica Genesis. Religion and the Politics of Moral Order* (Chicago and London: University of Chicago Press, 1997).

18 Nancy Ammerman, *Congregation and Community* (New Brunswick, NJ: Rutgers University Press, 1997).

19 Geoffrey Walker, "Mission Canada: reflections on a paradox," *Anvil* 16:1 (1991), pp. 19–29.

20 Luis Fontalvo, "Hispanic Pentecostals in a Canadian Anglo-French environment," *Pneuma: The Journal of Pentecostal Studies* 13:2 (1991), pp. 74–9.

21 Leslie Francis, "Evangelical identity among young people," *Anvil* 15:4 (1998), pp. 254–67.

22 Nicola Toulis, "*Belief and identity,*" Cambridge University, Ph.D. thesis (1994).

23 Harald Hegstad, "A minority within the majority," *Studia Theologica* 53 (1999), pp. 119–31; Ole Feldbaek, et al., articles on Scandinavian revivalism in *Scandinavian Journal of History* 11:4 (1986); Eila Heilander, "Naiset eivät vaienneet" (Helsinki: Suomen Kirkkohistoriallinen Seura, 1987).

Eila Heilander discusses the crucial role of female evangelists in the early years (1920–50) of Finnish Pentecostalism, and its subsequent diminution.

24 Simon Coleman, *The Word and the World. The Globalisation of Charismatic Christianity* (Cambridge: Cambridge University Press, 2001). The percentages of Pentecostals in Scandinavia are 2 percent in Sweden and Finland, $1^1/_2$ percent in Norway and 0.2 percent in Denmark (given in Steve Bruce, *Choice and Religion* (Oxford: Oxford University Press, 1999), pp. 220–1.

25 Salvatore Cucchiari, "Adapted for heaven: conversion and culture in western Sicily," *American Ethnologist* 15 (1988), pp. 417–41.

26 Mark Hutchinson, "The trans-oceanic triangle in planting Pentecostalism among Italian migrants to Australia 1907–1979" (Wheaton Conference papers, 1992).

27 Eugenio Stretti, "Il Pentecostalismo in Italia," *Protestantesimo* 51:1 (1996), pp. 45–52.

28 The politico-religious nexus in Argentina is very complex, especially in relation to Peronism. A fascinating background is provided in Loris Zanatta, "Dallo Stato Liberale alla Nazione Cattolica" (Milan: Francoangeli, 1996).

29 Diego A. de Posadas Montero, "Desde el Sur" (Montevideo: Solaris, 1995).

30 Ralph Della Cava, "Miracle at Joaseiro" (New York: Columbia University Press, 1970).

31 Hugh McLeod, *Piety and Poverty. Working-Class Religion in Berlin, London and New York 1870–1914* (London and New York: Holmes and Meier, 1996).

32 Olav H. Angell, "The role of religion in substance abuse treatment centres" in Paul Repstad, *Religion and Modernity: Modes of Co-existence* (Oslo: Scandinavian University Press, 1996).

33 There is a large literature on Italian communism and Democrazia Cristiana which I have consulted from time to time, but there is a useful background introduction in John N. Molony, *The Emergence of Political Catholicism in Italy* (London: Croom Helm, 1977). Recent comprehensive coverage, including political aspects, is provided in Roberto Cipriani, *La Religiosità in Italia* (Milan: Mondadori, 1995).

34 Alexandra Richie, *Faust's Metropolis. A History of Berlin* (New York: Carroll and Graf, 1998).

35 A useful background work is René Rémond, *Religion and Society in Modern Europe* (Oxford: Blackwell, 1999).

36 James Davison Hunter, *Culture Wars: the Struggle to Define America* (New York: Basic Books, 1991). For a rather somber account of religion in the USA, cf. James Davison Hunter, "When psychotherapy replaces religion," *The Public Interest* 139, pp. 5–21.

37 There are several ancillary debates which I have not felt it necessary to enter into here. They concern the cultural shift to post-material values and "spirituality," and the shift away from commitment to public institutions, including churches, as well as questions such as the extent to

which Americans exaggerate their piety, the "flakiness" of what they
believe and the actual extent of conservative reinvigoration. However,
in my view, none of this undermines the remarkable difference between the USA and Western Europe, and it seems clear that the quite
dramatic shifts among young people in Germany and elsewhere have a
relatively modest echo in the USA. Moreover, American religious institutions have a way of adjusting to "post-materialism" and individualized "spirituality." There is a large literature here by such distinguished
scholars as Steve Bruce, Rodney Stark, Robert Wuthnow, James Hunter,
and Ronald Inglehart.

38   Hugh McLeod, *Piety and Poverty*.
39   David Martin, "Unitarianism," *Social Compass* 44:2 (1997), pp. 207–16.
40   Athena Leoussi, *Nationalism and Classicism* (London: Macmillan, 1998).
41   Eugen Weber, *Action Française* (Stanford: Stanford University Press, 1962).
42   Antoine Lion, "Theology and sociology" in David Martin, John Orme
     Mills, and William Pickering, *Sociology and Theology. Alliance and Conflict*
     (Brighton: The Harvester Press, 1980).
43   Grace Davie, *Religion in Modern Europe: A Memory Mutates* (Oxford: Ox-
     ford University Press, 2000).
44   Marlène Albert-Llorca, "Renouveau de la Religion Locale en Espagne"
     in Grace Davie and Danièle Hervieu-Léger (eds), *Identités religieuses en
     Europe* (Paris: La Découverte, 1996).
45   Peter Robb, *Midnight in Sicily* (London: Harvill, 1998).
46   Roberto Cipriani, *La Religione dei Valori* (Rome: Salvatore Sciascia Editore,
     1992); Franco Garelli, *Forza della Religione e debolezza della Fede* (Milan: Il
     Mulino, 1996) and Salvatore Abbruzzese *La Vita Religiosa* (Rimini:
     Guaraldi, 1995).
47   Roland Campiche, *Croire en Suisse* (Lausanne: Edition L'Age d'Homme,
     1992).
48   Simon Green, *Religion in the Age of Decline* (Cambridge: Cambridge
     University Press, 1996).
49   Robert Currie, Alan Gilbert, and Lee Horsley, *Churches and Churchgoers*
     (Oxford: Clarendon Press, 1997); and Callum Brown, *The death of Chris-
     tian Britain* (London: Routledge, 2001).
50   John Wolffe, "To die is gain? Religion, the monarchy and national
     identity in Britain 1817–1910," in I. Brohed (ed.), *Church and People in
     Britain and Scandinavia* (Lund: Lund University Press, 1996).
51   David Martin, "Pink bishops and the Iron Lady" in Dennis Kavanagh
     and Anthony Seldon, *The Thatcher Effect* (Oxford: Oxford University
     Press, 1989).
52   David Martin, *Forbidden Revolutions: Pentecostalism in Latin America* (Lon-
     don: SPCK, 1996).
53   Attila Molnar, "Civil and ethnic religion: the case of Hungary," *Religion*
     (2001, forthcoming).
54   Hugh McLeod, *Piety and Poverty*.
55   Daniel Antal, *Out of Romania* (London: Faber, 1994).
56   John Anderson, *Religion, State and Politics in the Soviet Union and the Successor
     States* (Cambridge: Cambridge University Press, 1994); Irena Borowik,

"Religion in post-communist societies" in Irena Borowik and Grzegorz Babinski (eds), *New Religious Phenomena in Central and Eastern Europe* (Cracow: Nomos, 1997); Patrick Michel, *Politique et Religion* (Paris: Albin Michel, 1994); Steve Bruce, *Choice and Religion* (Oxford: Oxford University Press, 1999), chapter 4; Eila Heilander *Religion and Social Transitions* (Helsinki: Helsinki University Press, 1999), chapters 2 and 3.

57 Ghia Nodia, "Georgia's identity crisis" *Journal of Democracy* 6:1 (1995), pp. 104–16. I am grateful to Paul Freston for sending me this information.

Chapter 3: Latin America: a template?

1 Francis Fukuyama, *Trust* (New York: Free Press, 1993); Lawrence Harrison, *Who Prospers?* (New York: Basic Books, 1993); and David Harvey, *The Condition of Post-Modernity* (Oxford: Blackwell, 1992).
2 Jeremy Seabrook, *Victims of Development* (Guildford: Verso, 1993).
3 Manfried Kellner and Heuberger (eds), *Hidden Technocrats* (New York: Transaction Press, 1991) and Scott Lash and John Urry, *The End of Organized Capitalism* (Cambridge: Polity Press, 1987).
4 Andrew Chesnut, *Born Again in Brazil* (Rutgers University Press: Rutgers, NJ, 1997).
5 John Burdick, *Looking for God in Brazil* (Berkeley, CA: University of California Press, Berkeley, 1993).
6 David Lehmann, *Struggle for the Spirit* (Cambridge: Polity Press, 1996).
7 John Burdick, *Looking for God in Brazil*.
8 Elisabeth Brusco, *The Reformation of Machismo: Evangelical Conversion and Gender in Colombia* (Austin, TX: University of Texas Press, 1995).
9 John Burdick, *Looking for God in Brazil*, p. 67.
10 Alan Gilbert, *The Latin American City* (London: Latin American Bureau, 1994).
11 Bernice Martin, "From pre- to postmodernity in Latin America: the case of Pentecostalism" in Paul Heelas, (eds) *Religion, Modernity and Postmodernity* Oxford: Blackwell, 1998); Andrew Walker, *Restoring the Kingdom* (Guildford: Eagle, 1998).
12 An authoritative summary of this debate is provided in chapters 3 and 9 of David Hempton, *The Religion of the People, Methodism and Popular Religion c. 1750–1900* (London: Routledge, 1996).

Chapter 4: Latin America: ambiguity in different cultural sectors

1 Daniel Míguez, *Spiritual Bonfire in Argentina* (Amsterdam: CEDLA, 1999). Also useful for the development of high-profile mass ministries and interdenominationalism, cf. Matthew Marostica, "The defeat of denominational culture in the Argentine Evangelical Movement," chapter 7 in Christian Smith and Joshua Prokopy (eds), *Latin American Religion in Motion* (London and New York: Routledge, 1999), pp. 147–72.

2   Andrew Chesnut, *Born Again in Brazil: the Pentecostal Boom and the Patho-gens of Poverty* (Rutgers, NJ: Rutgers University Press, 1997).

3   Henri Gooren, *Rich Among the Poor* (Amsterdam: Thela, 1999).

4   Bernice Martin, "New mutations of the Protestant Ethic among Latin American Pentecostals," *Religion* 25 (1995), pp. 101–17.

5   Lawrence Harrison, *Who Prospers?* (New York: Basic Books, 1992), and *The Pan-American Dream* (Boulder, CA: Westview Press, 1997).

6   John Burdick, "Struggling against the Devil" in David Stoll and Virginia Garrard-Burnett (eds), *Rethinking Protestantism in Latin America* (Phila-delphia: Temple University Press, 1993), and John Burdick, *Looking for God in Brazil: the Progressive Church in Urban Brazil* (Berkeley: University of California Press, 1993), p. 189.

7   William Hewitt, *Base Christian Communities and Social Change in Brazil* (Lincoln, NE: University of Nebraska Press, 1991).

8   Rowan Ireland, *Kingdoms Come: Religion and Politics in Brazil* (Pittsburgh, PA: University of Pittsburgh Press, 1992), p. 5.

9   Ibid., p. 5.

10 Roger Lancaster, *Thanks to God and the Revolution* (New York: Columbia University Press, 1988), p. 90.

11 Blanca Muratorio, "Protestantism and capitalism revisited in the rural high-lands of Ecuador," *Journal of Peasant Studies* 8:1, Oct. 1980, pp. 37–60.

12 Roger Lancaster, *Thanks to God and the Revolution*, p. 90.

13 Ibid., p. 101.

14 Ibid., p. 107.

15 Edward P. Thompson, *The Making of the English Working Class* (Harmond-sworth: Penguin, 1968).

16 Roger Lancaster, *Thanks to God and the Revolution*, p. 115.

17 Ibid., p. 107.

18 Frans Kamsteeg, "Pentecostalism and political awakening in Pinochet's Chile and beyond," in Smith and Prokopy (eds), *Latin American Religion in Motion*, pp. 187–204.

19 Summarized in David Martin, "Evangelicals and capitalist society in Chile" in Richard Roberts (ed.), *Religion and the Resurgence of Capitalism* (London: Routledge, 1995).

20 David Smilde, "El Clamor por Venezuela: Latin American Evangelical-ism and a collective action frame" in Smith and Prokopy (eds), *Latin American Religion in Motion*, pp. 125–46.

21 David Smilde, "The fundamental unity of the conservative and revolu-tionary tendencies in Venezuelan evangelicalism: the case of conjugal relations," *Religion* 27:4 (1997), pp. 343–59.

22 John Burdick, "Gossip and secrecy: women's articulation of domestic conflict in three religions of urban Brazil," *Sociological Analysis* Vol. 51, No. 2 (1990), pp. 153–70.

23 Jorge Maldonaldo, "Building fundamentalism from the family in Latin America" in Martin Marty and R. Scott Appleby, *Fundamentalisms and Society* (Chicago: University of Chicago Press, 1993).

24 Cecilia Mariz and Clara Mafra, "Family and reproduction among Protest-ants in Rio de Janeiro" in Smith and Prokopy (eds), *Latin American Religion in Motion*, pp. 205–20.

25 Diane Austin-Broos, *Jamaica Genesis: the Politics of Moral Order* (Chicago and London: University of Chicago Press, 1997).

26 Salvatore Cucchiari, "Conversion and culture in Western Sicily," *American Ethnologist* 15 (1988), pp. 327–54, and "Between shame and sanctification: patriarchy and its transformation in Sicilian Pentecostalism," *American Ethnologist* 17 (1991), pp. 687–707; Nicola Toulis, "Belief and identity: Pentecostalism among first generation Jamaican women in England," Cambridge University, Ph.D. thesis (1994).

27 Andrew Chesnut, *Born Again in Brazil*.

28 Kurt Bowen, *Evangelism and Apostasy* (London and Montreal: McGill-Queen's University Press, 1996).

29 Patricia Fortuny, "Jehovah's Witnesses in Mexico. The right to be different?" Paper presented at the American Anthropological Association Meeting, Chicago (1991). Cf. also Patricia Fortuny, "On the road to Damascus: Pentecostals, Mormons and Jehovah's Witnesses in Mexico," London University, Ph.D. thesis (1995), and Site Report (2000) on the International Headquarters of La Luz del Mundo, Hermosa Provincia, Guadalajara (made available privately).

30 David Clark Knowlton, "Mormonism in Chile" in Douglas Davies, *Mormon Identities in Transition* (London and New York: Cassell 1996), pp. 68–79.

31 Patricia Fortuny, "On the Road to Damascus" For the Judaizing of the New Israelitas, cf. Damien Thompson, "A Peruvian messiah and the retreat from apocalypse" in a forthcoming volume on millenarianism edited by Stephen Hunt.

32 Bobby Alexander, "The contribution of the Latino church to resurgent ethnicity" (unpublished paper) and "A Pentecostal-styled Mexican mission in Dallas," *Journal of Religion and Culture* ("Listening") 33:3 (1998), pp. 175–87.

33 Damian Thompson, article in *The Daily Telegraph Magazine* (23/10/1999), and Michael Leatham, "Rethinking peasant decision-making in peasant Millenarianism", *Journal of Contemporary Religion* 12.3 (1997), pp. 295–310.

34 Susan Rose and Quentin Schultze, "An awakening in Guatemala" in R. Scott Appleby and Martin Marty, *Accounting for Fundamentalisms* (Chicago: University of Chicago Press, 1993).

35 David Stoll, *Is Latin America Turning Protestant? The Politics of Evangelical Growth* (Berkeley: University of California Press, 1990).

36 Tod Swanson, "Refusing to drink with the mountains" in Marty and Appleby, *Accounting for Fundamentalisms*, pp. 77–98.

37 Kurt Bowen, *Evangelism and Apostasy*.

38 Ibid., p. 123.

39 Grant Wacker, "Searching for Eden with a satellite dish" in Richard Hughes (ed.), *The Primitive Church in the Modern World* (Urbana and Chicago: University of Chicago Press, 1996), pp. 139–66.

40 Ibid., p. 147.

41 Ibid., p. 148.

42 Daniel Levine, "Protestants and Catholics in Latin America: a family portrait." Paper prepared for the Fundamentalism Project, November 1991, kindly sent by the author.

43   David Lehmann, *Struggle for the Spirit* (Cambridge: Polity Press, 1996).
44   John Burdick, *Looking for God in Brazil*.
45   Material drawn from Peter Clarke, "Pop-star priests and the Catholic response to the explosion of evangelical Protestantism in Brazil," *Journal of Contemporary Religion* 14:2 (1999), pp. 203–16, and Andrew Chesnut, *Competitive Spirits: Latin America's New Religious Market Place* (Rutgers, NJ: Rutgers University Press, 2000), chapter 4.

Chapter 5:   Indigenous peoples

1   Tod Swanson, "Marks of a Christian, marks of a Quicha modernity" in Martin Marty and R. Scott, Appleby, *Accounting for Fundamentalisms* (University of Chicago Press: Chicago, 1994).
2   James Dow, "Protestantism and development in rural Mexico." Paper presented at ISSR conference, Maynooth, Irish Republic, 19–23 August, 1991.
3   Duncan Earle, "Authority, social conflict and the rise of Protestantism: religious conversion in a Mayan village," *Social Compass*, Vol. 39(3) (1992), pp. 377–88.
4   Ibid., p. 377. The studies of Earle and Dow should be compared with Bowen's account of the evangelical movement in Oxchuc, a Mexican *municipio* where it made up over a third of the population, at least until – like their northern border co-religionists – they engaged in differential migration. Bowen points to the relationship between pressures on land and the decay of the old clan system and conversion, and stresses that it was the Oxchuceros themselves who did the evangelizing. *Evangelism and Apostasy* (London and Montreal: McGill-Queens University Press, 1996), pp. 47–50.
5   Timothy Evans, "Religious conversion in Quetzaltenango, Guatemala," University of Pittsburgh, Ph.D. thesis (1990).
6   Sheldon Annis, *God and Production in a Guatemalan Town* (Austin: University of Texas Press, 1987).
7   Timothy Evans, "Religious Conversion," p. 218.
8   Edward Cleary, "Evangelicals and competition in Guatemala," in Edward Cleary and Hannah Stewart-Gambino, *Conflict and Competition* (Boulder, CO & Lynne, London: Rienner Publishers, 1992). See also parallel comments in Amy Sherman, *The Soul of Development. Biblical Christianity and Economic Transformation in Guatemala* (Oxford: Oxford University Press, 1997).
9   Carlos Garma, "Pentecôtisme rural et urban au Mexique," *Social Compass* Vol.39,3, Sept. 1992, pp. 389–400.
10 Susanna Rostas, "Conversiones Protestantes en una comunidad tradicional de Chiapas," Proceedings of the Second International Conference of Mayanists, Centro de Estudios Mayas, UNAM (1990).
11 Lesley Gill, "Like a veil to conver them: women and the Pentecostal Movement in La Paz," *American Ethnologist*, Nov. 1991, pp. 708–21.
12 Andrew Canessa, "The Politics of Pacha," University of London, Ph.D. thesis (1993). Cf. Luisa Elvira Belaunde, "Epidemics, psycho-actives and

evangelical conversion among the Airo-Pai of Amazonian Peru," *Journal of Contemporary Religion* 15:3 (2000), pp. 349–59. The group studied here is a tiny forest people found near the border of north-east Peru. The author argues (p. 349) that Evangelicalism offers a ritual protection against cocaine and alcohol introduced by colonists and against sorcery linked to traditional psycho-active plants. In rejecting intoxicating substances, men and women aspire to return to an ancestral paradigm of sociality and eliminate conflict and death from among their people. Therefore, evangelical conversion does not imply an epistemological break from their cultural values, while it entails a reassessment of shamanism and Airo-Pai relationships with non-indigenous colonists. Evangelicalism halts violence and personal and social disintegration.

13   Rita Laura Segato, "Cambio Religioso y Desetnificacion: La expansion evangélica en Los Andes Centrales de Argentina," *Regiones Latinamericanas* 1: Jan.–June 1991 (IAHR, Mexico), pp. 708–21.

14   Fred Spier, "Rural Protestantism in southern Andean Peru" in Andre Droogers and Susanna Rostas (eds), *The Popular Use of Popular Religion in Latin America* (Amsterdam: CEDLA and Free University, 1993), pp. 109–25.

15   Frans Kamsteeg, "The message and the people" in Droogers and Rostas, *The Popular Use of Popular Religion*, pp. 127–44.

16   Roger Kellner, "Christian gods and Mapuche witches," Droogers and Rostas, *The Popular Use of Popular Religion*, pp. 161–78.

Chapter 6:   Africa

1   Thomas Spear and Isariah Kimambo (eds), *East African Expressions of Christianity* (Oxford: James Currey, 1999).

2   Henri Gooren, *Rich among the Poor* (Amsterdam: THELA, 1999); Rob Garner, "Religion and economics in a South African Township," Cambridge University, Ph.D. thesis (1998).

3   Alan Anderson, *Tumelo – the Faith of African Pentecostals in South Africa* (Pretoria: UNISA Press, 1993) and Alan Anderson and Walter Hollenweger (eds), *Pentecostals After a Century* (Sheffield: Sheffield Academic Press, 1999). In his contribution to the latter volume, Anderson stresses the black origins of Pentecostalism.

4   André Corten, *Le Pentecôtisme au Brésil* (Paris: Karthala, 1995).

5   Irving Hexham and Karla Poewe, "The new charismatic churches of Durban, Pretoria and Johannesburg," *Navors Bulletin* 17:9 (1987), pp. 32–6.

6   Ruth Marshall-Fratani, "Power in the name of Jesus," *Review of African Political Economy* 52 (1991), pp. 21–37.

7   Ibid., p. 21.

8   Ibid.

9   Ibid.

10   Birgit Meyer, *Translating the Devil. Religion and Modernity among the Ewe in Ghana* (Edinburgh: Edinburgh University Press, 1999), and "Memory and post-colonial mentality in Ghanaian Pentecostal discourse," *Journal*

of Religion in Africa 28:3 (1998), pp. 316–49. Meyer emphasizes growing political participation and uncertainty about its direction. There is further development of her analysis, covering both the political and the economic, in Birgit Meyer, "The power of money," *African Studies Review* 41:3, pp. 15–37, and "Commodities and the power of prayer," in Birgit Meyer and Peter Geshiere (eds), *Globalization and Identity: Dialectics of Flow and Closure* (Oxford: Blackwell, 1999), pp. 151–71. The core of the argument is that Ghana is popularly understood as a field of occult forces, which lie behind the local nexus of wealth and power and the vicissitudes of the global market place, and that Pentecostalism can alone defeat these forces by the power of the (global) spirit. "Goods" of every kind are desirable and dangerous, and the Spirit ensures a relatively safe negotiation of both the desire and the danger. Parallel reflections on the global and the local demonic are to be found in Rijk Van Dijk, "Fundamentalism and its moral geography in Malawi: the representation of the diasporic and the diabolical" *Critique of Anthropology* 15 (1995), pp. 171–91.

11 Miriam O'Neill, "A study of Pentecostalism in the Embu District of Kenya", University of London, BA dissertation (1995). I am grateful to John Peel for drawing my attention to this, and for much other background material. There is a further material on Kenya in "The local roots of the Kenyan Pentecostal revival: conversion, healing, social and political mobility" by Yvan Droz, forthcoming in *The Journal of Religion in Africa*. Droz links the expansion of Pentecostalism to the wider East African Revival, which was a sort of alternative to breakaway tendencies to religious independence, offering therapeutic conversion, lay participation, lively hymnody, and social mobility. The specific Pentecostal emphasis on experience increased its appeal to the poorly educated. Today Pentecostals are an amorphous grouping, drawing more from the better-off of the poor, and accounting for perhaps 10 percent of the population, i.e. nearly three million. They also entertain some input from transnational evangelists, American-style. Droz emphasizes a simultaneous symbolic and spatial migration to a fresh environment where the old ills can be overcome by a new faith and fresh power. Pentecostalism picks up elements from traditional sources for dealing with inexplicable fortune and transports believers to the conditions of an imminent terrestrial restoration.

12 Rosalind Hackett, "Pentecostal appropriation of media technologies in Nigeria and Ghana," *Journal of Religion in Africa* 18:3 (1998), pp. 258–77.

13 Matthews Ojo, "The charismatic movement in Nigeria today," *International Bulletin of Missionary Research* 19:3 (1995), July, pp. 114–18.

14 David Maxwell, *Christians and Chiefs in Zimbabwe* (Edinburgh: Edinburgh University Press, 1999), "Delivered from the spirit of poverty," *Journal of Religion in Africa* 28:3 (1998), pp. 350–73; and "Catch the cockerel before dawn," *Africa* 70:2 (2000), pp. 249–77.

15 Pierre-Joseph Laurent, "L'Église des Assemblées de Dieu du Burkina-Faso," *Archives de Sciences Sociales des Religions* 44:105, Jan.–March 1999, pp. 71–88.

16 Paul Gifford, "Prosperity: a new and foreign element in African Christianity," *Religion* 20 (1990), pp. 373–88.
17 Paul Gifford, "Chiluba's Christian nation: Christianity as a factor in Zambian politics 1991–6," *Journal of Contemporary Religion* 13:3 (1998), pp. 363–77, and *African Christianity. Its Public Role* (London: Hurst 1998), and Paul Gifford (ed.), *The Christian Churches and Africa's Democratization* (Leiden: E. J. Brill 1995). A sympathetic critique of Gifford is available in David Maxwell, "In defence of African creativity," *Journal of Religion in Africa* (forthcoming). Maxwell stresses (1) African diversity over against any primal "essentialist" Merrie Africa; (2) the emergence of a popular Christian youth culture offering economic opportunities; (3) the extent to which Gifford has a focus on politics, clerical elites, and their conferences and statements; (4) the importance of culture, especially local culture and its existential concerns; (5) the way Africans channel external resources to establish local bases; (6) the way faith teaching outside the urban megachurches creates spiritual and other securities rather than prosperity; (7) the extent of continuity between Pentecostalism and Independency, and their often shared hostility to tradition; (8) the importance of other bodies e.g. Witnesses and New Apostolics in Zambia.
18 For a discussion of the uses and misuses of the sociological meta-narrative of modernization, individualization, disenchantment, commodification, dislocation, cf. Harri Englund and James Leach, "Ethnography and meta-narratives of modernity," *Current Anthropology* 41:2 (2000), pp. 225–48. Particular reference is made to Englund's studies of Pentecostalism in Malawi. In this context rural–urban migration occurs back and forth; and though the usual suggested shifts are noted (individualization, the breaking of kinship bonds and obligations, modern attire, healing and exorcism in the power of the Spirit, and rejection of African medicine) these are also queried and qualified from a theoretical perspective. There are complex issues raised in this article which cannot be addressed here but it is worth drawing attention to the admitted limits on individualization, to the way Pentecostals are relatives in the Spirit, whose bodies are "corporeal signs of composite selves" (p. 235) – and to the greater resistance they encounter in the urban context in Malawi compared to the rural areas.

Chapter 7: Asia

1 Robert Frykenberg, "The Gospel, globalization and Hindutra" in Donald Lewis, *Christian Expansion in the Twentieth Century Non-Western World* (Grand Rapids, MI: Eerdmans, forthcoming 2002).
2 Susan Bayly, 1994: "Christianity and competing fundamentalisms in South Indian society" in Martin Marty and R. Scott Appleby, *Accounting for Fundamentalisms* (Chicago: Chicago University Press, 1994), pp. 726–69.

3   Blandine Ripert, "Christianisme et Pouvoirs Locaux dans une vallée Tamang du Népal Central," *Archives de Sciences Sociales des Religions* 99: July–Sept. 1997, pp. 69–86.

4   Alan Hunter and Kim-Kwong Chan *Protestantism in Contemporary China* (Cambridge: Cambridge University Press, 1993.

5   Ibid.

6   Tong Chee Kiong, "The Rationalization of Religion in Singapore" in Tong Chee Kiong et al., *Imagining Singapore* (Singapore: Times Academic Press, 1992), pp. 276–98.

7   Michael Northcott, "A survey of the rise of charismatic Christianity in Malaysia," *Asian Journal of Theology* 4:1 (1990), pp. 266–78.

8   Robert Hefner, "Of faith and commitment: Christian conversion in Muslim Java" in Robert Hefner (ed.), *Conversion to Christianity* (Berkeley, CA: University of California Press, 1993), pp. 99–128.

9   Edwin Zehner, "Thai Protestants and local supernaturalism: changing configurations," *Journal of South-east Asian Studies* 27:2, September 1996, pp. 293–319. Alan Alderson (Selly Oak Colleges) has supplied me with material by Chin Khua Khai showing a parallel situation in Burma. A Christian population there is just over two million (5 percent) mainly in peripheral tribal groups, and Pentecostals have doubled since 1975 to nearly 100,000 (0.2 percent), also among tribals, though with a modest expansion in Rangoon parallel in its way to that in Bangkok.

10   Edwin Zehner, "Merit, man and ministry," *Social Compass* 38:2, June 1991, pp. 155–75.

11   In this section I have relied on Mark Mullins and Richard Fox Young (eds), *Perspectives on Christianity in Korea and Japan* (Lampeter: Edwin Mellen Press, 1995).

12   Robert Weller and Julia Chien-Yu Huang, "Merit and mothering: women and welfare in Chinese Buddhism," *The Journal of Asian Studies* 57:2 (1998), pp. 379–96.

13   Jungja Ma, "Pentecostal challenges in East and Southeast Asia." Material deposited at the Oxford School of Mission Studies, Oxford, P.O. Box 70, but now available as chapter 9 in Murray Dempster, Byron Klaus, and Douglas Petersen, (eds) *The Globalization of Pentecostalism* (Oxford: Regnum, 1999).

14   Jae-Yong Jeong, "Filipino Pentecostal spirituality," Birmingham University (Selly Oak), postgraduate dissertation (2001).

15   Steve Brouwer, Paul Gifford, and Susan Rose, *Exporting the American Gospel* (New York and London: Routledge, 1996).

16   Alan Davidson, "The Pacific is no longer a mission field" in Donald Lewis (ed.), *Christian Expansion in the Twentieth Century Non-Western World* (Grand Rapids, MI: Eerdmans, 2002). Material here is largely drawn from this paper. Cf. Manfred Erst, *Winds of Change: Rapidly Growing Religious Groups in the Pacific* (Suva: Pacific Council of Churches, 1994).

17   Anne Stensfold, "A wave of conversion: Protestantism in Cape Verde," *Religion* 29:4 (1999), pp. 337–46, and Diane Austin-Broos, *Jamaica Genesis: Religion and the Politics of Moral Order* (Chicago and London: Chicago University Press, 1997).

Chapter 8:   Trying conclusions: a global option?

1   Andrew Chesnut, *Born Again in Brazil* (Rutgers, NJ: Rutgers University Press, 1997), pp. 77–7, 138–9.
2   David Martin, "Bedevilled" in Donald Capps and Richard Fenn, *On Losing the Soul* (Albany: State University of New York Press, 1995), pp. 39–68.
3   David Martin, *Does Christianity Cause War* and *Reflections on Sociology and Theology* (Oxford: Oxford University Press, 1997).

bibliography

Comprehensive bibliographies are to be found in:

Bastian, Jean-Pierre, *Le Protestantisme en Amérique Latine* (Geneva: Labor et Fides, 1994).

Chesnut, Andrew, *Born Again in Brazil* (Rutgers, NJ: Rutgers University Press, 1997).

Corten, André, "The growth of the literature on Afro-American, Latin American and African Pentecostalism," *Journal of Contemporary Religion* 12:3 (1997), pp. 311–34.

Dempster, Murray, Klaus, Byron and Petersen, Douglas (eds), *The Globalization of Pentecostalism* (Oxford: Regnum, 1999).

Lehmann, David, *Struggle for the Spirit* (Cambridge: Polity Press, 1996).

Martin, David, *Tongues of Fire* (Oxford: Blackwell, 1990).

Stoll, David, *Is Latin America Turning Protestant? The Politics of Evangelical Growth* (Berkeley: University of California Press, 1990).

Vasquez, Manuel, *The Brazilian Popular Church and the Crisis of Modernity* (Cambridge: Cambridge University Press, 1998).

Suggested further reading

Anderson, Alan and Hollenweger, Walter (eds), *Pentecostals After a Century* (Sheffield: Sheffield Academic Press, 1999).

Bowen, Kurt, *Evangelism and Apostasy* (London and Montreal: Queen's and McGill University Press, 1996).

Burdick, John, *Looking for God in Brazil* (Berkeley, CA: University of California Press, 1993).

Cleary, Edward L. and Stewart-Gambino, Hannah (eds), *Power, Politics and Pentecostals in Latin America* (Boulder, CA: Colorado Westview Press, 1996).

Cox, Harvey, *Fire From Heaven* (New York: Addison-Wesley, 1994).

Gill, Anthony, *Rendering Unto Caesar. The Catholic Church and the State in Latin America* (Chicago and London: University of Chicago Press, 1998).

Ireland, Rowan, *Kingdoms Come: Religion and Politics in Brazil* (Pittsburgh, PA: Pittsburgh University Press, 1992).

Maxwell, David, *Christians and Chiefs in Zimbabwe* (Edinburgh: Edinburgh University Press, 1999).

Meyer, Birgit, *Translating the Devil. Religion and Modernity among the Ewe in Ghana* (Edinburgh: Edinburgh University Press, 1999).

Miller, Donald, *Reinventing American Protestantism in the New Millennium* (Berkeley, CA: University of California Press, 1997).

Mullins, Mark and Young, Richard Fox (eds), *Perspectives on Christianity in Korea and Japan* (Lampeter: Edwin Mellen Press, 1995).
Percy, Martyn, *Calling Time* (Sheffield: Sheffield Academic Press, 2000).
Percy, Martyn, *Power and the Church* (London: Cassell, 1998).
Poewe, Karla (ed.), *Charismatic Christianity as a Global Culture* (Columbia, SC: University of South Carolina Press, 1994).
Smith, Christian and Prokopy, Joshua (eds), *Latin American Religion in Motion* (London and New York: Routledge, 1999).
Stackhouse, John, *Canadian Evangelicalism in the Twentieth Century* (Toronto: University of Toronto Press, 1993).
Stoll, David and Garrard-Burnett, Virginia (eds), *Rethinking Protestantism in Latin America* (Philadelphia: Temple University Press, 1993).

Other writing by David Martin

"Bedevilled" in Richard Fenn and Donald Capps, (eds), *On Losing the Soul* (Albany: State University of New York Press 1995), pp. 39–68.
"Evangelical religion and capitalist society in Chile" in Richard Roberts (ed.), *Religion and the Transformations of Capitalism* (London: Routledge 1995), pp. 215–27.
"The People's Church: the global evangelical upsurge and its political implications" in Peter Berger (ed.), *The Desecularization of the World* (Grand Rapids, MI: Eerdmans, 1999).
Forbidden Revolutions: Pentecostalism in Latin America and Catholicism in Eastern Europe (London: SPCK, 1996).

General background

Benavides, Gustavo "Modernity" in Mark C. Taylor, *Critical Terms for Religious Studies* (Chicago: Chicago University Press, 1998), pp. 186–204.
Berger, Peter (ed.), *The Desecularization of the World* (Grand Rapids, MI: Eerdmans, 1999).
Beyer, Peter, *Religion and Globalization* (London: Sage, 1994).
Bruce, Steve, *Fundamentalism* (Cambridge: Polity Press, 2001).
Casanova, José, *Public Religions in the Modern World* (Chicago and London: Chicago University Press, 1994).
Davie, Grace, *Religion in Modern Europe. A Memory Mutates* (Oxford: Oxford University Press, 2000).
Hervieu-Léger, Danièle, *Le Pèlerin et le converti. La Religion en mouvement* (Paris: Flammarion, 1999).
Hunt, Stephen (ed.), *Millennarianism* (New York: New York University Press, 2001).
Poloma, Margaret, *The Assemblies of God at the Crossroads* (Knoxville, TN: University of Tennessee Press, 1989).
Robertson, Roland, *Globalization: Social Theory and Global Culture* (London: Sage, 1992).
Walker, Andrew, *Restoring the Kingdom* (Guildford: Eagle Publishing, 1998).
Woodhead, Linda and Heelas, Paul (eds.), *Religion in Modern Times* (Oxford: Blackwell, 2000).

index